How now?

ROGER EVANS

Merlin Unwin Books

Merlin Unwin Books Ltd
Palmers House
Ludlow
Shropshire SY8 1DB
UK
www.merlinunwin.co.uk

The author asserts his moral

ISBN 978-1-913159-20-7

Typeset in 12 point Bembo by Merlin Unwin Books
Printed by TJ International, Padstow, England

This book is dedicated to my grandchildren
Rhys, Tomos, Katie, David and Hannah

6 January 2018

I was driving over some spring barley stubble yesterday afternoon and I saw a hare. Big deal! Well it was a big deal for me because it was the first hare I had seen for a month. Two years ago I would have expected to have seen about ten hares on the same field. But the number of hares is not the only difference. A couple of years ago, if I were to disturb a hare it would just sort of jog off, for about 50 yards then pause, and sit up on its hind legs, then wander off, all in its own good time.

The hare I saw yesterday put its ears back and bolted into the woods as fast as a hare can go. This was a hare that had been persecuted by hare coursers. It had no way of knowing if I were friend or foe and it was off. It probably owed its survival to its preference to run into the woods. Hare coursers' dogs hunt by sight and the hare would be very difficult to catch amongst the trees. It's all a big shame on two counts. I used to see lots and lots of hares here. I used to think that they were a sort of barometer, that if the hares were OK, everything else was OK and I knew that I was farming in a sustainable manner. The other shame is that they were docile enough for me to observe them – now they just bolt at the first sign of a vehicle. It could be that there are more hares about than I think and that they are all keeping their heads down.

It may seem a strange comparison, but you get a similar reaction in cattle. When, for example, cows are housed in the winter, they sometimes pack close together in large groups. They could be waiting to be fed, or milked, or they could be hanging about after they've been milked. They will stand together tightly like a flock of sheep. Sometimes you have to get past them, to open a gate perhaps. You can go on some farms and the cows will move away when you are within five yards. This is sometimes referred to as flight distance. Our cows don't have a flight distance, you have to squeeze past each one, sometimes you have to squeeze quite forcibly. The cows for their part just stand there, ignoring you, probably chewing their cud. Possibly, if they do move, they will tread on your toe! The cows have nothing to fear from us. There are no sticks in our yard. We sometimes have to get a stick when it comes to TB testing time but this is usually to give you more perceived width as you guide the cows towards the vet. You can tell a lot about a farmer if you know how his stock behaves.

★★★

My daughter does eyes. She says she is an orthoptist but on a need-to-know basis, doing eyes, is all you need to know. When she graduated I had a photo taken of me in her cap and gown, which is as close to getting a degree as I shall ever get. She does clinics and she goes around schools. Because we live in a very rural area she does a lot of driving in the countryside and one day she passes a lot of horse boxes on a grass verge. She assumes, not unreasonably, that there is a hunt about. A mile further on she is overtaken by an ambulance, blue lights flashing, 'I wonder,' she says to herself, 'if someone has fallen off a horse.'

A bit further on she meets a man on a horse who is leading another horse. The lane is narrow so she pulls in as best she can to allow him to pass. But he is not best pleased with her choice of stopping places and he waves his whip at her and his fist and hurls abuse at her. She doesn't hear the abuse, it's raining and she doesn't wind the window down, but she knows abuse when she sees it. It's quite interesting when you think about it. She was sympathetic to what he was trying to do. She's a farmer's daughter and a farmer's wife so she knows a bit about animals. I think if there were to be a referendum on hunting she would probably vote in favour of it. She knows a bit about horses. Years ago, when her children were small, they were given an old Shetland pony. His name was Flymo. The children used to feed him carrots and groom him. He was a wicked little thing. He would eat the carrots and then try to eat the children. Naturally the children wanted to ride him and my daughter told them they couldn't ride him until his coat turned black. As he was a palomino, this was going to take some time, but the children accepted it. It's the sort of thing I would tell my children so we don't need to wonder where she got that from. There she is, in a narrow lane trying to help and she gets abused. It's very difficult for those who hunt, to get good press. Getting bad press, on the other hand, is very easy. If this is how they behave, it's no wonder hunt saboteurs get so much pleasure in winding them up. Here's proof, if proof were needed, of where the saying, 'on his high horse,' comes from.

13 JANUARY 2018

I've just been watching a news item about A&E departments failing to reach their targets. It never used to be a problem. We all knew that staff in A&E departments worked hard and did their very best. That's as true today as it ever was. We all knew that they would get to us just as soon as they could and we understood that they had to make choices about who to treat next and whose case was more urgent. What's different today? I expect there are malingerers in the queue. I expect there always were, but I suspect there are more now – people have a greater sense of entitlement, and one person's cut finger means a bandage to some but to someone else it means a trip to A&E.

Years ago my son broke his ankle badly whilst taking his sons ice skating. In the ambulance he was offered oxygen to relieve the pain. He said that he was OK. They said that he must be either a farmer or a rugby player and they were right on both counts. That, in a way, brings us to the next problem for A&E. When my son broke his ankle, before he even got off the ice, before there was even a sign of a stretcher, he had to sign a waiver that the accident was his fault and he would take no further action against the ice rink. For A&E staff there must always be the fear in their minds that if they make a mistake or turn someone away, they will end up in court. Hospital beds are taken up by people they can't send home and the system backs up to the extent that people are waiting on trolleys in corridors and in ambulances. Then they criticise the ambulance for not hitting its targets. I'd like to see politicians hitting targets. But where would you begin?

★★★

It's probably a bit late for a turkey story but here goes: one of the regulars in the pub works on a farm that adjoins a cottage with a bit of land attached. The man in the cottage rears about 40 free-range turkeys for Christmas and this friend of mine gets about six for other regulars in the pub. He's a sort of middleman in all this. We had one last year and very good it was too. Every year about September I start asking him how my turkey is doing. 'Yours isn't growing much.' I ask for a photo but he always has an excuse for not taking one.

Come December and various others in the company are getting pressure from their wives who in turn are starting to fret about whether their turkey will actually turn up. 'I've done all the preparations for Christmas; all I've asked you to do is get the turkey.' They start asking when their turkey will be ready. So you go to the pub and enquire. 'When you do want it?' 'I want it on the 23rd at the latest.' And he gives a half smile, and sucks some breath in, 'Can't see it being ready by then.' 'You'd better not let my missus hear you say that.' Me, I'm not too worried, I know that he'll turn up one night with a turkey, that I'll give him a glass of port and a mince pie, and it will take another 2-3 months before he tells me how much I owe him.

It seems that most of these pub regulars cook their turkey on Christmas Eve. When they get home from the pub at midnight, their house is full of the delicious aroma of cooked turkey. It's late and they are hungry so they have a bit of a pick at this turkey. The result is that most of the turkeys in our village get to Christmas day apparently without any legs or wings.

Yet more turkey stories. On 22 December I was told that there wouldn't be a turkey for me because the man who reared them had broken his arm and so he couldn't catch them. I go to the pub on the 23rd. I was told that he had got a relative to catch them but there still wouldn't be one for me because he had got the count wrong and he was one short. But not to worry, a tin of ham was put on the pub table, 'That's your Christmas dinner,' I was told, 'We'll give you that.' At midday on Christmas Eve a very fine turkey turns up, it's huge, which is just as well because there's 14 family to eat it plus two others we invite because otherwise they would be on their own. We always have our Christmas dinner at night, after all the work and the milking are done. At midday, after half an hour's struggle, my wife and I decide we can't get it in the oven. We make various phone calls for help, but the only person to answer is the person who supplied it. 'We need help to cut the turkey up.' He's here in five minutes with the sort of motorised disc cutter that they use on building sites, but no worries, he has a clean saw in his truck. Sorted.

20 January 2018

I've decided that I could easily do without January in my life. The snow has gone but it's raw and damp and cold. I can't drive around the fields, they are too wet. The nights are slowly getting a bit lighter but I'm sure the mornings are getting darker. These big old farmhouses are nice and cool in the summer but, boy, are they cold in the winter. My daughter's farmhouse is older and colder than ours and she has taken to wearing a hat (that looks like a Christmas pudding) inside the house. I jumped out of bed when the alarm went this morning, just so I could get into the kitchen to get warm.

★★★

A reader has sent me a book about hares. I couldn't find an address so I use these pages to say 'Thank you'. The reader tells me the book is heavy-going and that they gave up on it halfway through. I've always got a book on the go, I read in bed before I put the lights out, there's two big piles of books in the corner of my bedroom. I rarely look at the title, and most of the books are given to me so they are of all sorts. I can only remember not finishing one book because it was rubbish, so this 'hare' book will probably be read. I've also been given a hare calendar for Christmas. I've got more hares in the house than I've got in the fields. You can imagine what I think about that. If it was badgers that were being hunted, there would be a public outcry. It's all very strange.

Thus far this year I have seen just two hares. That's good. Or it would be good if they were not dead, freshly dead, torn to pieces and thrown into the bottom of the hedge. Hare coursing is climbing up the agenda of rural crime which is to be applauded but it's too late for most of my hares. The police have a very difficult job, most of the registration plates of hare coursers' vehicles are from cars that were scrapped years ago, so the perpetrators are almost impossible to track down. The police measure crime by how much it is reported, so if I see any suspicious activity I will report it right away. I used to dial 101 but that has been upgraded to a 999 call.

Hare coursers can rarely resist a bit of theft as a part of their remit, so with a bit of luck, if they are not caught coursing the hares, they might be caught in pursuit of something else. The local population don't seem too bothered about the hares, which I find disappointing, but if, for example, someone takes power tools from their garden shed, well, that's a very serious matter indeed.

The local wildlife groups are strangely quiet and inactive on the subject, which I also find odd. If I were to plough up some lapwing nests or if someone was after badgers, there would be a public outcry, and they would be leading it. Why the double standards? The strangest thing of all is that the hare is such a lovely inoffensive creature compared with a badger. In the same way, it's the easy option to target farmers. Much easier, for example, than looking out for hare coursers, who largely live beyond the law and who have scant regard for anybody.

★★★

I go to the gym on Tuesdays and Fridays because of my health. When I started I used to go in the mornings but I soon discovered that it was quieter in the afternoons, and you get nicer people there. Mostly when I go there's about four others but as the clock moves towards 3, they start to leave and I often spend my last quarter of an hour on my own. I go on the first Friday of the new year and it's full up, eleven people in there! One of the instructors is married to one of my nephews so I ask her what's going on, are they having a happy hour? 'You should have seen it this morning, there were twenty here!' Eleven is plenty. Gym people behave a bit like children in a toy shop. They are constantly on the move from apparatus to apparatus. They do about 30 seconds on one piece and then they seem to think, 'That next one looks good, think I'll try that.' This often means that they go up to a person already busy on a machine, 'How long will you be on that?'

Nobody tries that with me, I've got a scowl on that keeps them well away. A lot have new gym clothing on, they all have obligatory water bottle. I have neither, I'm in my dirty working clothes, which is probably another reason why people keep their distance. A family come in, mum and dad and two teenage children. They all have new gym outfits on. They do some coordinated stretching exercises before they move to the apparatus. The exercises are the sort worthy of an athlete about to attempt a world record. Whilst I am there, the instructors have four other couples turn up to be shown around with a view to joining the gym. Why this sudden escalation of interest? Then it dawns on me, New Year resolutions!

27 January 2018

It's a funny old month, January. Lots of people are short of money, because the true cost of Christmas dawns as their December credit card statements arrive. Others are having a 'dry' alcohol-free January, which I suspect is as much to do with the credit card statement's arrival as it is to do with abstinence. Anyway the pub is nearly empty some nights.

January is a very important month for vegans. They're having a go at livestock farming in January as they encourage people to try their lifestyle as a part of their New Year resolutions. The big hope is that people will try vegetarianism and like it so much, they will also become vegans in due course. They embrace their chosen lifestyle with an evangelical zeal and seek to convert everyone to their way of life. Vegans have the remedy for saving the world: no livestock, lower greenhouse gases, they see it as a win–win and as a result are positively glowing with self-righteousness.

But, and there is a big but, they have driven up world demand for quinoa and avocado and thus prices. These are, or were, staple foods in South America, and the poor there can no longer afford to buy them. They don't tell you about that, do they? Chicken, in some parts of South America is now cheaper them quinoa and avocado, so some poor people are now eating more chicken. Those that can't afford quinoa or avocado or chicken are really struggling. The rush to grow more quinoa and soya is leading to more deforestation. Well done, vegans. Apparently new converts drop off being vegetarian and vegan just as quickly as all those 'new year's resolution' people at the gym, whose decline in numbers by the end of this month is in free fall.

★★★

I've just returned from doing the morning school run. It's a horrible morning, wet and cold. The outside temperature on the car shows one degree, there's a lot of stuff falling out of the sky and some of it is white. I'm very glad to get back to a warm kitchen and breakfast. Everything in life is relative and our kitchen only seems warm if you compare it with what's going on outside. As I scramble from car to house, I spare a thought for my neighbour's new-born lambs which are two fields away down the road. Lambs were meant to be cavorting in the sunshine, not pictures of abject misery, backed up against what shelter the hedge provides with their chins resting on their front feet. I used to enjoy a bit of cavorting myself. Haven't done any for a long time.

★★★

The lambs are in a steep field that slopes down to the road. When I was in my 20s my brother came to stay with us. One night there was a goodly fall of snow so after we had done all our work we decided to go sledging. First we had to build a sledge, which took us over an hour. We thought we'd made a fair job of it, we even found some metal strips to fix to the wooden runners. The nearest field suitable for sledging was the one where the lambs are today. It's not our field, but no matter. We walked to the very top and both got on the sledge and away we went. The combination of the steepness and the combined weight of two 20-year-olds meant that we were soon going quite fast. Then we hit a frozen molehill that completely destroyed the sled.

I've never been one to give up easily but the sled was beyond repair so we went a bit further down the road, to the blacksmiths, to see if he could help. For someone who has spent his life mending things for grumpy farmers, this was a welcome diversion. He was so enthusiastic I thought at one time he would want to come with us. He found some square metal tubes and made us a sledge in about half an hour. He put some metal mesh on top for us to sit on and we were soon climbing back up the same field. Off we went and soon reached speeds we had previously only dreamt of. It's about 300 yards down that field and when we reached the bottom we were going so fast there was no way of stopping. Under the barbed wire we went, through the hedge, across the road and through the hedge on the other side. We eventually stopped about 30 yards into the flat field the other side of the road. By the time we had removed briars and blackthorns from faces and hands, it was time to go to milk again.

We only had the one ride on that sled that day but my children used it for years and it was sturdy enough to carry bales of hay about the yard when there was snow on the ground. We've still got it, somewhere, although I haven't seen it for over 20 years!

3 FEBRUARY 2018

I'm reading a really good book at the moment, it's about a farmer and his efforts to grow crops on one field and at the same time, enhancing nature, both flora and fauna. He reports that the presence of hares is a good barometer of the well-being of how you farm.

I learn that a red legged partridge female lays two clutches of eggs, one of which is hatched out by the male. I never knew that. But there is no end to what nature has to teach you and you never stop learning, which is part of what makes it such a delight. I suppose the partridge sees it as a sort of a baker's dozen, a bit extra to ensure that some chicks are reared. I know, for example, that if there are winged predators about (and there's an abundance of those), the red legged partridge will head for cover whilst the wild grey partridge squats down where it is and is easily picked off. That's another of the choices or balances that wildlife organisations have not come to terms with. We are forever being told about the demise of the grey partridge. The RSPB refuses to link it to the proliferation of birds of prey, whose numbers escalate year by year. There's lots of red legs about here. You see large coveys scurrying along the lanes. Most shoots rear some. I often ask keepers why they don't rear some greys as well (you can buy them), but they all say it is a waste of time, they would only be rearing food for birds of prey.

★★★

When I was involved at the village school, which was many years ago now, there were over 70 pupils and three full-time teachers. In recent years it's struggled for numbers. Not because I'm not involved any more, but because it's a sad biological fact of life that the many retired couples who have moved in to the area rarely start a new family. Attendance drifted down to the 20s at times and the school was amalgamated with another village school about three miles away. I'm not sure how that works, I think they share Heads.

But there have been two significant changes lately. Pupil numbers have gone back well up to the 40s, this taking away any closure threat. The biggest visual change has been outside the school. There have always been some pupils from outside the catchment area and you see lots of cars outside the school doing the school run. There is probably a mixture of reasons why people take their children out of town schools and put them in to village schools. I'm sure the smaller class sizes are attractive, why wouldn't they be? But perhaps there is a social status benefit to be had as well. Whatever the reason, these out-of-catchment children have kept many a village school alive. But there has been one dramatic change. I don't know where they come from but there are now about three mothers collecting children on foot and they have pushchairs with them that presumably contain even younger children. It's the most heart-warming thing I've seen outside the school for a long time. Perhaps we've got our living village back.

★★★

When you go to secondary school in a rural area, it could well be that the school is a fair way away. I went about eight miles to school, which gave you the chance to do your homework on the bus on the way to school. The downside was that your best friend at school might also live eight miles away, in another direction. It made contact outside school very difficult. My children had to go six miles to secondary school. When my son was 12 or 13, he used to breed ferrets and he sold a ferret to a classmate who lived ten miles away in the other direction. It was decided that there was no better place for the ferret to be handed over than at school. My son took the ferret to school, fast asleep amongst his books, in his school bag. The prospective purchaser refused to take delivery of the ferret until school finished for the day. My son was totally unperturbed by this request and carried the ferret all day long in his bag from lesson to lesson. At the end of the school day, animal and money changed hands and the ferret went safely off on another bus journey. I was always quite proud of my son for doing this.

10 FEBRUARY 2018

I've never really sought to air my medical problems here but if you will indulge me a while you will discover there is a purpose. I've got this condition that has taken away my balance. The biggest effect has been I've had to stop going to international rugby matches,. I still get to do a lot because people are so kind and thoughtful. For example I can get up the six or so steps into the pub, but I need help to get back down them. I usually get offered a brawny tractor driver's arm. The other big downside is that once or twice a month I will have a fall. And it's a fair old fall, there is no warning and it's so sudden that you just go down in a heap. It's very important where you fall. Onto a bed or a settee is OK, concrete not so good. Last week I had a fall backwards onto the toilet. And the seat was up so I fell onto the rim. I landed on the small of my back and it was the most painful thing I can remember. I had to go to bed for three hours but as soon as there was a grandson about I went downstairs to the safety of my armchair.

Now it's time for a bit of self-diagnosis. Everything is working OK, so I decide its muscle damage. If I go to the doctors he will send me to A&E and do I need to spend 12 hours on a trolley in a corridor? No I don't, so I decide I will tough it out which is why I spend the next three days in the armchair and why I end up watching Prime Minister's questions. After about ten minutes I decide I would never make an MP. Call it pride, call it what you will, but I could never bring myself to ask such stupid questions. Yet there they all are, bobbing to their feet, dozens of them, trying to get 'called' by the speaker. And if I couldn't think of a better question to ask than they do, I'd stay well down in my seat. 'Will my honourable friend join me in congratulating a rugby club in my constituency, on their 40th anniversary?' Of course the PM will, and graciously acknowledges the importance of physical activity. Big deal, what's all that about? Is it just to use up time in case someone should have a real searching question? What a way to run a country!

Then there's the speaker, who is central to all this. He's a self-satisfied preening sort of fellow. There's a saying around here 'He's as slick as a mole.' It is reserved for those who have about them the sleek velvety smugness of a mole. That probably describes him very accurately but I also think he looks a bit like a carrion crow perched on the top of a hedge in springtime. He's cleared out one nest of song bird fledglings and now he is looking for the next opportunity. The whole scene in Parliament also reminds me of a noisy, dirty, sea lion pool at a zoo. The Speaker is the keeper distributing fish, in the form of the opportunity to ask a question. The MP's are the very noisy sea lions, bobbing up and down to catch his eye. That's got to be enough analogies for one day. For a few seconds I am forced to admire his ability to know everyone's name. Then reality kicks in – he probably doesn't know everyone's name, he only calls the names he knows. Only he knows the answer to that and I bet he keeps that very secret.

After three nights I venture back upstairs. And decide to stay in the B&B wing – fewer stairs to climb. Big mistake. I awake at about 3am in agony. I try every position known to man and I can't get out of pain. I can't make anyone hear me, I can't get down the stairs on my own, I'm just stuck there. By the time the house gets up I'm at a pretty low ebb. Perhaps the self-diagnosis was wrong, perhaps it's more serious than I first thought. We decide that I can't sit in the car and I need an ambulance. Ten minutes later there's two big men stood at the end of my bed. One is an ambulance driver and one is a paramedic. I can't praise them enough. They get me downstairs, give me a really thorough examination, speak to my GP, arrange for prescription pain killers, arrange a GP appointment for next week and decide I had torn back muscles which had started to heal and I'd torn them again. If they can employ nice people like this, who are so good at their job, it must be the system that is wrong. And I think I've sold one of the ambulance men two hens.

17 FEBRUARY 2018

Although my mobile phone is only about two years old, (the last one fell out of my pocket into the brown stuff), it's quite a simple one. It is used to make and receive phone calls, it sends and receives texts and its alarm function gets me up in the morning. Very, very, occasionally it is used to take a photograph. That is all I use it for. It does lots of other things but they remain a mystery to me. Not for me, one of these phones with a touch screen and all the functions that come with them. I despair of people spending time in company, staring at their phones when they should be making conversation or listening to gossip.

But one night in the pub it was particularly noisy. If you have ten or twelve people in a room and they are all talking at the same time, the only way they can get themselves heard is by talking louder than everyone else and the whole scenario gets out of control and the volume escalates. We had just that sort of scenario recently. It was so noisy that me and the person next to me had long given up trying to make conversation. He gets his phone out, I'm not too pleased about that, but in the circumstances I don't blame him. He lays it on the table, presses it a few times and then points for me to have a look. I soon forget any misgivings I may have, he's activated a function that measures decibels! There's a needle going back and fore as the conversation volumes ebbs and flow. There's a portion of the needle's travel that is in a red zone, presumably this is the area where you can suffer hearing damage. The needle measure is mostly on the edge of the red and every extra shout and peal of laughter sends it well into the red. Here comes the irony. When they introduced 'quiet' cabs in tractors, the maximum decibel level was around 180. The noise in the pub was way beyond that, and many of the people making the noise were tractor drivers and lorry drivers. They are making more noise than the big diesel engines they drive.

★★★

A friend calls by for a chat and a cup of coffee. He has been to take some sheep to a small local abattoir. The sheep were born and bred on his farm, the abattoir is only ten miles away, the meat will be sold in his brother's butchers shop, which is also local. This is an example of local food provenance of the highest order but he probably doesn't see it like that, he just sees it as common sense.

He is in reflective mood so I just sit and listen. He tells me that the countryside has gone quiet. He farms alongside a minor road that travels from the valley floor to the top of the hill, where the hill farms are, a journey of about three miles. When he went to school, (admittedly over 50 years ago), there were 21 places that sold milk along that road. Now there is only 'me'. 'That was 21 families and the place was alive.' He tells me that years ago, when they went out of the house, they could always hear a tractor working somewhere. They would all stop and listen, and they could mostly identify the make of tractor and hence whose it was and what he was doing. 'Sounds like Sid Jones mowing his clover piece.' 'These days when folk are busy they call in a big contractor with big machines and all you can hear is tractors roaring for 12 hours. Next day we are back to silence again.'

He recalls threshing. At an early age he was allowed to stay home from school so that, with his terrier, he could catch rats and mice. 'The threshing drum would arrive early; it often took over an hour to get it all ready. It had to be blocked up dead level. If it wasn't level it wouldn't work properly and grain would be lost and belts would fly off. When it was all ready, we all went in the house where Granny had cooked us a huge breakfast.'

He pauses to take a swig of his now cold coffee and I tell him of some of my threshing experiences. As the boy on the farm where I worked I was frequently sent to help neighbours at threshing time. The food was always plentiful and good. The trouble was that, as the boy, I was always fed last. The first-fed men would be mopping up the last of their gravy with a piece of bread almost before I had speared my first potato. As they returned to work one day, and me with half a plate of food, one of them jabbed his forefinger in my back and said, 'I don't begrudge you your food but I begrudge the time you are taking to eat it!'

24 FEBRUARY 2018

My eldest grandson, who is I think about 24, has been working on the farm for about six month and he's moved in with us. He moved in with us because we have plenty of room. It's quite a handy arrangement as he is close at hand if I am struggling with my laptop, which is most days. The only downside is that he gets better food than me. One day he says to me 'I'm thinking of getting a dog.' He means he wants his own dog to work on the farm. It's half a statement of intent and half of it that says 'I live with you so will that be OK?' The query comes out of courtesy because he is not the sort to do otherwise. I don't think he realises just how important getting your own dog is, in the process of growing up. One of the first things I did after getting married, was to buy a dog. I'd been back at home living with my parents for two or three years before I got married and if I had wanted a dog then I would have had to ask them. So when I did buy that dog there was a sort of freedom involved, I just went out and bought it, I didn't ask anyone. I didn't even ask my wife for her permission. I thought it best to start like that and, as I went on, not ask her for support in any big decisions. It's a yardstick that has served me well over the years.

The next time the boy mentions a dog, he's bought a puppy and it is arriving on Sunday. He shows me photos of it on his phone. He asks me what he should call it. This is an important issue, and I tell him that for a working dog, a name with only one syllable has much to commend it, as it is easier to shout instructions with a short name. I once knew a gamekeeper who had a lot of Springer spaniels, they were a particularly lively strain (which is very lively if you are talking about spaniels). He always used men's names for his dogs that had an old-fashioned ring to them. He had an Adrian and a Neville and a Jonathon. I suggest the name, 'Dog', which has much to commend it, but the best name comes from the very end of one of my favourite films, 'Babe'. Then you could stand next to your dog and say, 'That'll do Pig, that'll do.'

★★★

It's a sad irony regarding working dogs, that if you get a really outstanding dog it will meet an untimely end. If you rear a useless dog, it will sleep on your yard until it is at least 20 years old. Even my favourite dog Mert, who was a really good worker and lived until he was very old, met his end under the wheels of late night teenage traffic. To most livestock farmers, a good working dog is indispensable. Some rely on the combination of dog and quad bike, a few seem to manage with just a quad bike, but they can't have the pleasure and satisfaction of having a really good dog.

Then there are those who don't have either. I knew of such a farm. They had quite a lot of sheep to look after but their dog was run over. It so happened that there was another farm that was only a couple of hundred yards away. They had a good dog. This dog was always free to come and go as he pleased and when he wasn't working he would roam about at will. Part of his roaming would take him down the road to the other farm, just to say hello and to see what is going on. One day they are getting their sheep in at the 'dog-less' farm. Because they are dog-less, there is a lot of noise involved. Shooing and cursing and the like. Two hundred yards away the dog hears all this noise, he vacated his cosy refuge amongst the bales and goes down the road to the other farm, to give them a hand. He stays there until the sheep are returned to the field and his help is invaluable. They are quite taken with this help and start feeding this dog with titbits so that he starts calling several times a day. If he is not about and there is sheep work to do, they live near enough to call him and he soon comes running. They use their neighbours' dog in this fashion for two years but one day his owner needs him, can't find him, and drives to his neighbours to ask if they have seen him. He finds his dog busy helping with the shearing, he's so busy he's almost exhausted. The owner is not best pleased. And that, as they say, was the end of that.

★★★

Our local town is built on the side of a hill. It means that some of the streets are quite steep. It is always ironical to me that the vets' is on a level business park at the edge of the town but the doctors' surgery is at the top if the steep bit. This was once explained to me that the doctors was built at the top of the town in order that old people, struggling up the hill to the doctors, would die before they got there. I struggled to get in there yesterday and once I was sitting in the waiting room I announced that the doctors and vets should swap over premises.

A lady nearby disagrees, 'If the doctors was down there, we wouldn't have such a nice view from the waiting room.' But I get support from a farmer's wife sitting in the corner. 'I think he was referring to the access.' Our local scrap metal dealer comes in, he's a good friend of ours, he's obviously popped in during his working day because he is in full, filthy working outfit. He's not there long as he goes in to see the nurse. I just hope her hands are cleaner than his.

★★★

The dog Gomer had a knitted pig for Christmas. I think he's just killed it.

3 MARCH 2018

I had occasion to phone a company I'd never had contact with before, none of whose employees I knew. When we finished our conversation the lady who had answered the phone called me, 'Sweetie.' 'Thank you Sweetie.' It registered with me because it's quite unusual these days for someone to say something like that. I've never been really sure what political correctness means, I just plough on regardless, tell it how I see it. I wasn't offended by it, in fact I quite liked it. Could it be that society is taking itself a bit too seriously these days?

★★★

There's this very large farm with a lot of employees. It is decided by the owners to make some changes to improve efficiency. One of the things they want to do is bring in outside contractors to do some of the tractor work. This will involve some redundancies and all the staff are called to a meeting, which is part of the consultation process, in order to explain what is going to happen and why. After all the reasons are explained, the staff are asked if anyone will volunteer for redundancy. Half the staff look at the floor and the other half look at the ceiling. There is no eye contact. The boss wants to move things on a bit, truth be told he is probably as uncomfortable about the whole process as his men.

He turns to the oldest employee, 'What about you Fred, you never seem to be very busy, you always seem to be pottering about.' Fred is the stockman, he works quite hard in the winter when the cattle are inside, but in the summer he rides slowly about on his tractor from field to field to see that the stock is OK, and he makes sure that this takes all day. Fred draws himself to his full height. 'You can't be much of a farmer if you can't afford to keep one man who doesn't do anything.' There was no answer to that and Fred survived the cull.

★★★

It's a bright sunny day today, following several days of wet and cold. The weather thus far this year has been miserable. January is to be endured but it's not unreasonable to expect

February to be better. It's the month when the harbingers of spring start to turn up. It depends where you live and in particular your height above sea level, just how many of these harbingers you actually get. But eventually spring will turn up, it always does, so it's best to be ready for it. One of the things we have to do is get the electric fence ready: we use them throughout the grazing season. We have fairly modern solar charged units. They work very well but I admit to being a bit scared of them. I've always been a bit scared of electricity; it's OK in the right place, the right place being not through me. Years ago we had an electric fence unit that worked off the mains and I will always remember fetching the cows one dark wet morning, the fence wire was sagging a bit, the dog brushed against it, and it fetched a spark the length of the dog's back. It frightened the life out of me, and the dog didn't reckon much to it either.

When I was a boy, one day a local farmer took some of us to market. He had to call at the machinery dealers. The man behind the counter asked if he'd seen these new electric fence units. 'They are not like your old one. No moving parts, it's all transistorised.' Transistors were once the future, they were as modern as you could get. There was one of these new units on the counter. The farmer switched it on, held the end of the lead and said, 'It's not working.' The man behind the counter was amazed, 'Of course it is.' He grabbed the end of the lead and received such an electrical kick, it nearly put him on his back. Of course the farmer was one of these rare individuals who can receive electric shocks and they have no effect on them. I don't know how that works but their greatest delight is to grab hold of an electric fence and grab hold of you at the same time – you get a sort of enhanced shock. They never tire of doing this.

This same farmer had an old Bedford lorry, it had a six-cylinder petrol engine. He used to let us boys use it to cart hay bales. There were usually four of us. Two would pitch by hand, one would stack the bales on the lorry and one would drive. We took it in turns to drive so in theory the harder we worked, the sooner we would get our turn to drive the lorry.

One day the farmer came out into the hay field to see how we were getting on. I was driving, he listened to the petrol engine and said 'she' was only going on five cylinders. He undid the side of the bonnet to expose the spark plugs. The plugs didn't have plastic caps on them, they had metal screws that held the leads and plugs together. He put a finger on each plug in turn and said, 'This one is not working, switch her off'. He got his tool kit out, took out the plug he had identified, and sure enough it was caked up with bits of carbon. He cleaned it up, put it back in, 'Now fire it up.' He put his finger onto the plug he had cleaned, 'She is going OK now.' I haven't a clue just how much electricity was coursing through him when he did this. But best to keep well clear. On no account let him grab your hand.

10 MARCH 2018

Pheasants always seem to know when the shooting season finishes. Within two or three days there are pheasants everywhere. The shoot that I allow on my land catch up some of these pheasants. The hens produce eggs to hatch next year's pheasants and any surplus cocks are released in a wood that is fairly central on their shoot, hoping that they will still be there for next season. We get a lot of pheasants hanging about our chicken sheds. This is not ideal for biosecurity so I suggest that they put a catching pen by our sheds. In three days they catch 53! Where did they all come from?

★★★

We were talking about driving tests in the pub the other night. One of our regular companions works for a local auctioneer and he has to drive the tractor about the market when they are cleaning the pens out. They make him take a tractor test to prove his competence to do just that. Never mind that before he went to work at the auctioneers he had worked for over 30 years on a large arable farm, as a tractor driver! It all has a health and safety agenda feel to it. I tell them that my grandson has just been on a loader competence course. That he had to go over 40 miles to get there, it took two days and he had to go back on the third day to sit a test. All that at a cost of £400. You have to do all this because if there should ever be an accident it is important to be able to show that you have taken the issue of safety seriously, and have taken the trouble to train to prevent accidents. We all think £400 is too expensive but we can't do anything about it. There were several doing the course at the same time, which is several £400s. Most unpopular is the trailer test they want you to take. It's apparently OK to drive a tractor on the road with 20 tons of trailer behind it. But if you have a stock trailer behind a truck, they want you to take a trailer test. These tests cost £600 and I know of only a few farmers who have done one. If you have done this sort of work for a long time, you achieve a sort of 'grandfather's right' to carry on doing it. That's is why I often drive calves to market with my grandson sitting beside me, looking over hedges, which is what I should be doing.

The conversation in the pub moves on, as it always does, to motorbike tests. I passed my test on a motorbike in Newport. What they did in those days was that you went to the test centre and the examiner gave you a map of the town centre with a route clearly defined. You had to study that route and the examiner told you to ride around it repeatedly. He would walk around the route while you did it. 'I will be watching you at junctions and traffic lights, you may not see me because I will be hiding in shop doorways and the like. At some time during the test, when it is safe to do so, I will step

out in front of you and you will do an emergency stop.' Seems
so old-fashioned today. This reminds me of a story I heard
on the radio many years ago. Listeners were invited to call
in with amusing stories relating to driving test experiences.
Someone phoned in and said that he had been for a motorbike
test. He was instructed in exactly the same way that I had
been, the only difference was that the examiner was going to
test two motorcyclists at the same time. The two motorbikes
set off at intervals and our caller drove around the course as
instructed but saw not a sign of the examiner or the other
bike. He drove thus for over an hour and a half, and as his fuel
was getting low, he drove back to the test centre. When he got
there he was told that the examiner had stepped out in front
of the other learner in order for him to do an emergency stop,
and the other learner had run him over.

17 March 2018

It's Friday, it's bad weather and I haven't been out of the house
for two days. Do I feel guilty? Not a bit. I've probably done
my share of bad weather farming. A succession of people come
to the kitchen every morning to fill watering cans with hot
water. I make them cups of tea and tell them my stories of bad
weather; my bad weather stories are much worse than what's
outside today, but I can tell they don't believe me. They want
the hot water to thaw out cattle drinking troughs. I used to set
fire to straw to do this — it had the added benefit of warming
me at the same time. This wasn't without its disasters though.
The fire would occasionally burn through the blue plastic
water pipe so I would have a plumbing job to do as well.

The worst winter for me was the winter of 1963. I
was herdsman at a farm about three miles from where I lived.
The '63 winter seemed to go on forever. It was three weeks
before I could drive to work, so for three weeks I had to walk
to work. This used to take a good hour. When I got there

I had all the milking parlour to thaw out, I had to milk the cows and I had to try to get all this done by seven o'clock. Why seven o'clock? Seven o'clock is apparently the time that the good people of Cardiff get up in the morning and put the kettle on. Electricity supplies would struggle to cope and as that hour approached, you could hear the electric motors that ran the parlour were getting slower and slower and by seven o'clock they would stop altogether.

The most frustrating aspect of the 1963 winter was when the roads were reopened. I could drive back home fine but there was a short steep hill to negotiate and time after time I would fail to get up the hill because other vehicles were already stuck. If you were stuck you had to back all the way to the bottom and about 100 yards back along the flat in order to give yourself another run at it, to give yourself the momentum needed to get to the top. Time and again the vehicle that had thwarted me would try to start off at the bottom, get ¾ the way up, and get stuck again. I often spent my entire one-hour lunch break trying to get up that hill.

Some parts of the country this morning have snowy roads gridlocked with traffic at a standstill. Probably because someone at the front of the queue has done something really stupid and hasn't got a clue how to drive in snow. You get a similar sort of problem most days around these narrow lanes. You can be driving a tractor and trailer, or truck and livestock trailer and meet a car. There may well be a passing place just 30 yards behind them but they just sit there, they haven't got a clue how to reverse but expect you to back a vehicle and trailer 300 yards or so to reach a passing place.

★★★

A young lad who is doing an apprenticeship here comes in for some hot water. I make him a cup of tea. Whilst he is drinking the tea, and warming himself at the Rayburn, I tell him my stories of the '63 winter. I can tell by his eyes that he's not really listening, he's only pretending to listen while he drinks his tea. I can remember when I was his age having a similar experience. There was someone living in our village who had worked on farms in Canada for 20 years. There was no way that you could beat him on stories of cold weather. He had seen our struggles in the winter of '63, and it was no consolation to be told that it was so much worse in Canada. 'Big bulk carrier ships would pull up into the rivers and anchor in mid stream. It would be so cold that night that the river would freeze over and next day you could drive lorries laden with grain across the ice to fill the ships up.' This was usually received with sceptical eye-rolling from his audience, so he would go a bit further, 'It was so cold at night, the milk would freeze in the cows' udders.'

When things get back to normal, as they always do, there will be competitions at the pub – who had the deeper snow drift or the lowest temperature. Quite why they should differ I don't know; they all live within three miles of each other. Perhaps I can win the day if I recycle the Canadian stories. 'When I was young, I worked in Canada for ten years, it was so cold at night....' They don't know it's not true. Besides I once went to Vancouver for five days.

24 MARCH 2018

I told you that I had had a fall and injured my back, so slept two nights in the chair before I went back to bed. Bed was the worst thing I could have done – at least the chair provided support. I had to have paramedics to get me back downstairs and I slept in my armchair for over another three weeks. I'm back in bed now and going again to the gym, I'm nearly back on full power. I noticed 'they' have put a whistle next to my bed. It's the second time I have been to bed with a whistle. Many years ago, three of us went on safari in Zimbabwe. We were flown in a four-seater plane to a remote landing strip where we were collected by the safari staff. The camp was designed to emulate going on safari many years ago. It was spartan, but probably all the better for that. We were the only guests there that week. On our last day the staff told us that when they received notice of our arrival, they had looked at our ages and written, 'Three grumpy old men', on the paper, but admitted that they'd had more fun with us than they'd had for years. I'd bought myself a khaki shirt, long khaki 'shorts' and a pith helmet. The safari staff struggled to hide their contempt when they first saw me. We were each given our own tent but only had running water and electricity for ten minutes when we got up and when we went to bed. The tents were pitched on the banks of the Zambezi and although they were only ten yards apart, you couldn't see the next tent because the bush was so thick. My companions were a bit quicker than me and made sure that I had the tent furthest into the jungle and furthest from the centre of the camp.

I shall never forget that first night in the tent. You lay there in total darkness, but all about you was the nocturnal noise of African wildlife. You could hear insects that sounded as big as large birds. It was probably the only night in my life when to say I never slept would be true. The noise of lions roaring was never far away and we had to wear whistles around our necks in case we needed help from the armed night guards. The most dangerous animals were the hippos. They come onto the banks to feed at night and you could hear them crashing about in the undergrowth. They have a sort of roar which sounds a bit like a chainsaw being started up. I kept awake because it was all so scary.

But it was more scary than we even knew. There was a really nice lad at the camp. He was having a year out between school and university. Two or three weeks after we were there a lioness got him out of the tent and I don't think he was ever seen again. We were in a national park which meant that vehicles could not go off the tracks and so we walked miles. We arrived at midday, had some lunch, and set out in a truck, to see what was about. What was about was a bull elephant about 100 yards from camp. He was browsing in some bushes. We left the truck and walked closer to him. The rangers said, 'If he charges, stand your ground'. We got about 30 yards from the elephant who suddenly got wind of us and came out of the bushes acting all aggressive. He made three or four charges at us. I decided I was off. I thought to myself, I'm a farmer, I know more about animals than these others, he is going to attack. I looked over my shoulder at the truck and decided that there was a straight line between elephant, spectators and truck. 'If I run now the elephant will get to all the others before he gets to me,' I thought. I was just going to make my dash for freedom when a big hand clamped on my shoulder. 'Stay where you are.' So we stood our ground and after a bit more aggressive posturing, the elephant wandered off. There was no loss of face for humans or elephant, but there nearly was. Another day we were out walking in a grassy area and we came upon a large pack of wild dogs hunting. We lay in the grass and they came right up to us and sniffed at our feet. I wasn't a bit scared, I've always liked dogs, liked them more than elephants.

And that is my tale of two whistles.

★★★

In the pub on Sunday night, there's only five of us hardy souls in there and we are talking about the weather! I'm told that we had to throw away 3,000 litres of milk because the lorry couldn't get through. This is news to me. We are on night collection and the lorries were not sent out on one night, but we have room in our tank for two days' milk and it was all collected next day. I don't tell anyone that. If you are getting free sympathy, why not milk it!

31 MARCH 2018

We had not had a 'real' winter for years, so just to remind us what a real winter is like, nature sent us one. It was so much worse because nature sent a bad winter at the beginning of March and not in January, which is the proper time for winter. Farmers came out of it all OK. The media was dominated by snow stories and time and again farmers were praised for their work, clearing minor roads so that isolated hamlets and homes were not cut off more than was avoidable. I know that some farmers are contracted to put snow ploughs on their tractors and to try to keep minor roads clear whilst the authorities concentrate on main routes, but lots of farmers turned out voluntarily, to clear snow drifts and the like. One of the difficulties with narrow lanes full of snow is that there is no room to 'plough' it out of the way and it needs to be put over the hedge whence it came. Farmers are much better equipped to do this than they were 20 or so years ago. Most of us now have purpose-built loading shovels with telescopic booms that can lift a big bucket full of snow and put it back over a hedge or fence. These are magical machines. They rarely go wrong whilst they are under warranty, but after that, watch out. If they are approached by a mechanic bearing spanners and a laptop, several thousand pounds will subsequently disappear from your bank account!

I remember many years ago, we had a big snow and there was an elderly lady who wasn't well living in an isolated cottage on the top of a high hill. She needed the district nurse to give her her medication and put her to bed comfortably for the night. You could only get up there by Land Rover so every night for over a week, I would drive to pick up the nurse and take her to her patient, wait for her, and then take her home. It used to take about two hours. The patient's family and the nurse were so profuse in their thanks that it almost became embarrassing. I just saw it as a job that needed doing,

I could do it, so I just got on and did it. Which is what most busy people including farmers do all the time. So if you are stuck behind a tractor this summer, remember there are times in the winter when you are glad to see them. You can't have it both ways.

★★★

I'm at the gym, I'm on the exercise bike. There's a lady on the bike next to me who is talking to another lady who is standing close by. They are talking about farmers. I can tell by their accents that they are not from around here. At some point in their lives, they 'escaped to the country', a concept that has much to answer for. 'Farmers will ruin the countryside around here.' Around here is very beautiful. There are trees and hedges everywhere, all planted by farmers and foresters.

They are talking about hedges. They think that farmers should be banned from cutting hedges. Their idea is that hedges should be left to grow unchecked. This illustrates, to me, that they don't have a clue what they are talking about. If you leave a hedge uncut, in the fullness of time you will end up with a line of trees. Hedges were planted to keep livestock in a field, and to provide a wind break and shelter for those animals. If you allow hedges to grow unchecked they will do neither of these functions. Their argument is that if the hedges were left to grow unchecked they would bear more berries and food for the little birds.

On my farm, we are in a scheme that only allows us to cut hedges once every three years. I have my doubts about the benefits of this. The biggest danger to small birds around here are the bigger birds that predate them. If a hedge is short and dense, eggs and fledglings are safer than they are in an open straggly hedge. When I'm on the tractor in the spring I see this corvid hedgerow predation going on all about me.

But in the gym I don't contribute to the conversation. Twenty years ago I would have, but I have learnt that these people are so sure that they are right that there's no point. I move off to the treadmill. I do most of my winter walking on the treadmill. I am yet to find a treadmill that is covered with the mud, stones, snow and ice that is to be found walking about our yard. One of the instructors walks past, she is married to my nephew which makes her a sort of auntie. 'You OK on that treadmill Roger?' 'Fine thanks.' 'Well done.' Well I should be OK on a treadmill. Been on one all my life.

★★★

My daughter had a man stay for bed and breakfast last week. After he had gone she is putting clean linen on the bed and she discovers half a portion of fish and chips under the pillow. They are not wrapped up tidy, they are half eaten and just lying there, wide open. You couldn't make it up could you?

7 April 2018

For most farmers who keep sheep around here, the traditional time for lambing is March. The theory is that if you get all your lambs born by April, your ewes will milk well on April grass and you lambs will thrive. Of course you have no way of knowing what the weather will be like when you put your ewes to the tup. Once the tups go in the die is cast. It will not have escaped everyone's notice that March this year has not been a good time to have ewes lambing. If, you example, your preferred lambing date is 1st March, there will probably be lambs arriving a week before that. The week before lambing can test the resolve of the most dedicated shepherd. If any ewe is going to abort dead lambs, it will often occur during this week. The live lambs that are born are in theory a bit premature, so they will take just a bit more looking after. If the weather is mild, most ewes are lambed indoors, and after two or three days they are moved outside on to grass. If it's really mild they can go outside the day they are born. If the weather is terrible, as it has been twice this year in March, and you have to keep ewes and lambs inside just as long as you can, all sorts of problems can occur. Lambs lose their mothers, ewes lose their lambs and if a ewe loses sight of her lamb for just a short while, they can't always be successfully reunited, especially, as is normally the case if the ewe has two lambs and is quite happy to devote her care to the one she has kept by her side. Instead of being able to move ewes and lambs outside in an orderly fashion, your system backs up and everything becomes overcrowded and chaos quickly follows.

The sort of snow that has been falling has made matters much worse. We have all had the fine sort of snow. Even if you are not a sheep farmer, you will have seen the effect of high winds and fine snow. It blows off fields and fills up roads and lanes. The sheep farmer might have chosen a perfectly good shed to lamb his ewes in but this sort of snow will find its way in anywhere. It will get through ventilation ridges in buildings, it will get in through gaps in the eaves, it will get in through keyholes. As a result there has often been as much snow in the sheds as there is outside. This eventually melts making the straw wet and new-born lambs damp and cold. A new-born lamb is at its most vulnerable until it 'dries off'. It's difficult to dry off if you happen to be covered in snow.

The obvious solution is to have pens that will dry these lambs but if the weather is at its worst and you have ten such pens available, you can bet you will have seventeen ewes to lamb. That's how things usually work. I have met three different sheep farmers recently. I know them to be conscientious in the care of their stock and they have worked endlessly throughout the bad weather. Each one has told me that they have probably lost over fifty lambs. They have used the number of 50 as a guess. I know shepherds well enough to know that they are only guessing, they will not have counted the dead lambs because they didn't want to know the real answer. All they could do is do their best for each lamb and that is what they did. I called to see my daughter one day in the snow. Their farmyard is laid out so that you drive through the farm buildings to get to their house, buildings which have evolved over the years. As I left, my daughter went off to bottle feed some lambs. It wasn't actually snowing but she went off down the road in a blizzard of snow that was being blown off the fields and roofs. It was so bad she soon disappeared from sight. I've seen farmer's wives in adverse conditions before. They call it living the dream.

★★★

I've had a birthday this week. My wife says she hasn't bought me a birthday card because I haven't yet opened the Christmas card she bought me. This is very true. Christmas cards have gone right off my agenda. I haven't sent one for years. A few years ago I was sending about 70 and my wife was sending over 100. This was getting out of hand and so I stopped altogether. Now I phone about twenty friends in the run-up to Christmas and I give the money I used to spend on cards and stamps to a children's charity, and it feels a much better way of doing things.

My son was way ahead of me on this. Years ago I was looking through the chaos in the back of his van for a particular spanner. I found a box of Christmas cards, all stamped and addressed. It was August. I tell my wife that there is no need to buy me a birthday card and that she can give me the Christmas card instead. She likes this idea and it puts her in a good mood. But she can't find the Christmas card so she is soon back to normal again. The family clubbed together and bought me a new armchair. I can remember a time when they clubbed together to buy me new rugby boots. Every picture tells a story.

14 April 2018

Truth be told, I have been about the farm less this year than I usually do. We were about four inches down on our average rainfall but nature, as it usually does, has been playing catch-up. The ground has been saturated, I don't think I've ever known it so wet in the early part of the year. As I need the truck to get about anyway it would make a mess on the grass with its wheel marks, something I can't bear. I can't bear it if others do it, and I can hardly criticise them if I do it myself. The worst case scenario would be to get stuck and have to phone for help. The eye-rolling of the person who came to pull you out would be spectacular. We have one field that is quite long and narrow and slopes down to the wood, we call it sideland, so to cross it in the truck you are driving across the slope. One part of the journey crosses a particularly steep bit so it's best to keep your wits about you and keep tight to the top fence. One wet day, early in the year, I didn't do either: I wasn't concentrating and I didn't keep up tight to the fence. I had an old Discovery at the time, (as good on wet going as you can get), and 'she' set off sideways, down the field to the wood. It's a funny old feeling, going sideways down a field. You are totally out of control. Try to drive out of your trouble and it only goes faster. It seemed to take an age to get down the field and your main hope is that you don't hit a rut and turn over. 'She' didn't turn over, and nestled into the fence at the bottom, rather than hit it too hard. I had to phone for a tractor to pull me out and the driver didn't roll his eyes at me that day because it was so slippery he could well have joined me in the fence.

There's a stone track that we use to access the other fields but this is at right angles to the wind and was blocked for days with spectacular snow drifts. The few times I have managed to get up there, I have only seen one hare. It's always within about 200 yards of the same place, so I think it's the same one. This is devastating. At one time, about three years

ago, I could take people up there and there would be around
ten hares in each field. The hares would be so preoccupied
with the business of producing even more hares, you could
park in the middle of the field and just watch them for ages.
If there is only one hare left up there it will have just its own
shadow to box with this year. It's all very sad, but there only
seems me bothered about it. It's all down to hare coursers and
the local wildlife 'lovers' who told the world, via Facebook,
that there were a lot of hares up there. Thanks for that.

One day, when I did get up there, I let the dog, Gomer,
out for his exercise. He found the hare and set off in pursuit.
Gomer is not built for hare chasing. He has turned into quite
a big dog with very short legs. If I describe him as 'sturdy', it's
being kind. His body is quite large, probably because he eats
a round of toast and marmite for breakfast every day. I don't
think it's the toast or marmite that has made him grow but
probably the thick layer of butter that lies in between the two.
Most people around here buy me a stick of rock if they go
away somewhere. Gomer has half of this and that's probably
not helping. He is black all over with white on his chest; he has
a lot of wiry hair which owe its origins to the Border terrier
in his ancestry somewhere. He has something of the badger
about him. I wouldn't be without him for the world. He is my
constant companion, he has his head on my feet as I write this
now. He just loves it when I take him for an adventure in the
truck and he stands in the back and looks between the front
seats and whimpers in delight and excitement, I just wish he
wouldn't lick my ear. The hare and the dog have done a lap of
honour around the field and the dog didn't get anywhere near,
even though he cut the corners. The dog cuts the last corner
and heads straight for the truck – he knows when he is beaten.
The hare sits about 100 yards away and looks as perplexed as
a hare can look. It adjusts its whiskers, it's probably used to
being chased by greyhounds and lurchers, so being chased by

a slow terrier with its tongue hanging out is a new experience.

What of the hares? If there is only one left, and there could be, it will probably seek out another from somewhere or one will come and join it, that's how things work. Will numbers recover? I hope so but we are starting at a very low base. The only plus I can see is that only one hare is hardly worthy of the attention of the hare coursers. It's a very tentative plus because as sure as you can be, they will find some other hares to terrorise on someone else's fields.

21 APRIL 2018

For people of my age, the gym phenomenon is a bit strange. People paying money for repetitive exercise seems very odd. This is probably because those of us, of our age, who worked on farms had plenty of repetitive exercise in our daily lives. I can remember helping my father-in-law with his hay harvest; he had 150 acres and I had 30. Two of us would go out and load about six trailers through the day and I pitched most of the bales by hand. A gang of us would unload those trailers first thing next day and the trailers would all be empty for us two to start again. Later in the year there would be 100 acres of corn to harvest and that would all be in two hundred weight bags that the combine would leave on the ground. Carting the straw bales are lighter than hay and a lot lighter than two hundred-weight sacks of corn. No wonder we were quite strong.

There were about 12 farmers in the rugby team I played for and if the ball ended up in what is called a maul, very few teams could get it off us. In my time I have owned my own exercise bike and my own rowing machine. I preferred the rowing machine because you can wind more 'grunt' into a rowing machine. I lent the bike to someone, who denies it, so I suspect that ended up on eBay and I think my son has the rowing machine. Rowing machines or exercise bike, used in the home, have one thing in common – they are both deadly boring. At least now I go to the gym twice a week. They are still boring but you have other people to watch, which can be a welcome distraction.

When I think of repetitive exercise I remember with awe a man who used to work for me. He was retired when he worked for me but when he was younger he had been a lorry driver and one of his regular jobs was to haul basic slag from the steel works in Port Talbot. Basic slag was a bi-product of the steel industry, it is a dense black powder rich in phosphates and all farmers used it a lot because phosphate enhances the growth of legumes like clover. The downside is that it used to be sold in one hundred-weight paper bags, like bags of cement, and you used to get filthy handling it. I've not seen it advertised for some time, wonder where that went to? Jack told me that he had to back his artic up to an elevator. Lorries were not so big then but I bet he was carrying 20 tons. The bags of slag would arrive at shoulder height and he had to carry them the length of the lorry, stack them and be back at the elevator before the next bag arrived. If the bag left the elevator it was yours so if you weren't there to catch it, it probably burst but still had to be paid for. As your load was filled, you didn't have so far to carry the bags and it got a bit easier but the load still had to be sheeted and it all had to be unloaded by hand when it eventually got to the farm.

My own exploits with hay bales are as nothing compared with Jack's bags of slag. Handling hay bales by hand soon declined as mechanisation moved on apace in the late1960s and early 1970s. I think the biggest difference was the move from hay to silage. Silage was easier to mechanise and it was less at risk to the vagaries of the weather.

Jack was a hard man, even when he was in his 70s. During the war he had been a farm worker and there were five of them working on the farm and the army turned up one day and said one of them had to join up. Jack was the only single man there so he volunteered. He hated his basic training. One day, at parade, they said 'Step forward if you want to earn an extra two shillings and ten-pence a week?' Jack thought that anything had got to be better than this, so he stepped forward. A few weeks later he was jumping out of a plane over Arnhem. He was holed up for three days in a wood. The wood was shelled consistently throughout that time. Jack had a bad stammer. 'I didn't stammer before I went into that b b b Bloody wood.' After three days he reckons there wasn't a tree left standing and the third night he slipped into the river and swam downstream for several miles until he was back behind allied lines. I bet he never went to the gym.

★★★

There's usually two ways of looking at things. On *Countryfile* last night we were told that 1% of the population is now vegan. Turn this around and you could say that 99% of us aren't. Everything in is relative. Someone told me the other day that the reason vegans make so much noise is that their diet doesn't agree with them.

28 April 2018

I finally paid for our Christmas turkey last night. I never found out how much it cost, I wasn't told, but I took the good friends who gave it to us out for a meal. They're good friends of ours and that was a very pleasant way of paying for a Christmas dinner. I hadn't been to this restaurant before; we sat down in front of a very good fire to look at the menu. There were three very fine settees arranged around the fire. The only criteria on which a settee should be judged is its suitability for sleeping on and these were gold medal standard. Sharing the fire with us was the most beautiful young tri-coloured corgi bitch. When the landlady came to take our order we talked about corgis and our love of the breed. We were so taken with this bitch that both my wife and I were thinking perhaps we should stretch to another. Then we asked the big question. How much did you pay for her? £1,200! That is just too much of a stretch.

★★★

I got up the track to the top field yesterday. I gave the dog his usual run at the very top. There's 14 ewes up there and one of them, a black ewe, has had two black lambs in the night. They were all OK, which is good. None of them is mine, which is not so good. Gomer goes close enough to put them back through my neighbour's fence, whence they came, but I know they will soon be back. I get the dog back into the truck, he is still a bit confused by the black lambs, they look so much like him, he is not sure why they won't play with him.

I go into the next field where there have been 12 lapwings, but I can only see three today. I park up and watch them. They are wheeling about, as only lapwings can, over some stubble we left over winter. Adjacent to them are about five acres we left in wild bird food mix and next to that are four acres we left specifically for lapwings. The idea is that you drill a crop, a root mix to provide cover for the birds, but you leave bare patches within the crop, which you call scrapes, that the birds can easily land in. Both the wild bird crop and the lapwing crops have been beaten down by the weight of the snow but we can't do anything about that, we are where we are. But there's not just me watching the lapwings. 50 yards away to my left, sitting on a fence, are four carrion crows. They are not watching me, they are watching the lapwings, nothing new there then. It's early in the year and spring is forecast to arrive next week but there might just be an early lapwing for a carrion crow breakfast.

★★★

I was writing last week about the repetitive work we used to do on farms, years ago, especially handling small hay bales. I particularly remember when I was in my late teens helping a good friend of mine carting hay bales from a field about three miles from his farm. We had a tractor and trailer each and had to load the bales by hand. We fetched two loads in the morning and two in the afternoon. We had our tea and decided there was still enough daylight to fetch two more. We went and put the two loads on, by which time it was getting towards twilight. We started for home but there was a pub just along the road and you have to stop and try one, don't you? After all, we had worked hard all day.

When we came out it was darkish. We each had a little grey Fergie tractor and only one had any lights and they were only at the front. But we were resourceful in those days, resourceful and just a little ingenious. Just up the road were some road works. Do you remember, years ago, they used to surround road works with these red oil lamps with hooked handles on the top? We drove as far as the road works, 'borrowed' two oil lamps and hung them on the back of my trailer. It all seemed quite logical and reasonable.

We set off tight together – he drove the first tractor the one with the lights on the front and I drove behind him with the trailer with the red oil lamps at the rear. We were safely illuminated front and rear. There was, however, one factor we hadn't allowed for. I can't remember if I had a bigger trailer than he did and therefore more bales, but his tractor was a lot faster than mine. By the time we had gone a quarter of a mile he was a hundred yards in front of me! He had no way of knowing what was happening because he couldn't see me because I didn't have any front lights; he had a load of bales behind him so he couldn't see behind him and wing mirrors on tractors were still light years away. I drove the last two miles in splendid darkness.

If you were caught doing something like that these days goodness knows what a catalogue of misdemeanours they would contrive. They would probably start with theft and end with dangerous driving with several other transgressions in between. Probably would have ended up in a young offenders' facility. Except in those days, we called it Borstal.

5 MAY 2018

I'm driving home from the pub lateish one night and about half a mile from where I live there are two hares on the road. This is good because it's one more than I have seen in my fields thus far this year. What is not so good is that hares are notoriously bad at road sense. Sometimes they will travel quite long distances on the road in front of you. They will zig zag about so sometimes it is tempting to try to overtake them. But it's best not to as they will zig onto a grass verge and just as you think it's fine to overtake, they will zag back out and right under your wheels. If you put any value on the life of a hare, and you should, give them space and time if they are running on the road in front of you, day or night.

Now that the ground is drying up and we are getting on with some tractor work, word comes in that we don't just have one hare, we have several. We don't have the abundance of hares that we used to have, but several is a big improvement on one. There is still a long way to go for numbers to recover to what we had before and there are plenty of challenges ahead in the form of predation and I expect the hare coursers will be about come harvest time, but let's hope not.

★★★

When we moved here, all those years ago, we had a fair bit of work to do within the house. What is now our kitchen was a sort of scullery with a wash boiler and a baking oven. If I knew what I know now, we would have kept some of these in place and made features on them. There weren't any taps but there was a stone sink with a hand pump over it with a wooden handle. On good days, with a bit of effort, you could sometimes get water out of it. There was such a gap under the door that, if it snowed the sort of fine snow we have had this year, it would blow under the door and form drifts right across the room. I have to think where everything was because it's all so long gone now. But I remember so well that there was a board in the corner that had about six little bells on it. At sometime, they would have been connected to different rooms in the house and would have been used to summon the servants. I quite fancy the idea of sitting in my armchair and pulling a cord and ordering a cup of tea. Knowing me, I probably fancied the same thing all those years ago and probably passed a remark to that effect. We were newly married then so there were markers to set down. When we got around to working on the kitchen my wife made sure that the board with the bells on was one of the first things out of the door. I've regretted that ever since. It would have made a nice feature. If we had got all the bells working, and whether I could have used them to get a cup of tea, I doubt very much.

12 May 2018

This week on the news it was the turn of organisations that wanted to highlight the plight of unwanted horses. I saw some harrowing footage on the TV lunchtime news. Particularly disturbing is the dumping of horses that need veterinary attention because the owner can't or won't pay for that treatment. Immediately after lunch and I was out and about in the truck and listened to a radio phone-in on the same subject. A farmer phoned in to say that he was going around his farm and saw a plastic sheet in his field, under which he found two dead horses. Someone phoned in to say that they rented a field for their two horses and people kept dropping off unwanted horses; there were so many that they had to get the RSPCA to feed them, they ended up with 75! Apparently you can get, 'buy one get one free' with horses, buy a mare and get last year's foal for nothing. There are free horses on social media, kittens are dearer than horses! Then a man phones in and says he has the answer. He says he locates a free horse on social media then he sends it for proper slaughter, has it cut up, puts it in the freezer and eats it. You could immediately tell that everyone, interviewer and listeners were aghast at this story. It was clear that amidst all the horrific tales of cruelty and neglect, the concept of eating horses was by far the worst. But the man had a point. If a species, however much it is loved, has no monetary value, people are reluctant to spend money on it. Whether it's food or vet, they will dump the horse somewhere else rather than spend any money. It's mostly because they don't have enough money. If the horse is worth nothing and you have to spend £250 on it at the vet, and it's still worth nothing afterwards, they don't bother. Some years ago, Princess Anne suggested that if horses were eaten it would put value on them and they would be less likely to be neglected. Her idea then received about as much support as the man on the radio did.

★★★

Hardly a day goes by but we don't hear a plea for more money for the NHS. I find this just a bit irritating because I am always left wondering: just how much of the money they presently get, do they waste? I'll explain. Thus far in my life I've been very lucky, with my health. Because I've been lucky, I've not had to take much in the way of medication, in fact 'pills' have always been a very last resort. I now find that I have to take four prescription pills a day, as sure a sign of aging as there is. The first pill is a statin to reduce my cholesterol. My cholesterol has always been well below average, but 'they' tell me that some of my cholesterol is of a bad sort so statins will bring that down. Besides, everyone else takes statins, according to the newspapers. I suspect that it will only be a matter of time before they put statins in the water supply so everyone is on them, very much as we medicate our chickens.

Next on my list of pills is one for my heart. When I went for my last annual check-up (which was three years after the previous one) they said that my heart was beating too fast so they put me on beta blockers. Personally I thought it was more to do with the steep steps up to the surgery, but what do I know? But your heart is serious stuff so I check it twice a week on the exercise bike at the gym. These bikes have digital displays which show your heart rate. The one bike says my heart is beating at around 180. The other bike says it stopped beating some time ago. But if you take the average of the two, it's just about right. That's two of my four pills accounted for.

Don't you hate it when someone only tells you just half a story? I take the other two for issues, down below, in the water works department. On a need to know basis, that's all you need to know. That's four pills a day, regularly, and I have a repeat prescription so that I don't have to bother my GP. Trouble is that the repeat prescription gives me two months' supply of three of the pills and one month's supply of the heart pills. I've told the doctor and the chemist about this but nothing happens. I think that the heart pills are the most important ones, so at the moment, if I want to get them, I end up with twice as many as I need of the others.

How many times is this sort of error repeated throughout the country? What if it is antibiotics that are over-prescribed? If it is, and it easily could be, it's no wonder that antibiotic resistance is such a problem. Despite my best efforts, I am accumulating a stockpile of unused pills. Pity to waste them: I sense a commercial opportunity here. There could be a chance to sell them on. What about 'The Farmyard Pharmacy?'

19 MAY 2018

I warn you, I'm not happy, not happy at all. We were ploughing some stubble and found two lapwing nests. In each nest were four chicks. We ploughed up to the chicks, stopped operations, and gently coaxed the chicks onto the fresh ploughing. This wasn't the easiest of jobs and took over an hour but we eventually had the chicks settled on the fresh ploughing. They ended up in indentations in the soil so they were less visible than they were previously and their mothers were soon back brooding them. What's not to be happy about? I'll tell you what. The lapwings were sharing the field with ten kites, 25 buzzards and a host of carrion crows and magpies. What chance of survival do those chicks have? I would say none. You would be forgiven for thinking that things can't get any worse but they can. A millionaire who describes himself as an environmentalist is on the Ministry for Environment board of advisors. Amongst his aims is the reintroduction of wildcats to the countryside; he has offered to pay for this himself.

Wildcats exist in Scotland and the biggest threat to their survival is their inclination to breed with ordinary feral cats. It erodes their gene pool and you lose the pure wild cats and after a few years you would end up with feral cats that are bigger and nastier than the ones we have now. Even I know that. This person is reported to have said, 'Find me someone who wouldn't like to see wildcats restored to the British countryside.' Well here's one for a start and I don't expect lapwings and other ground nesting birds will be too pleased about it either. Call me naive but I suspect that wildcats would eat the eggs and young of ground nesting birds and their decline will be accelerated.

How someone with such a minimal understanding of reality became an advisor is beyond belief.

★★★

Whilst technology continues on its amazing march forward, I sometimes think that we take it for granted. I readily admit that much of it has left me behind. I still marvel at the sat nav. I left my first one attached to my windscreen whilst at a rugby match in Cardiff and someone swapped it for a rock, which to be fair, they left on the front seat. I've still got the rock, I kept it as a souvenir and put it in the garden. My point is that if my parents were still alive, can you imagine explaining to people of their age that you could easily buy a device that would direct you accurately around anywhere. They simply wouldn't believe you. Especially if you told them it would give you the names of all the side roads you passed as you drove along a main road. I don't use mine very often. If I am travelling far I look at a map and use the sat nav for the last few miles to help me find wherever it is that I am going. I sense that those who use sat navs all the time don't really know where they've been.

★★★

Nowhere do you see more trends than in farming. I've often said that if your farming remains the same, you will be a pioneer for ten years, you will be the same as everyone else for ten years, you will be hopelessly out of date for ten years, but not to worry, next year you will be at the forefront, a pioneer again. This year 'they' want us to take about six cuts of silage instead of the dairy farmers normal three. This means cutting grass every three or four weeks and takes no account of a wet week. We will stick with three. Arable farmers are encouraged not to plough but to drill into what was left by the last crop: this is called 'min till'. It was quite popular around here 30 years ago (that 30 year cycle again), and lots of farmers bought big robust drills that drilled into the stubbles. Better crops were being grown on land that was ploughed conventionally and the practice lasted about ten years. No one wanted the redundant big drills and they found themselves in the scrap yard or the nettles.

26 MAY 2018

One of the fitness instructors at the gym is married to my nephew and she lives next door, so I know her quite well on two counts.

Over half of the people at the gym, when I am there, are referred there by their local GP for reasons of mobility or excess weight - so she is mostly helping them with their exercises. But sometimes, if she is not too busy with people, she can be seen in her Marigolds, giving the exercise kit a wipe over with a wet cloth, all the time chatting away to whoever is there and keeping an eye on them in case anyone needs help.

She is getting towards the end of her shift so she comes across for a chat. I'm on my last exercise on a bike, it's a very comfortable bike with a backrest on the saddle so I can relax and chat as well. I always tease her about her cleaning role and she always teases me because this is the bike that says my heart is beating too fast.

She is off now with her bucket but she shows me a polythene bag that is full of chewing gum that she has removed from different apparatus. What a filthy nation we have become.

I suspect the young; the only sticky stuff the older ones are likely to put in their mouths is to put their false teeth in. The sort of people who put chewing gum under the seat of equipment at the gym are the sort of people who think nothing of throwing fast food containers out of car windows, and society is knee-deep in that sort of waste.

★★★

Stephen, who works with us, calls in for a cup of tea. He's been away for nearly three days – he's been with a local contractor in a silage gang (we put a tractor and rake into the gang). He tells me how things went. He doesn't tell me things like how many cows they have or how much milk they send off.

What he does tell me is, in a way, more interesting. They were working at just one farm and they had to leave uncut five acres in five different patches because there were curlews nesting there. There were five pairs of curlews nesting there last year; they left the grass uncut but they didn't rear a single chick. Badgers, foxes, kites and buzzards had the lot.

This year the curlews' eggs are taken away and replaced with hens' eggs, (to keep the curlews laying) and the curlews' eggs will be incubated and the chicks reared artificially.

The farmer is quite happy to co-operate in all this. The sound of a curlew as it flies off is one of the most joyous sounds of the countryside. While so-called environmentalists clamour to protect predators, the farmer is involved in something far more positive, something that will make a real difference.

★★★

We were discussing holidays in the pub last night. There are women there that are going on a mini three-day cruise to France this week. This will be their third break thus far this year. The journey to Southampton by road will be longer than the hour they, and 2,000 others, will make on the ship!

We have nothing planned for this year. I did well last year. I went to Suffolk, Exmoor and Ireland. It's lovely around here in the summer, but I do enjoy travelling and seeing new places. One of the women in the pub went to Ireland with us last year and still has painful memories of it. We went to Kilarney and one day we went to the Gap of Dunloe, which is a spectacular road that goes up a pass between two mountain ranges. You can drive through OK in a car but that's not entering into the spirit of an Irish holiday.

There's a sign that says, 'No cars beyond this point,' and if you want to go further they like you to go on horseback or on pony and trap. This woman, who is with us, asks how much it costs to go in the trap. '20 euros'. 'How much on a horse?' '10 euros'. She says she will go on the horse. I go in the trap. I'm too old to fall off a horse, especially one with a cardboard saddle and a bridle made of baler twine. I'm sitting next to the owner of the trap and soon build up a good rapport with him. The Irish are ten out of ten when it comes to building rapport. I tell him I'm a farmer and have 160 dairy cows, and he's really interested. He tells me he has two traps and five horses. There is no doubt in my mind at all that his five horses make more profit than my 160 cows.

When we get back, the woman goes to pay for her ride on the horse. Turns out that it wasn't ten euros for the ride, it was ten more than riding in the trap, which made it 30 euros. The trouble was she paid him with a 50 euro note. Once he had that note in his hand it was his prisoner and there was no negotiating to be done. The experience still rankles with my friend and one mention of Ireland and she goes on endlessly about it. She reckons she will go back to Kilarney just to try to get 20 euros back, which as long shots go, has to be a very long shot indeed.

2 JUNE 2018

I'm mowing the lawn and our two cherry blossom trees are in full flower. They are a picture. Ours are a bit later than most places because we are up in the hills and you don't have to go far from home in the spring to see trees in full flower a month before ours. The biggest problem always seems to be that just as soon as they are in full flower we get high winds that blow the blossom off and so their beauty is short-lived. There's a stiff breeze blowing now and as I drive the mower past the trees I am driving amongst all this pink blossom. My Dad planted the trees when we moved here and they remind me of him.

There's another reminder in the kitchen. He made us a box to cover up the electricity meters and the fuse boxes. He was a better gardener than he was a carpenter and it is not difficult to find faults in his box. Over the years various trades people have pointed this out and offered to replace it with something 'tidy'. Like the trees, I don't think the box will last forever but it is OK for now. The breeze picks up in strength and I drive through even more pink petals. Perhaps it's not pink blossom, perhaps it's radio-active snow. Nothing would surprise me these days.

★★★

For about 12 years, my lawn has been mole-free. But not anymore it isn't. First there was only one mole hill and so I thought there was only one mole. But now when I cut the lawn there are about ten mole hills and, because we have quite a lot of lawn, the hills are dotted about all over the place so I assume there are several moles at work. I'm not a great gardener but I like the lawn cut tidy. Cutting the lawn is my job and tidy is the order of the day. I always say that the views from our garden are so spectacular in every direction, there's no need to keep the garden tidy because everyone is looking at the view not the garden. Most people seem to agree with me; as far as I know the only one who doesn't is my wife.

Apart from being unsightly and thus spoiling my tidy intentions, they, the mole hills, are no big deal. I don't pick up the grass but leave it behind, and I cut the grass often so that I don't leave a lot of cut grass in my wake. At this time of year I cut it every three or four days. We have had a ride-on mower for years so when I come to a mole hill I just plough right through it and the soil is nicely scattered by the blades. My son, on the other hand, whose lawn I also cut, has been plagued by moles for years but he's never seemed to be bothered about it. As far as I can make out, there's only one mole there this year. My conclusion is that the others have all died of old age.

Patience, apparently, is the thing.

9 JUNE 2018

I've got this bank account where my pension and other bits and pieces of money go, as opposed to the farm account. The branch is ten miles away and I've just had a letter to say it is closing. As I have only been there six months (and they moved me there because my branch six miles away also closed) I could feel a bit indignant, but I don't. I miss the original one because the cash point was handy, but life goes on. The branch where the farm bank account is, is also closing but that is 60 miles away and I'm not bothered where that is. Soon our world will be full of empty banks, monuments to internet banking.

Here's something in the paper: it says you shouldn't sleep next to your mobile phone as it will affect your sleep patterns. I always sleep next to mine as I use its alarm function. I text my daughter, 'Get me a cheap simple alarm clock.' I don't do internet shopping, I use her, so I'm just as culpable. I shall need some new 'going out' trousers before long. I always wear navy blue trousers from Marks and Spencer, always have. When the time comes she will get those as well, as we are discovering, it is easier than shopping. So I am as much to blame for all those stores closing as anyone else. I don't think I've been in a shop for two years and that was a charity shop. The nearest I go to shopping is when I pay for diesel but I pay for that by the door, so I don't count that.

Two days later my daughter turns up with a tiny alarm clock. 'What do you want that for, you always use your phone.' So, like a worldly parent, I explain about interrupted sleep patterns. And she, like a worldly child, says 'I think that only applies to modern phones with touch screen access to apps and the internet, not to phones like yours.' The 'phones like yours' bit is patronising but I ignore it. I've got my alarm clock next to my bed, where it should be. But I haven't a clue how to switch my phone off. Not that I'm admitting that to anyone.

***

We have finished our first cut silage so I am driving around the outside of the cleared fields just to have a look. I loose the dog out for his run. The first field I go on is a big field, over 40 acres, so if I take him all around that he will have a good run. At the bottom side of this field is what we call a six metre margin which we leave uncut. These margins are much loved by wildlife enthusiasts, who call them wildlife corridors. If you go on uphill, the margin goes to several pieces of woodland and if you go downhill the margin connects up with other margins in other fields so that in effect we have margins the length of the farm. It is intersected twice by the road but because there is a stream running parallel to the margins, wildlife can cross under the road via culverts, just as long as they don't mind getting their feet wet.

I get paid for establishing these margins, I wouldn't pretend otherwise, but I don't have to do it. I do it because enhancing wildlife is important to me. Because the margins are uncut throughout the year, the grasses in them go to seed and thus provide valuable food for the birds during the winter to come.

Enough of this, there is drama afoot. The dog Gomer is running about ten yards in front of the truck and about ten yards in front of him, a fully grown hare bursts from cover, out of the margin, and Gomer sets off in hot pursuit. For every ten yards Gomer runs, the hare goes about 30, so it is hardly a coming together of equals, but Gomer is doing his best; he looks over his shoulder to see if I am watching him and the hare moves even further ahead. Fortunately there is a diversion at hand. There is a bit of a dogleg in the margin and as we go around that there are six mallard out on the field, three ducks and three drakes. They are close together and the hare runs right through the middle of the group. The dog is not dull and tries to pretend that it was the ducks he was after all the time. I don't know where these ducks came from, probably from a shoot in the area. Twenty yards away over the hedge amongst the trees there are two pools and they have set up home there but there is no sign of them breeding. Ducks reared for shoots soon become semi-domesticated and these only fly about 30 yards away before they come back down. The dog chases them several times, gets nowhere near them and soon gives up, exhausted. He climbs back over my lap into the truck. His look says, 'I could have caught those ducks but I knew they were out of season.' His look doesn't say anything about the indignity of chasing the hare in vain, which is the way with terriers. The ducks are busy feeding 30 yards away completely unperturbed. They have been chased into flight about five times but they have never been more than ten feet off the ground. Previous experience tells them that any higher than that, and they will be shot at.

16 June 2018

As the local banks close, the real challenge is for the staff that lose their jobs. They still have their commitments to family and to all that that entails. And they have to find another way of making ends meet. I can remember all this starting with the arrival of cashpoints. They are a familiar part of our lives now but I can remember when they first turned up. Once or twice a month I would go to my local branch to get some cash for my pocket money. I used to know all the girls behind the counter and I knew their families as well. I used to go in brandishing a cheque to cash and we'd have a bit of banter, but they would always say, as I was leaving, 'You don't need to cash a cheque in here anymore, you can get cash outside in the machine with your card.' And I would say 'The day that I don't come in here to cash a cheque, they won't need you to sit behind the counter, will they?' They would all laugh but I was right, wasn't I?

★★★

I can't remember a time when I didn't want to be a farmer. My mother wasn't impressed. She wanted me to get a job in a bank, 'You get a job in a bank and you'll have a job for life. If you work on a farm you'll work long hours and be out in all weathers.' She was right about that bit!

23 JUNE 2018

I don't go to church very often; weddings and funerals are about it really. The weddings are getting fewer and the number of funerals is increasing. One Christmas day, I had finished work quite early, the house was empty, everyone else was out distributing tidings of comfort and joy. I know, I thought, I'll go to church. I shan't make that mistake again! Everyone came up and said how surprised they were to see me there.

Because we all live in a small community, I've got a fair idea of what goes on at the church. For example, I know that a few years ago, they put a toilet in the vestry. This was a very contentious issue at the time but eventually they went ahead. I would be mortified if I couldn't manage my life better and I had to use it. I had always assumed that it was there for older people that were caught short, there being nowhere else in the vicinity that they could dash to. Not a bit of it. I've seen it used three times, twice by teenagers and once by a 20 something, and they have taken leisurely strolls down the length of the church and twice, as the background to a hymn, and once during a sermon, we have heard the sweet sound of a toilet flushing. You can't hear it flushing during a hymn but you can hear it between verses and it can be heard clearly during a sermon.

I get called for my tea. It's curry; she must be in a good mood. Before I can start she says she has a very serious question to ask me. I'm on full alert now, what could it be? I say if it's that serious, can I eat my tea first and she says yes. This is an important concession; it gives me time to try and guess what the question is and to think of a suitable answer. We've been getting on quite well lately so I don't think she wants to leave me but if it's a question perhaps she wants me to go. If I had to choose I would prefer, she went, it would be less disruptive. There are endless possibilities and I am only guessing, but I decide that whatever it is it will probably cost me money. I finish my meal, it's time to bite the bullet. 'Go on then!' 'Instead of buying me a birthday present, [August] and buying me a Christmas present, [December] will you buy me a new dishwasher now?' 'How old is the one you have?' I hate appliances becoming obsolete after a short life. '20 years!' That' s good, more than I thought. 'Yes, but only if you put a sign on it that says I paid for it.' 'OK!' Phew, could have been so much worse.

30 JUNE 2018

I've been using my alarm clock for three nights before I find out how to switch my phone off, and that was by accident. The mobile phone signal around here ebbs and flows like the tide and I often get texts when I am in the bedroom at the top of the house. That's how I discover that you can only switch it off when it is unlocked. Truth be told I think I am sleeping better with the phone off. Not that it's the alarm that first wakes me. My bedroom is right under the eaves and we always have a lot of martins nesting under the guttering. It's a good place for martins to nest because it's only 30 yards from the pond in the field which is quite handy if you need mud to build a nest.

I sleep with the window open and at the first light, almost before it's dawn, the martins start up. I can hear the chicks clamouring and I can hear the wings of the parents as they come and go. It's still more dark than light so I presume the parents are catching moths that are making their way home after a late night. This goes on for an hour then they go quiet and we all go back to sleep again. When they start up again it seems that I have only been asleep for five minutes but I am sure it's longer than that. I am well used to being woken up by rural noises and I've never minded, it's all part of the package.

★★★

We are at my daughters for a pre-Father's Day meal. She does farmhouse bed and breakfast like us and she has two guests for the weekend. The guests are a bit different to your normal guests in that they have brought four chickens with them to stay as well. The chickens arrive in pet carriers, two in each, and the guests bring with them a coop and run. The coop and run fold down into a flat pack for travelling but are soon erected and the chickens are quickly installed. I've never been in an Ikea store, I didn't know that they made chicken coops, but you live and learn. As the chickens don't come into the house and she doesn't have to feed them, my daughter lets them stay for free. The coop and run are placed in my daughter's hen yard where she has four chickens of her own and a drake. They all come across to inspect the visitors. The drake, who is wifeless at the moment, has romance on his mind, to the consternation of the visitors. But it takes all sorts to make a world, and isn't that just grand?

7 July 2018

My car needs a service, it also needs a couple of new tyres and it needs a wound on its front corner attending to. I've been waiting over a week for the car to go for its service, but it's not that simple. I'll explain. Thirty or so years ago I bought a second-hand car from a dealer but the car was full of faults and eventually they gave me my money back. This left me in the position where I could buy a car without having a part exchange to worry about. I was looking for a second-hand

Ford or Vauxhall when I see this very cheap Saab advertised. (Saab was prestigious in those days). The vendor lived 60 miles away so we met halfway and did a deal, and I have bought all the cars I have had since from him and he's become a good friend. All the family have bought cars off him and there's five cars in the family now. He doesn't have a garage and he doesn't have a showroom, he's a one-man band and works from home. He is a brilliant mechanic and never fails to diagnose faults correctly which as most of us know, can save a fortune.

I've booked my car in with him and been waiting over a week to meet him halfway. The procedure is that I meet him and he lends me something while he has mine. Most car traders do this, they call it a courtesy car, but his are different. In the past his only criteria would be to lend you something that was taxed but now this is not an issue for him. You never know what you will get as a loan. Over the years I've had jags and other luxury limousines, I've had all sorts of ordinary cars, I've had clapped out vans and once even had a motorhome.

I understand that, because he's a one-man band, he sometimes has to stay at home if someone is coming to see a car. My family say that I show my dealer friend infinite patience but that I have none for them. That's probably because he takes all my patience and there's none left for anyone else. My daughter calls him Lord Lucan, because he never turns up. He has just phoned to ask me to meet him, wonder if he'll be there and what he will lend me? I quite like an element of uncertainty and excitement in my life.

★★★

I've got this friend who deals in timber. Dealing in timber involves him in driving his eight-wheeler lorry about the countryside. He's driving down this narrow lane, they've not cut the verges around here yet, they've just tidied up the junctions to improve visibility. The banks along this narrow

lane are a profusion of cow parsley and other roadside plants
that overhang the lane and reduce its width. The growth is
touching the lorry at both sides so that in effect the lorry fills
the lane. He sees a cyclist approaching and so he stops. There's
a gateway about 30 yards in front of the cyclist so my timber
friend assumes the cyclist will pull in there, but the cyclist
ignores the gateway and rides right up to face the lorry. They
both sit there looking at each other for a minute, eventually
the cyclist comes around to the driver's window. He asks
'What are we going to do now?' My friend suggests that he
takes his bike back to the gateway. 'You should have stopped
there.' The cyclist is a bit belligerent, 'If you pull onto one
side I can cycle past.' My friend is amused by all this, which
is just as well because he can do belligerent along with the
best of them. He indicates that the lane is 'full of lorry' and
asks where he can possibly pull onto the side, repeating his
suggestion that bike and rider should go back to the gateway.
The cyclist says that if he will leave the lorry stationary he will
push the bike past.

You need a bit of luck to turn an ordinary story into a
good one. And here we are blessed with two pieces of good
luck. Firstly the cyclist was wearing shorts and secondly, on
the side he chose to push his bike past, there was a big clump
of nettles growing in the bank. My friend watches his progress
in his wing mirror, the cyclist goes quite steady until he gets
to the nettles and he pauses and then has to go for it. He gets
past the rear of the lorry, the bike is flung against the bank
and as my friend drives away, he can see the cyclist frantically
rubbing his legs hopping from one foot to the other, which are
presumably covered in nettle stings. Living in the countryside
can be tough but occasionally little incidents happen that help
you along the way.

14 JULY 2018

We were on second cut silage this week, we were chopping it to put it in a clamp. We had to abandon that because the grass became too dry to go through the machine. I've never heard of that before but the driver says it can happen. There's about 20 acres still to do and we have got to bale that into big round bales and wrap them in plastic. I'm on my way to see how baling is going. As I go down the narrow lanes I come across a swan. The swan is walking in the same direction as me but he stands on one side for me to pass. I pull up alongside him (or is it she? you have to be careful these days). Swans are usually the epitome of serenity.

This one wasn't, its beak was open as if it was panting and it was dirty and unkempt, as if it had been in a fight. Ann wants a swan on our pond so I decided it will be a simple matter to scoop it up and put it into the truck. There's a high hedge next to where it is standing and over the hedge is a large pond in a large garden and a nice house. I assume that the swan lives on this pond but if I decide to take it, I won't be seen because of the high hedge. I am quite taken with the idea, not least because my wife will be so pleased and I will accumulate untold bonus points.

I scrutinise the swan and the swan scrutinises me. Then I remember something I was told as a child. 'You want to be careful of swans, they can break your arm.' This advice has always intrigued me, as if it was something that swans did on a regular basis, as if they wake up, stretch, and say to themselves 'Think I'll go and break a human's arm today!' I decide that I'll give it a go but the swan, as if it can read my mind, launches an attack on the truck. I pull my head back inside the truck and wind up the window. Think I'll pass on swan catching for today.

★★★

I drive on the to the field where the grass is. Stephen has just started to put it into rows prior to the contractor arriving to bale it. He stops and I ask him what time the baler is due. 'Ten o'clock' he says. It's now five past, but I'm not too worried. The contractors we use are very reliable. In the past, 'Ten o'clock' could quite easily mean 10 o'clock today or 10 o'clock tomorrow! Just by the gate there is a bunch of grass that the rake has missed, and Stephen picks it up and throws it onto the swathe to make sure it is baled too.

It's little more than a handful but it reminds me of my late father-in-law. Fodder harvesting for him involved making quite a lot of hay into those small bales. He would spend all day in the hay field, with about five of his men there as well, one putting the hay into rows and one operating the baler. The baler had a sledge behind it that would gather the bales and then leave them in random heaps. There would then be two or three men stacking these bales so that they could be picked up with a loader and put onto a trailer. This loading of bales onto a trailer was the first important step along the road that was to see the mechanisation of an arduous and demanding job of harvesting fodder. It seemed no time at all that the parcels of hay and straw moved to large round bales and big square bales that had to be hauled by loaders, both in the field and in the yard.

Back to my father-in-law, he was in the hay field because there was a team of men there to supervise and he was on hand should there be decisions to be made or if anything broke down, and at regular intervals he would test the weight of the bales. Too light, and you would use too much string, too heavy and the men couldn't lift them or the hay would go mouldy and spoil. While all this was going on he would prowl the field endlessly, looking for any hay that the rake or baler had left behind. Mostly, it would be a mere handful, he would gather it up and put it onto the next row of hay that was due to be baled. He used to say, that these bits of hay that he picked up in his various fields would add up to enough to feed the bull all winter. Of course we didn't know if it would be enough to feed the bull, there was no way of telling, but rather it was the action of a man who had lived and farmed through the depression years of the 1920s and 30s and waste of any sort could not be countenanced. What people of his generation would think of the wasteful society of today, goodness only knows.

21 July 2018

I'm going to write about dry weather. The consensus in the pub last night was that this hot dry spell would last until the end of September! It is inevitable that comparisons are drawn between the present hot spell and the dry summer of 1976. There used to be a steam engine rally near here and in those days it was customary for the steam engines to make their own way to the rally.

Steam engines under their own power dispense large quantities of cinder-type red hot soot. If you combine this with a parched hot landscape, you get fires. Most of the fires started in the dry bottoms of hedges but quickly spread to grass fields and to standing corn. It was frightening just how quickly these fires could spread, and cottages that were half a mile away from where the fire started would be under threat in no time at all.

For their part, the drivers of the steam engines would be charging patiently on, blissfully unaware of the havoc that they were leaving in their wake. After the rally they returned home and thus were able to set fire to anything they had missed on their outward journey. It was as if a retreating army had carried out a scorched earth policy. If I said that there was more corn around here burnt than there was combined, it would be an exaggeration, but only just. The next year, steam

engines had to arrive on lorries but that was well and truly
bolting the stable door after the horse was long gone.

But I've got a better story than that of dry weather. I
know of a row of cottages on an estate that had a water supply
that came off a hill, half a mile away. It was the same dry year
and the owner imposed a hose pipe ban. This was serious
stuff indeed. Each cottage had a small garden at the front
with a little square of lawn and nice flower borders. But at
the back they had quite large gardens that were given over to
the growth of vegetables. Traditionally these vegetables were
an important part of the family's budget and the well-being
of the vegetable garden was the source of much pride and
there was clearly a competitive element involved between the
various families that lived there, and to be fair, the gardens
were a picture of neatness and productivity.

I had a friend who lived in the one cottage, so we will
let him take up the story: 'I was really pleased with my garden
that year and I used to water it every evening after work, but
after the hosepipe ban I could see it 'going back' every day as
the dry weather took its toll. Then after a week I noticed that
my next door neighbour's garden was still flourishing whilst
mine seemed to wilt more and more each day. I was puzzled
by this.

'A couple of days later I was just going to bed and I
heard my neighbour's back door slam. He usually goes to bed
early so I went to my bedroom window to see what was going
on. He was on his hands and knees in his potato patch, there
was a hose pipe snaking behind him. He got well into the
potatoes, turned over on to his back and he was completely
hidden by the potato tops. His arm appeared, he waved to his
wife, she turned the tap on and I could see the jet of water
working its way over all the vegetables. When he had watered
them all, he repeated the procedure and crawled back into the
house.

'Next night I was waiting for him. I had my "catty pult" with me [I know you don't spell it like that but that's how he said it. In his youth he was a prodigious poacher, he was accurate and the catapult was silent and couldn't be heard by a gamekeeper]. He watched his neighbour get settled with the hosepipe and he put a small stone into the potato tops about a yard from him. 'The hosepipe paused for a while and then recommenced its work so I put a stone about a foot from his head. His head shot up out of the rows and he looked all around him. Whilst he was looking around I put another stone as close to him as I dared. He leapt to his feet, all ideas of concealment long gone, and he beat a hasty retreat back into the house, taking the hosepipe with him.'

28 July 2018

We started selling organic milk on 1 July. Becoming organic was a journey we started two years ago, so for two years we haven't used any artificial fertiliser or done any spraying. And we like it. One of the reasons we have gone organic is that the milk attracts a premium and we were halfway to organic anyway. We were using a fraction of the fertiliser we were using ten years ago, relying instead on the increased use of farmyard manure. We had kept spraying to a minimum anyway. The biggest challenge to organic farming is weeds, especially docks, in crops, so we have stopped growing crops and are all grass at the moment. The advantage with grass is that you can cut it and therefore, at the same time, you cut the weeds before they seed. We are still on a sort of learning curve with all this but we will try to grow some kale later this month for winter feed.

There will be two challenges here. Just ploughing the hard ground will be one. The other is the depredations of the flea beetle. Flea beetles can wipe out a crop in 24 hours, even if you have the option of spraying them, which we don't. At the moment we think we will sow a mix of seed and will assume that the flea beetle is more partial to some than others and it will consume them first, then, whilst its back is turned, the plants you really want, the kale, will flourish.

There has been a mix of reactions from my friends and neighbours. Most of them have been cynical. They have looked at the quantity of my silage crops, and been surprised. They have had a bit more grass than me, but not much. They know, and I know, that their crops have received several hundred weight of expensive fertiliser, so they don't comment. It doesn't matter how you farm at present, none of us is growing any grass. Organic or conventional, all grass needs rain now and again. Some have asked me outright how much more I get for a litre of milk so I tell them I get an extra one pound. This is ten times more than I actually get, but they don't know that, and they slink away as they try to guess how much milk we are selling and then multiply it by a one pound. Serves them right for being so nosy. Others have quite openly accused me of jumping on a bandwagon, but, as I have said, it was a decision we took two years ago. Besides, in my experience, if you see a bandwagon it is too late to jump on it anyway. Any opportunity is usually long gone by then.

★★★

One thing you are never short of on a livestock farm, in summer, are flies. Flies are a given but I don't think they have ever been so bad as they have been this year, during the hot dry spell. They plague your livestock and give them no peace. I always used to reckon that afternoon milking in the summer, during hot dry weather, was the worst milking of the year. You would put the milking cluster on a cow and then you would see a fly land on her lower leg, and she would kick away at the fly and off would come the machine. You would soon end up with a bad-tempered milker and a herd of bad- tempered cows.

There are lots of ways to alleviate the fly problem, for example you can have a continuous spray of water that the cows have to go through to enter the parlour. Flies don't like to follow the cows through a curtain of water. Or you can fit a large fan that will blow a constant flow of air down the parlour which flies don't like either, and then there are a multitude of fly zappers and baits you can use as well.

But that's not the half of it. We like to leave our kitchen doors open in the summer, the flies see this as an open invitation. We use those old fashioned sticky fly papers to catch them. We put up fresh ones every morning and after 24 hours they are nearly full and the flies have a job to find somewhere to land. They have to adopt a holding pattern like they do at Heathrow and there are flies stacked up and flying in circles awaiting their turn. We used to have one of those electric fly zappers but that broke down. I'm toying with the idea of getting another as there's a certain satisfaction to be had when you hear a fly being electrocuted.

4 August 2018

I can't put a figure on it but it seems that more than half the people in our parish have moved here to retire. For the most part they seem to be in their early sixties and took early retirement. They are usually still very fit, and it is good to see that the villages are growing. At the parish council we have a plan that focuses itself on the long term viability of the village: school, shop, pub, that sort of thing. But since most are retired, I often think that we should be concerning ourselves with care in the community, day care centres, stuff like that.

Some of these people who have moved here took a life-changing decision to live in the countryside, but there are lots of things that are countryside norms, which come with the package. Those who like to see cattle in the fields have to get used to the sound of mooing and cattle on the road, being moved to a new field. And tractors on the roads too. Those individuals don't like it when tractors drive past their houses, (there is one resident who will come out and stop tractors as they drive past his house, on a council road, and tell them not to come past again). He doesn't like tractors driving through the village, some especially don't like it if the tractors are carting farmyard manure – and should they be carting poultry manure, there could be a petition! At present there is a lot of straw moving about, as the cereal harvest starts, and bits of straw blow off loads. Some don't like that either. They don't like it to be too dry because tractors then leave dust. I am left to conclude that they would prefer you to have a wet harvest, with all the difficulty and expense that that involves.

But they are not all like that, some seek to assimilate themselves with the locals. They go to the pub on Thursday because Thursday night is farmers night. I was there last Thursday and was the only farmer there. A local resident came in and asked where everyone was. I told him that they would all be working still. I could tell by his reaction that this had never crossed his mind. It was gone 9.30pm but they would still be hard at it. Of late it's been hard work and long hours for those who work on tractors, especially for those who do some contracting. The hot dry weather has meant that one harvest has merged into the next with little respite in between. Second-cut silage was quickly followed by wholecrop silage and as soon as that was done the winter barley and the oil seed rape were ready. 12-hour day has followed 12-hour day and they are starting to look tired.

Contrast that with the retired person's life. He hasn't had to mow his lawn for a month, it's been too dry, it's been too dry for the weeds to flourish in his flower beds. His biggest job during the day time is probably switching the TV on to see if there is any cricket on. When it cools down in the evening he takes the dog for a walk, and the length of that walk depends whether they go into the pub using the front door or the back door.

★★★

We've just had two hours of rain, but we probably need two hours of rain every day for a month to make any difference. At present our cows are eating six big bales of silage a day and that will surely increase. They were all bales that were meant to be fed next winter. It will all catch up with us at some time.

★★★

Understatement of the year. Two friends of mine are driving to work one morning in a van. They are driving down a lane and come to a B road. The junction is at one of the acute angles back to the left where it is difficult to see if it is clear or if anything is coming. But they go this way to work every day, taking it in turn to provide the van. Driver: 'Is it OK to go?' Passenger: 'If you are quick.' The driver pulls out onto the B road there is a blast on a horn, a squeal of brakes and a lorry slams into the back of the van, propelling it up the road with an acceleration it has never achieved on its own. Passenger: 'Quicker than that.'

11 August 2018

When I get back from the gym I have to sit down for an hour to give my knees chance to recover. It's always time to switch the TV on. I just love to watch the Tour de France cycle race. It's all very complicated to follow, I know that the cyclist wearing the yellow jersey is in the lead, but what I really like is the view of the French countryside that you get as well. I like to see at what stage their crops are at, and the helicopters that cover the race direct their cameras to places of interest. In this way I feel I've travelled quite a lot of France and just love it.

★★★

My phone rings. It's the farmer next door who grows a lot of corn. I have bought two fields of straw off him. He combines the crop and I buy the straw that the combine leaves behind. He is phoning to say that the combine has just gone into the field of oil seed rape I have bought, that the stems are a bit green and it is probably best to leave it to dry out for a couple of days. This absolutely typifies farming and how you have to cope with the vagaries of the weather. The forecasters are predicting two very wet days, starting tonight, with all the confidence that they have predicted it being hot and dry for the last two or three weeks. Therefore there is no choice but to let my straw get wet and to hope that it will dry out on its own.

Straw is very expensive this year and in short supply and I have only been able to buy two fields whereas I usually buy four. If you have to go in with a machine to turn it, to dry it, it can break up and you can lose some and that's the last thing you want to do. Farming teaches you to be pragmatic. It teaches you not to spend time worrying about things you can do nothing about, especially the weather. And what if I have a field of straw getting wet? The rain is doing untold good in all the others.

★★★

There was a car rally around here last night. There's one every two years or so. The organisers go to great lengths to call to see you beforehand in case you might be affected, which is to their credit. We have three fields that have a council road running through the middle and they like to use these. Every time they offer to put marshals on the gates but we always move livestock away for the night to avoid any mix-ups. And I support any group having harmless fun. I am awakened by the first car and I hear every car until the last. Except that you don't know it's the last until the world falls silent and you drift back to sleep again. I know every car's progress from about a mile away because I can hear every gear change and every time they touch the throttle, because their exhausts are so noisy. It's no big deal but if they were to fit normal exhausts like everyone else, you wouldn't know they were there at all. It all reminds me of when I was a child and I used to fit a piece of stiff cardboard to my bike with a clothes peg so that it rubbed against the spokes and made a noise that I pretended sounded like an engine. But I grew out of that.

18 AUGUST 2018

When we went into broiler production, all those years ago, it was a very new experience and there was a lot to learn. About the second lot through, I was horrified when a few of them started feather pecking. This sounds innocent enough but it starts with the feathers of a victim and then the skin and then the flesh until the unfortunate victim dies and they find another. It is nothing to do with having thousands of birds in one shed because the first time I saw feather pecking it was among the 20 or 30 hens I kept free range when I was at school. I've never seen it here since, just that one lot.

One of the causes could be boredom so I bought a box of cabbages, scattered them about, the birds picked away at them instead of each other and that was the end of that and we didn't lose a single bird to pecking again. But it wasn't the end of it, word gets around very quickly in the broiler world. 'You will never guess what, Roger Evans is buying his chickens cabbages!' There was much laughter at this, the laughter of derision, which is much less friendly.

If we move on to the present, we don't produce birds for the table anymore, we produce point-of-lay pullets that are destined for free range egg laying units. We produce these to RSPCA Freedom Foods standards. A part of this is that we put a lot of coloured plastic balls in each shed and hang some blank CDs up for the birds to peck at. This is to give the birds something to distract them. Now they can eat, drink, sleep and play. Come to think about it, that's all any of us want. It could be that when I bought those cabbages all those years ago, I was ahead of my time. It could be that I am not as thick as I look, which is very fortunate.

★★★

Just in case any of you are interested, I sent my car for a service and for some Botox on the front corner. It's due back this afternoon, that's five weeks tomorrow since it went in! During that time I've had the use of a 4x4 pickup truck and the car I part exchanged 18 months ago. That car is very high mileage but still goes well and I only swapped it because I couldn't drive it about the fields in winter. Still, five weeks is a long time for a service by any standards. It won't surprise me if it's had a 500 mile test drive.

★★★

There's these two men I know who have worked in the woods together for years. They are as different as chalk and cheese but they get on and work together really well. One is very lively and full of fun the other is very slow and deliberate in everything he does or says. A couple of years ago they planted a 40 acre wood and for the first couple of years they go and cut off the weeds that have grown to give the trees a chance to get established. They were doing this one year and the slower one needed a day off, so the other went on his own. He's a bit of a gourmet and his journey to work takes him past a very good fish shop and he buys a crab to eat with his sandwiches.

There's a little stream runs alongside where he parks his van and he puts the remains of the crab, shell and claws, in the water and arranges them to look as life-like as he can. Next day his friend is back at work and he parks his van so that the friend has to get out next to the stream and where the crab is. There's a sort of magnetism to water and he sees his friend pause as he spots the crab. He looks at it for ages and then says to the crab, 'Hello you're a long way from the sea.'

25 August 2018

The increase in rural crime is making headlines this week. It's never been a problem around here before – just a few years ago it was nil but it's on the increase. Fifteen years ago we didn't take keys out of cars at night. Now we would lock the kitchen door at night, if only we could find the key! We have had the tractor diesel stolen twice but the nozzle is padlocked and the key is so well hidden that I can rarely find it myself. Each time the padlock has been intact but the diesel has gone. It's a case of putting two and two together and getting four but you still need proof.

A friend of mine put one of those cameras on his yard that are triggered by movement, he wanted to see if there were any badgers about in his cattle buildings at night. There were no badgers but there was someone from his village stealing his diesel on a regular basis.

We have a four bay shed where we store feedstuffs and the end bay is devoted to what we laughingly call our workshop. All the tools are open to be stolen, there is nothing in there that we paid a lot of money for but if you had to replace them all together it would come to a tidy sum. My lawn mower lives in there, I managed to buy a good one second-hand one last year but you can't rely on doing that again.

We will have to raise our security game but I resent having to spend money on doors and cameras. There has been a metal shipping container doing nothing on our yard for years so we have dragged it out of the nettles and we are starting to put stuff in there. My inclination is to use natural security and there is little better natural security than a big nasty dog.

But if the dog is nasty enough, that brings its own problems so the dog would need to be locked, with your valuables, in a secure compound. And if the compound is secure enough, why would you need a nasty dog anyway? We know that a flock of free range turkeys would do a good deterrent job but residents would be in as much danger as would-be thieves. Geese and guinea fowl are good watchdogs but at night time, when most thieving takes place, like the turkeys, they will be roosting somewhere cosy.

★★★

I like going through yesterday's paper as I wait for my breakfast. I find a story about an alpaca that has failed its TB test. The ministry want to slaughter it and the owners query the accuracy of the test. There's all bar an inch of a whole page devoted to this story but there is no mention of the 40,000 cattle that are slaughtered every year which are subject to the same testing regime and the same slaughter policy. This, in a way, puts the whole matter in perspective. Lots of farmers are dissatisfied with TB testing, fat lot of good it does them. I wish I could get a picture of 40,000 cattle. Only then would the general public truly realise the enormity of it all.

Every time my wife sees a picture of an alpaca she says, 'I want one of those.' Alpacas have such an endearing, perpetually, quizzical expression on their faces that I can see where she is coming from and she has one at the top of her wish list. I've got them on a list as well. A no-chance list.

1 SEPTEMBER 2018

I go to the pub on Thursdays, Saturdays and Sundays. Thursday night is farmers' night, Saturday nights you get more ladies there. Sundays can be an odd sort of night, you never know what to expect but I am a creature of habit and go anyway. Last Sunday it was quiet. Quiet is a relative term; if last Sunday was quiet you should just see Sunday nights in January and February! But it was also remarkable, there were only eight of us in there but six were in their working clothes and they had all been working until 9 o'clock, harvesting. For two hours we chatted about the private parts of combines, in intimate detail, and important things like the difficulty of baling the huge swath of straw left by today's gigantic combines. What is so remarkable about that? Everyone there was involved in farming and we talked, uninterrupted, about farming matters.

★★★

I didn't build our house; some of it is about 500 years old, which means that some of it is older than me. Our house is built on the rock. They say it was a wise man who built his house on the rock, implying that he was sensible and thought about things. What I also know from personal experience is that the wise man who built his house on the rock didn't have much of a garden. Shallow dry soil does not produce much of anything. When we came here there was a walled kitchen garden but a dry summer and no water meant that it was a waste of time. You can still see where the walled garden was but we have built on bits of it and over the years have used it as a dog pen, a pig pen, a hen and turkey pen, to calve cows in and at present it is a wilderness.

But we are never short of fresh vegetables; others have an abundance at this time of year and knowing we don't have any, they bring some to us. Thus far this week, on consecutive days, we have received courgettes, tomatoes, runner beans and more courgettes.

It is also time to show vegetables at local shows. Showing vegetables can be emotive and highly competitive. It makes me think of fishermen as arms are outstretched to demonstrate how big various vegetables are. I am minded of some photographs in a pub I used to visit. By some photographic sleight of hand they had a series of photographs depicting local characters with gigantic vegetables. I remember one man with an onion that filled his wheelbarrow, two men cutting up a huge potato with a six foot cross cut hand saw and six men carrying a single runner bean on their shoulders, very much as you would carry a coffin.

People can get very competitive about growing vegetables, which I suppose is all part of the pride in having a tidy allotment or an immaculate vegetable patch, and it gives those who don't farm, at least an insight into the hard work, pride and the eventual harvest of being a farmer.

A good friend of mine is a renowned grower of fruit, flowers and vegetables. He used to have a proper cottage garden in that he had a pig sty at the bottom of his garden. The pigs provided manure for the garden. Any waste from the vegetables and any food waste from the house was recycled via the pigs and it was a perfect recycling solution. He hasn't had pigs for ten years now, neighbours don't like pigs, they don't like the smell and they don't like the noise.

One year he was very pleased with his broad beans. 'They were the best I have grown for 50 years.' He entered them at a big show, it wasn't at Chelsea, but it was the next level down. He had to enter nine pods, so he took them across early on the day and went in the afternoon to see how he had got on. He hadn't won a prize but there was a note from the judge. 'Pity you didn't read the rules.' And the reason? His nine beautiful pods were down to 7. He assumed two had been removed by another competitor. Life is like that, people mislead other people all the time, but why would you want to mislead yourself?

8 SEPTEMBER 2018

It's not for everyone, but the young men around here are mostly going out one night a week, foxing. They go out with lamps and rifles that are very effective. I've never done it myself but

I can't believe how many foxes there are about every year. At this time of year there is a lot of foxy traffic as this year's cubs move about seeking to establish new territories.

I don't have a lot of compassion for the fox. When I was at school, I used to rear 12 cockerels a year for Christmas. I built them a small shed with a run of wooden slats outside. About two weeks before Christmas a fox took all their legs off through the slats. I had to kill them all as there is not a lot of demand at Christmas for chickens without legs. The cockerel money was to buy me a bigger bike as I had out-grown mine, and I had to wait another six months and buy a second hand one.

When I was first farming I put 60 ewes and 120 lambs onto some good grass under the wood. They were only there two nights and by the time I moved them again, I only had 100 lambs. Three vixens used to sit out on the field up by the wood watching me feed them. Fox lovers will always tell you that a fox will only ever take weak and sickly lambs. My lambs were ten to fourteen days old and would not have been there if they were weak and sickly. They had all been through a process of holding pens and orchards that ensured that they were as fit as fiddles before they were introduced to the real outside world, and as I said at the beginning, I had turned them onto some good grass I had saved to ensure that their mothers had plenty of milk. So there were no easy pickings for the foxes.

And now for some good news. The anti-fox activity on my land today is all to do with protecting this season's pheasant poults but as they go about that part of their business, apart from foxes, those involved with the shoot see what else is about as well. They report seeing a lot more deer than last year, but it's the keeper that has the best news. He has a new sight on his rifle, I don't fully understand it, but it has a device that identifies heat, so if an animal is in cover, you'll still know where it is because the new sight can detect it. 'Boy, there's a lot more hares about than I thought. As soon as they hear a vehicle they are off into the woods or crops there but there are lots there that I didn't know about.' Before the hare coursers came, our hares were relatively tame. You often knew where they like to squat, I think they call it a form, and you could drive alongside them and they would just sit there. Now they are a lot more wary and don't hang about, which can only be a positive for their own preservation. I don't get the pleasure of seeing them all but that is because they are trying to keep themselves safe, and that can only be a good thing.

15 SEPTEMBER 2018

A friend of mine has been off work for a week because a cow kicked him on the hand at TB testing time. He is probably the best stockman I know, he knows what he is doing, but he sustained broken bones and needed stitches in cuts. The trouble is that cattle are being tested so many times they are starting to get a bit prickly about it, they know that when you get them in, someone is going to stick a needle in them and they don't like it. People have died handling cattle and the more you handle them the more people will die. It's just one more cost to TB in cattle that doesn't make the statistics.

★★★

I've been keeping an eye on a friend who lives on his own and who has had a new hip. I go every morning to make sure he hasn't had a fall. I don't think I could pick him up but I could call the fire brigade. He has two of those devices that are a bit like litter pickers in case he drops something so he can pick it up without bending. I always thought that their main purpose was to pick up your boxer shorts when you were getting dressed so you could lasso the foot on the leg you couldn't bend.

But there's a 2p piece on his kitchen floor and he picks that up very skilfully. I was telling someone this and they say it would be handy should he drop a £1 coin. I say that he wouldn't be inclined to get a £1 coin out of his pocket let alone drop it on the floor.

★★★

I've not written much about Gomer this month. We've not seen much of him lately because he has been in love. He's slept outside with my son's collie's bitch. The rest of the family think there's too much difference in size for anything to happen, but I'm not so sure. He's come home now and we've rewarded him with a new flea collar.

22 SEPTEMBER 2018

We were invited to two weddings in five days. It's unusual for us to get invited to weddings – we mostly go to funerals. They were both superb but the one was at a hotel and the ceremony was conducted outside in beautiful gardens on a lovely sunny day. There were sweeping lawns, a stream, ducks and swans, a fine view and the faint aroma of poultry manure. Farmers really should take more care. We spread poultry manure but if it's within a field or where someone lives, we do it when it's raining, the rain seems to take the smell into the ground and anyway the manure works better if its washed in right away.

Years ago I went to a niece's wedding in a country house hotel overlooking Cardiff. After the reception folk went outside to see the view, which was spectacular. A mile or so away was the M4, then the urban sprawl of houses, then the city centre and beyond that the sun was glinting on the Bristol Channel. They didn't stay outside long to admire the view because within 30 yards of the front door there was a grass field and the farmer was spreading slurry on it. I ask you, who in his right mind would spread slurry on a Saturday afternoon just outside a popular wedding venue? There could have been some spite involved as well.

Anyway, back to the wedding in the garden and the sunshine. Just next to the stream was the most beautiful weeping willow tree. Weeping willows are one of my favourite trees. I've tried, three times, to grow one. Each time they have grown in a sort of half-hearted fashion for about ten years, and then they have died. That's 30 years I have tried to grow one, and failed. My son-in-law has a beauty which he prunes with his chain saw about every three years; it stands close to their home so they don't want it to get too big. He cuts every branch off until there's only the trunk left, but still it flourishes and recovers in no time. Under this tree at the wedding were a group of musician friends of the bride's who played background music. What better than sitting in the sun, drinking Pimms and listening to good music?

When we were planning my daughter's wedding we went, about three months prior, to a wedding where there were some musicians playing and we thought how nice it was. The next week we made enquiries as to how much they cost but it was too much. My daughter's wedding was very much a 'do it yourself' affair. My wife made the wedding and bridesmaids dresses, she had help to prepare the food and she had friends to serve it on the big day. There were 150 invited in the afternoon and about 250 at night; trouble is the ones invited in the day don't go home so there were over 400 there in the evening. The biggest expense was the marquee and its floor and the chairs and tables but Barclays paid for that on the farm overdraft, though they never knew.

The thought of some live background music was still nagging at me. Then I had an idea. There was, at that time, a lady in our area who lived on a farm, up in the hills. But when she had first arrived she had appeared on a grass verge in a traditional caravan, drawn by a horse. We called her 'Gypsy Jo'. She used to go in the pub on Saturday nights and we became friends. Then someone said to me that Jo was an accomplished concert pianist; nothing surprises me about the people around here anymore. I asked her one night if this were true, she said it was, so I asked her if she would play at the wedding. She said yes, and she would bring her own piano.

I hadn't seen Jo for a month and thought she had forgotten but the afternoon before the wedding we were laying the tables when there was the roar of a tractor outside the tent and next thing we knew, Jo was backing a battered Fordson Major into the tent. There was what we call a box on the back of the tractor and in the box was a piano. She backed in and sent tables and chairs flying, she couldn't see behind her because of the piano. We manhandled the piano onto the small stage we had constructed and next day she proved that she was indeed an accomplished concert pianist. I paid her in food, beer and cash.

29 SEPTEMBER 2018

I can't remember my wife, who is a fine seamstress, ever darning any socks. If I have a button off a shirt she says I've got plenty more shirts, which is true. I've got two pairs of going out trousers. They take it in turns to be washed or worn. One pair is too long and I've worn a bit off the backs because I walk with my heels on them. The other pair is so short that they show all my socks. If my late mother-in- law saw a man whose trousers were too short, she always said that they were at half mast because the cat had died.

6 OCTOBER 2018

I'm not a fan of Chris Packham, so when I came across a two-page article that he had written in our Sunday paper, I read it, fearing the worst. I find him patronising. I suspect that Chris Packham has an agenda to be the next David Attenborough when the time comes, but he'll never even come close. Back to his article, there wasn't much there that

I took exception to. I'm always a bit sceptical about numbers of birds: who counts them and how accurate is the count? Chris says that 44 million birds have disappeared since 1966. I've just been reading a book that tells me that cats kill 55 million a year! (figures from a study in 2003). We are told that the house sparrow numbers are down 66% but the cat is the most common pet in cities. Surely those statistics are not unconnected, but there is no public outcry about cats.

Chris Packham says that hedges continue to be removed, I doubt that. You need planning permission to remove a hedge and if you remove a hedge without permissions, woe betide you. I suspect that there are more hedges now than there were 15 years ago. Most hedges were removed by large scale arable farmers, big machinery needs big fields, I have not removed a single hedge in over 50 years of farming and I resent being tarred with that particular brush. It's what isn't said in the article that jars the most. Cats weren't mentioned. But just as important are the proliferation of the birds of prey that eat the eggs and young of small birds whenever they get the chance. I have been banging on about this for years.

Just to confirm this, a neighbour calls by, and without any prompting, tells me that he was planting corn the other day and that his tractor was being followed by 24 red kites, 14 buzzards and so many carrion crows he didn't bother to count them. The birds that are under the most pressure in this area include grey partridge, curlews, lapwings and sky larks, all ground nesting birds, birds that are under the most pressure from the winged predators that follow my friend's tractor. And when he is planting corn, so is everyone else, so there could be 20 tractors working within the parish and every tractor will be followed by birds of prey. But Chris Packham's list of birds that are in demise is longer than that. Some of these birds, in fact most of them, nest in the hedgerows that he thinks are so important. When their young fledge, and they are making their first faltering attempts at flight, they are picked off by the birds of prey, I've seen it happening countless times. If birds of prey are part of the problem — and they are — some control of their numbers has to be part of the solution.

★★★

There are too many people in this country. Fact. No matter where they come from, there's probably 10-15 million too many. The pressure this puts on infrastructures such as schools, hospitals and roads is well chronicled elsewhere and it puts pressure on wildlife. I don't advocate a solution but merely that the fact should be acknowledged. At this time of year my travels in support of my local rugby team often take me in to suburbia. Street after street, road after road, I see houses that have turned their front gardens into places to park their two or three cars. I'm not criticising this, I'd probably do it myself, but 30 or 40 years ago these gardens would have contained lawns and flowers. Where you get lawns and flowers you also get birds, insects, bees and butterflies and hedgehogs. People have chosen cars over wildlife and you can't have it both ways, you rarely can.

It seems that for years I have read of the elusive Croyden cat killer. Turns out the unknown stalker that kills and mutilates cats is a fox or foxes. The outcry that someone should put the blame on an 'innocent' member of the wildlife fraternity is almost equal to the outcry that greeted the killing and mutilation in the first place. Like Packham and his birds of prey, these people are in denial. But there could be worse to come. Chris Packham is an advocate of rewilding. If he has his way, the wolf at your door could become a reality. Like foxes, wolves will soon discover that there are rich pickings to be had in urban areas. Wolves won't only eat your cat, they will eat your dog, your child and your granny. Much of the Packham plan for the countryside is stupid and that's enough off my chest for one day: normal service can resume.

13 OCTOBER 2018

One of our pub regulars is busy calving quite a lot of beef suckler cows. He is calving them outside in a field. This is much the best way at this time of year, it is better for cow and calf. The only drawback arises if there are any complications, in which case the cow has to be brought inside for assistance. But the cows he has are noted for easy calving so, although they are checked several times a day, it mostly goes without too much trouble. That's not to say he doesn't have incidents and adventures, and he tells us all about them. He's going around the cows one morning and one has just started to calve under a tree; the calf's nose is showing but it has a membrane over its nostrils. He leaps off his quad bike (at least he says he leaps) and removes the skin from the calf's nose. The cow is not best pleased at his arrival and gets to her feet and proceeds to chase him around the tree. He says he was chased for ten minutes, it was probably not that long, but being chased by an angry cow is no laughing matter so it could easily seem that long. During the chase and its exertions, the calf is born, it drops out onto the grass, the cow turns all its attention to the newborn calf, and peace is restored. He tells this story as if he is some sort of hero, which in a way he is, and seems to expect some understanding and sympathy from his audience. He gets neither, the concern in his audience is that she couldn't be much of a cow if she couldn't catch him in ten minutes.

★★★

I'm having my breakfast when Stephen, who helps us, arrives at the kitchen door. He is offered a cup of tea but says 'No thanks' as he has just had his bait. Everyone who comes here is offered a drink, lorry drivers who get here in the snow get a bacon sandwich as well. I sometimes say to visitors 'Would you like a drink?' 'Yes please.' 'Tea or coffee?' Some visitors always say, 'Whichever is easier for you.' And I always think to myself, 'It would be easier for me if you would make your mind up, it's only a spoonful of one or a tea bag in a mug for the other.' I said it out loud once and the recipient of my sarcasm looked so crest-fallen that I shan't say it again.

Anyway let's get back to Stephen. There's quite a big window opposite where he is standing and he can see, in the distance, a field of my neighbour's that slopes up from the stream to the woods beyond. My neighbour, runs his yearling heifers here every summer. Over to Stephen: 'There's a dog chasing those heifers.'

We all have a look and sure enough, the heifers are clearly being chased. Then we have a closer look and it's not a dog that's doing the chasing, it's a fallow deer stag. But he's not really chasing, it's as if he's trying to round them up. It reminds me a bit of when we were in Killarney last year, lots of cars and coaches had stopped to watch a stag and a group of hinds in the middle of a filed. He was circling them constantly to try to keep them together, and with good reason because around the outside of the field were several other stags waiting an opportunity to steal a hind or two. He had to chase the bolder ones off continually and whilst he was doing that, others would sneak in to steal what hinds they could. If you are a stag deer and it's rutting time and you can't get a group of hinds, the next best thing is apparently a group of Holstein heifers. Stag and heifers disappear behind some trees but we've been watching them for a quarter of an hour. He could be quite pleased with himself but I suspect that all he'll get for his trouble is unrequited love.

★★★

I've been waiting about ten years to tell you this story. It concerns my eldest granddaughter who is learning to drive. She failed her first test (no bad thing, I know it's disappointing but it shouldn't be too easy). All those years ago I was watching her on a tricycle together with her other grandfather (now departed). He was a good friend but he was also a glass half empty sort of person. If you had an early warm day in spring, he would say, 'We'll pay for this sometime.'

But we are both watching Katie terrorise the farmyard on her tricycle. Dogs and cats have sensibly slunk around corners long ago and she is now chasing hens (who take longer to work things out). He says, 'Just look at that girl on that bike, she's got no fear at all. She is going too fast, she could easily fall off but she doesn't care and if she carries on like this she'll kill all those hens. When she's a grown woman and passes her test, there'll be no one safe in this village.' Time will tell.

20 OCTOBER 2018

We've gone down with TB again. We had a cow that went to the abattoir and they found it in her. They bought our annual test forward as a result and found six more! In practical terms that means that we can't sell anything for four months, and that's the best-case scenario. It's a serious blow. It's not been a good year to be a dairy farmer, a late spring followed by a drought, and now this. I know that most people think that farmers are constant whingers, and I try not to fall into that category. But you need ten out of ten for resilience just to survive. The most frustrating thing is that TB is not a problem that is going to go away anytime soon. There's nothing we can do that says that we won't have six more next year and so on for years to come. In the 1950s and early 60s we managed to clear up TB in cattle at a time when it was endemic in the UK herd. What's the difference now? We all know what the difference is, even those in denial know what the difference is.

A friend of mine has just been on holiday to Burnham for a week. We went to stay on a farm in that area when I was a little boy and it's one of my earliest memories. What I can remember is that it was my first memory of cows being milked. Every morning, as the rest of the family slept, I would stand at the bedroom window and watch the morning milking, which took place out in the field next to the yard. There were only about six cows to milk, they were milked by hand, and the cows were assembled close to the yard and the farmer and his wife did the milking. I can remember the cows standing there patiently until it was their turn to be milked, I suspect that their back legs were tied together (hobbled) to restrain them and can't remember any dramas. What I do remember is that the milkers used stools with one leg. It was a substantial leg to stop it digging into the ground and should the cow move slightly, the milker could tilt the stool a bit to follow her. I also remember it was a very wet week and the cows and milkers were out in steady rain. They didn't have such good outdoor clothing in those days, but I found the whole process fascinating. Still do.

★★★

I used to get acres of paper information when I had a role in the dairy industry. One of these reports used to concern statistics on consumer buying trends with regards to food. I always thought this was very important. If you produce food, you need to know what the people who buy it, want. The one sector that showed growth, year after year, was the sale of ready meals. This always intrigued me because television is awash with cooking programmes and lots of people must watch. But they clearly don't use these programmes to teach them to cook or why else the increase in sales of ready meals? I eat two ready meals a week: my wife buys me two curries when she goes shopping, very good they are too, one not being enough for a growing boy.

The next two generations in our family eat out a lot more than we do. They eat lots of bar meals, burgers and chips are very popular. Lots of people I know always go out for Sunday lunch. If you want to, around here, you usually need to book up in good time. One popular pub has to do two sittings, one at midday and one late afternoon. My eldest granddaughter used to waitress at a pub carvery and they used to regularly serve 200 lunches.

We only go out on Sundays two or three times a year, always on the occasion of birthdays or anniversaries, probably because we are of a generation where eating out should be a treat not a norm. If you go out for Sunday lunch and it's excellent, that's fine. If it's average or mediocre, what's the point? You wish you had stayed at home. We went out a few weeks ago, it was my wife's birthday. There seems, as far as I can tell, a competition to see who can make the biggest Yorkshire pudding. These were huge, as big as the plate and about six inches high, they were served if you had beef, chicken, fish or pork. A diner on the next table, unsure how to tackle his Yorkshire, picked it up with both hands to take a bite out of it. Trouble was he didn't spot that is was full of gravy and that went all down the front of his shirt front. Bet he wished he'd stayed home.

★★★

Today I report on something we got right. After the drought most farmers have a wary eye on fodder supplies for the winter. Should you run out it fodder, will be expensive to buy. If you are organic, like us, organic fodder could be difficult to locate and if you did find some you wouldn't want to think of the price. We still had our third cut silage to do but the grass was still growing so we left it and left it. I was starting to get a bit twitchy about it all, as three wet days and we are into winter.

Then the forecasts said that yesterday would be the sunniest and hottest October day for years so we cut it all down, about 120 acres. We put 105 acres through the chopper and clamped it and 15 acres into round bales of silage. I've watched these self propelled choppers at work lots of times but still can't get over how quickly they work. It did over 100 acres in one day, with ease. You mostly get lighter crops when they are organic but it is all safely gathered in and in the dry and it could be a life saver at the end of the winter. It was raining this morning. Phew, that was close.

3 NOVEMBER 2018

Now the fields are cleared of grass I can drive all over them, and recently I did so with a purpose. This is also the dog Gomer's exercise time. He is covering the bits of field that I don't cover in the truck, at least as much of it as his little fat legs will allow him to cover, but he has a good nose so between us it takes over an hour to do what I'm about and the conclusion is quite remarkable. Between us we haven't found one single hare. Five years ago I guarantee we would have found 10, but it could just as easily have been 20. Hare coursers and their activities have removed that massive pleasure from my life. All I can hope is that there are hares about but that they are hiding in woods and root crops. That would be good but if I can't see them, where's the pleasure in that?

Just when you think things can't get any worse they usually do. I read somewhere that hares in the eastern counties of England are suffering from a form of myxomatosis, and it's spreading. I worry about that becoming endemic and that it will wipe out large numbers of hares as it has rabbits. But I only worry a little bit. One of the lessons of life I have tried to take on board is that there's no point in worrying about things you can do nothing about. If my hares get a myxomatosis-type disease, there's absolutely nothing I can do about it, so why worry? Just to contradict myself, it seems that there's nothing to be done about hare coursers either, but they, and all the negatives they bring, really wind me up.

★★★

Here we go again! As shooting has started again and as most shooting is on Saturdays and as that means that most beaters are in the pub by 3.30 on Saturday afternoons, there are stories to be had on Sunday nights. Here's one. One man is fast asleep in the early hours of Sunday morning when his mobile phone rings. He tries to ignore it and it stops. But straight away it rings again. Reluctantly he answers it, it's his wife, who is in bed. 'Where the hell are you?' 'I don't really know.' 'Don't you think you should find out?' 'OK.' He is well awake by now so he arouses himself sufficiently to take stock of his situation. He remembers walking home from the pub, he remembers he made it home with some difficulty. Seems he made it safely just as far as his favourite armchair which is where he is now. Satisfied, he rearranges the cushions and goes straight back to sleep. Then his phone rings again, it's his wife, 'Have you found out where you are yet?'

★★★

I've been signing books lately. I apologise if that sounds pretentious, but it's a part of the story. Because my handwriting is so bad, every signature is different, but they are all authentic. It's the Michaelmas Fair in our local town and I'm at the shop of Jane, my friend the florist. Jane's main job is to get me safely down the steps at the pub when I go home on Saturday nights. Jane and I have been drinking together on Saturday nights for years. Halfway through the evening she buys a packet of cheese and onion crisps for us to share. Because I'm afraid of her, it took me ten years to tell her that I didn't like cheese and onion. She still buys them but she doesn't share them anymore.

Jane is using the occasion of the fair to raise money for a cancer charity. She has two small doorways into her shop and she has me sitting at a table just inside the one. It's raining quite hard. If it was just ordinary rain she would have me outside in it, signing books alfresco, as it were. In the other doorway she has loudspeakers and amplifiers because she is also a very fine singer and is known as the Singing Florist. She usually sings better on Saturday than Sundays, it depends how much we have had to drink on the Saturday night. She always starts the Michaelmas Fair off by entertaining the crowds for 40 minutes as they go by. Today she's in good voice, never better. She starts off with, 'It's a long way to Tipperary,' and you can see the passing crowd picking up their feet in time to the music. Forty five minutes later she concludes with 'Will you still love me tomorrow?' Of course I will.

10 November 2018

My son has just changed his truck and I'm having a look at it. He only changed because the previous one had a faulty diesel tank and needed a new fuel pump. The new parts were over £1,000 and goodness knows what the labour would be. His truck was only worth about £2,000 and that would be part exchange value. It's the sort of dilemma many of us face, when do you say enough expense is enough? His 'new' truck is 15 years old and it was bought from a local scrap dealer. I did find him a ten years old truck to try but he said it was too posh. As a family we have never been much given to buying shiny new machinery and cars. We know two local scrap men, good friends both, and we are just as likely to buy vehicles and machinery from them as anywhere else. The last new machine we bought was a slurry tanker, but that is a job you have to keep on top of, for obvious reasons.

The one car I've always fancied is a Range Rover. I did have one years ago but it was only for six weeks so you can't really count that. It was over 20 years old and it had a gas conversion on it, that was the only reason I thought I would try it. I thought it would be cheap to run. As it turned out it used more oil in the engine than ever it used petrol or gas so after six weeks the dealer took it back and gave me my money back. After tea, on the day it arrived, I asked my son, who was still living at home, if he fancied going to the pub. I was not bothered about going to the pub but I did fancy driving the

Range Rover. We were using the pub in our local town at the time so we parked outside on the road. It was quiet in the pub but one of our friends gets up to get another drink and whilst he is waiting to be served he turns his back to the bar, rests his elbows on it, and looks out of the window.

'Look at that', he says, 'there's a Range Rover outside, wonder whose that is?' Neither my son or I say anything, there's a bit of a stigma to having a Range Rover, however old it is. 'She looks in good nick. Good God, her's off down the road!'

I think that the handbrake on Range Rovers works on the transmission so 'she' didn't gather speed, she just went down the road sedately; there were cars parked either side but she didn't touch one, and she eventually came to rest gently against a wall about 50 yards from where she had started with just a bit of a graze on the wing to show for her adventure.

But things were about to get worse. In the next two weeks my son had broken his ankle and I had broken my collar bone badly. As neither of us could do much work we decided it would be a good time to have a family holiday. We went to Scotland for five days, in the Range Rover, we got as far north as Fort William. Because of our various incapacities I drove all the way, with one hand, and my son did all the gear changing. I think that he had lost his driving licence for 12 months, at the time, but that was just a technicality!

Two years later, different car same me, and things took another turn for the worse. I'm chasing a pea hen and her chick, (that's yet another story), I vault over a gate, (there was a time when I could vault a gate), land on a large stone and break my ankle. A week later and I can't drive but I'm looking at my truck. I can get people to take me places I need to but I can hardly ask them to take me pottering about the fields, can I? Then it occurs to me that if you are driving an oldish tractor, and you match engine revs to forward speed, there comes a time when there is no load on the engine and no load on the gearbox and you can change gear perfectly smoothly without using the clutch. But this only works if the vehicle is moving. After a bit of practise I find that I can operate the clutch using my crutch and once moving I can change gear.

With this new-found freedom I range far and wide and it works OK as long as you don't go anywhere near a steep hill. One day I go into our local town and as I drive home I can see that I am being followed by our local policeman, who follows me up the yard. 'I've seen how you start that car off, if I see you driving again I'll have your licence off you!' That was the end of that. Next time I changed car I bought an automatic. You never know when you might need one.

17 November 2018

On the first day of the shooting season the beaters seek out every pheasant that there is. The pheasants could be hiding in woods, hedgerows, root crops or game crops but they are sought out wherever they might be. Most beaters have a spaniel so it is very rare that a pheasant is not found. The idea is to put all the pheasants over the guns. Nobody wants to see them all shot but it is the guns that have paid to rear the pheasants so the keeper wants to put on a bit of a show so they can see what a good job he has done. The whole process is like a search party going out over my fields. That is why I am in the habit of texting the keeper next day after the first shoot to see how many hares there were about.

Five years ago I remember the keeper texted back and said, 'You have 130.' That was a memorable day. This year he didn't text, he phoned, he was indignant. 'We didn't see one.' I told him I had recently seen two. 'If you want to see them, they are dead by the gate into the Lea Bank field, hare coursers have cleared you out, they came three times last week.' The police are too stretched so I think it's a job for the army. It's just what they need. There would be the surveillance, these coursers are aggressive, they are beyond the law, sounds like anarchy, never mind the cruelty. It looks as if the hare chapter in my life has come to an end.

★★★

It's Sunday evening and we've been out all day at an 80th birthday party. As it happens two of my lady friends were doing the catering so I got better food and better service than anyone else. I'm reading my weekly farming paper and the phone goes. It's a near neighbour, they tell me that they haven't got any water. We are all on mains water but they get their water off my supply so I am their first call. I tell them that there is probably a burst main somewhere.

In the next hour I get three text messages from the water company to say that there is indeed a burst main somewhere and they are doing their best to fix it. I also get further phone calls and raps on the door from near neighbours about not having water. We, as farmers, are more pragmatic about things going wrong. Stuff happens! It slightly amused me that these people were agonised about not being able to fill their kettles. I don't think it occurred to them for a second that further up the yard there were about 150 cattle and tens of thousands of 14-day-old chicks. They like water as well.

★★★

We have some friends come to stay the night. It's a nice dry, sunny afternoon so I take them for a ride over our top fields. They are farmers as well but where they farm is very flat so this is very different to what they are used to. The views, in the sun, are spectacular. I never tire of seeing them, and I see them every day. We are going across this grass field and there is a solitary sheep in the middle. 'I didn't know you kept sheep,' he says. 'I don't, these are 'visitors', there's visitors here most days.'

Boundary fences can sometimes be contentious. A good rule is that you should fence against your own stock, whoever's the fence is. In this case it's my neighbour's fence and it's his sheep, there's been three sheep in one of my mowing fields all summer but we don't get too uptight about it, they are always there, life is too short. Two winters ago there were 20-30 sheep there. Once they had eaten all my grass they broke into the adjoining wood and ate all the wheat in the pheasant feeders, the keeper wasn't best pleased.

My companion has a story to tell. He knew a dairy farmer who didn't keep sheep but who had a neighbour who had a lot. They were good friends and in most respects they were good neighbours. The only reservation was that most days there were about six sheep eating his grass. They weren't always the same sheep and they weren't always in the same field but it was a norm in their lives that every day there were sheep in their fields, although they didn't have any sheep. He thought it was about time to do something about it. He invited his neighbour and his wife over for Sunday lunch. The host bought a nice leg of lamb for the occasion.

The guest is tucking into his share and says what nice lamb it is and asks which butcher did they buy it from. He is told, by his host, that they like lamb very much, but they don't get it from a butcher, although they take two or three to the abattoir every year and this is one of those. The visitor goes quiet and he is not eating his lunch with as much relish as he was previously. You don't have to be a genius to guess his train of thought. He knew very well that his host didn't have any sheep. If he took any lambs to the abattoir they could be his own lambs, and the roast lamb he had in front of him could indeed be his own.

Next day the neighbour and his son could be seen repairing the boundary fence; they did some fencing every day for a week and they didn't have sheep straying ever again.

There's a moral to this story. You can resolve, with a bit of subtlety, something that could easily turn into a dispute.

1 December 2018

Yesterday afternoon was spent in the kitchen. First one friend arrives for a chat, shortly followed by another, who was there for the same purpose. After about an hour I suggest that one of my guests, who is fleeter of foot than me, makes us a cup of tea. I should qualify this by saying that it is normal practice in this house, when making a cup of tea, to put a tea bag into a mug. My friend put the tea on the table and I have a sip, there's a sort of scented tang to it that I don't particularly like so I don't drink it all. I idly wonder why has she started buying Earl Grey? Much later in the evening my wife asks if I have made a cup of tea in the teapot. I instinctively answer no, always a good practise in order to keep a happy marriage, but in this case it is perfectly true. She tells me that someone has. 'It must have tasted awful, I've just put two dishwasher tablets in there to take the tea stain off.'

★★★

One of the friends is a timber merchant so we spend a lot of time talking of all things wood. He reckons that the timber industry is in chaos and that demand is unprecedented. Why so? He says that there is a huge demand for firewood that is driven by the use of wood burning stoves but that is as nothing when you compare it to the amount of woodchip that is used to heat industrial premises. Factories, warehouses, large country houses, they are all using it. In this area most poultry houses use woodchip to heat them. The reason is that because wood is considered a renewable, it attracts a huge subsidy. Some poultry sheds are making more money from using woodchip than they are from rearing poultry. Some industrial premises kept the heating on all summer, even in the hot weather, because the more woodchip you use, the more subsidy you get, (though they had to keep doors and windows open and, bizarrely, fans running). If there was ever any truth to the adage, 'a licence to print money,' this is it.

But it gets worse. If you buy cut timber, and most do, and you chip it and dry it, because it doesn't burn properly unless it is dried, you get paid to dry it and you get paid to use it. Just how green is this after you have used huge machines to chip it and a proportion of your dried woodchip is used to dry other woodchip, is open to question. But it's all OK because timber is a renewable so the green lobby is happy, never mind the waste or the detail.

And when we've used all our timber, as we surely will, there's plenty of timber elsewhere in the world, even if it has to be brought thousands of miles. There is only one more question. Who pays for all this subsidy? You and I in our electric bills. There's a call on the news to grow more trees, fat lot of good if we are presently cutting them down and burning them faster than they can grow.

If you look at a map of the world, our island is only a tiny speck. If you planted it all with trees, wherever a tree would grow, no sheep and cattle, no arable crops, how much difference do you think that would make in the global scheme of things? While elsewhere in the world they carry on using fossil fuels as if there is no tomorrow. Yet there are plenty of those that would sacrifice UK agriculture on such a folly. What would we eat then: leaves in summer and hibernate in winter? The green lobby have their eyes fixed on the horizon and the final solution to global warming. They don't look at the waste and the chaos they cause whilst we get there. I've no problem with the ideal but as in solar panels and wind power and now woodchip, fortunes are being made and that are paid for by ordinary folk like you and me. As always, a sense of balance is the way forward.

8 December 2018

When my friends in the pub say that they are going shooting, what they invariably mean is that they are going beating. They just love it. They like working their dogs, we are just as likely to hear an amusing anecdote about someone's dog committing a shooting day misdemeanour as we are some prodigious retrieve. But what I sense they like above all else is that on the shooting day itself, shooters and beaters are all treated as equals. It's a good day out as it's a good social experience, they all eat together, drink together, and tractor drivers form good friendships with captains of industry, and obviously vice-versa.

Because the day is conducted in a friendly manner, our beaters take it in turns to take a bottle of drink with them so that they can have a 'livener' between drives. Their preferred choice is a swig of port and sometimes the occasion is enhanced by someone producing a piece of Stilton from the depths of a shooting jacket pocket. The customary drink between drives had been thrown into confusion because the person whose turn it was to buy the port, forgot and brought a bottle of sweet sherry he had found in the cupboard, instead. They much prefer port to sherry. After three days' shooting there is still a third of a bottle of sherry left. The consensus opinion is that they will try sherry one last time and if there is still some left after that they will use if to clean the guns.

After shooting they all go off to the pub.

15 December 2018

When someone irritates you by something they have said or written, you usually have two options. You can reply publicly and attempt a counter argument or you can just keep quiet and allow them to continue, until, in the fullness of time, they say too much and, with a bit of luck, bring about their own downfall. For satisfaction, the second option is much to be preferred. There is a person who writes, every two months or so, letters to our local paper about badger culling. I can tell, by how and what they write, that they trawl the internet for facts and figures that suit their argument, to the extent that what they write is misleading, possibly deliberately so. 'Someone needs to reply to that letter,' people say, and mostly it has been me.

I thought I would try the second approach and leave a letter unchallenged. I like to think that this person was thus emboldened and wrote a second letter in which they said that the TB problem in cattle was due entirely to poor biosecurity on farms, and they proceeded to set out a regime that would solve the problem. That's when they went that bit too far. Their final biosecurity measure is to advocate that on farms where a reactor is found, the whole herd is slaughtered! We had six reactors who went off for slaughter in October and that was upsetting enough — but for someone to seek to slaughter the lot is beyond belief, about 200 cattle!

There's quite a bit of TB around here at the moment and if I count the affected herds and you slaughtered all the cattle on those farms, you could be talking over 2,000 cattle, most of them dairy cows. There's only one sector of society that wants to see an end to livestock farming and that's vegans. Now we know they are using badgers to achieve their other ambitions.

★★★

Just gently, but with increasing urgency, I have been making enquiries, in the pub, about our Christmas turkey. The turkey comes from a friend of a friend who rears only 40 and as far as I can make out they are reared on a diet of grass and apples which, presumably, is OK if you are a turkey. All he will tell me about my turkey is that this year he is getting me a special one, 'Yours was born with one leg.' This alludes to the problem we had last year when we had to call him round on

Christmas morning to cut a leg off because we couldn't get it in the oven. It was still a squeeze but getting it back out wasn't easy either. We need a big turkey because there will be around 16 of us. Three of those would otherwise be on their own all day. I always think that when they see how grumpy I can be at Christmas, being on your own wouldn't seem so bad.

★★★

It's become a bit of a ritual, in our family, me being grumpy at Christmas, and I make every effort to not disappoint them. Just between you and me, I enjoy it more than I used to. We go around to Jane the florist for a drink in the morning, which is a lot of fun. And I don't have to milk in the afternoon. But wish I could. I've always thought that the most miserable place to have your Christmas lunch would be on your own in a motorway service station, especially on a cold wet day. I used to threaten to do this.

When my grandchildren were small they used to take the threat seriously and beg me not to go. Now that they are older they say, 'You go,' and I think they mean it, which is not the response I would be looking for, and is a bit of a blow. Quietly, I've thought about it and I suspect that a motorway services wouldn't be that miserable anyway. All the staff would probably be cheerful because they would be getting extra money for being on duty, but I don't expect they would be very busy. It would get them out of the house which they would probably see as a bonus anyway, and I bet they wouldn't all be wearing those ridiculous Christmas jumpers.

We always have a Christmas lunch at the rugby club to coincide with a home game, it's a good 'do' and I always go. But over half the people there wear these jumpers and parade them as if they were some sort of trophy. There's a sprinkling of professional people there and they seem to be the worst offenders. The more successful the person, the more ridiculous the jumper. The motif on the front is usually distorted by an ample paunch. I've got a jumper to wear at the Christmas lunch. It's plain navy blue.

We always have what we call a staff Christmas dinner, we have one full time employee and one part time but with family and partners there's usually 12-14 of us. We haven't booked a date yet but there's no rush. We've often had it after Christmas. One year we had it in March. Someone in the pub asked what was all that noise in the dining room, and someone said that's Evans' Christmas party. 'Is that last Christmas or next?' 'Last of course.'

22 DECEMBER 2018

It's important in life to plan ahead. Already I'm planning for the festive season in the pub. For several weeks now I have been sitting in the same seat in an inaccessible corner. Now if I go into the pub and it's a bit crowded, someone always says, 'Roger always sits there,' and someone moves for me to sit down.

You can't be too careful: Christmas and New Year is a time of much kissing. I've given the matter some thought and on a sort of balance I would prefer not to be involved. If I sit tight in my corner I can watch it all going on without having to take part. I can watch the men approach women with their lips puckered up, hoping for lips in return, and getting a cold cheek instead. Some women kiss everyone in the pub except me, because they can only reach me if I lean forward and they take one look at my face and soon work out that I don't intend to do that! It's not a sexist thing, I avoid the men too, they are all high fives and man hugs. I've never done either and don't intend to start. If I had to choose I would prefer to kiss the women.

Perhaps it's just me. I can't do that bit in church where you are supposed to turn and greet those in the pew behind you. I've been to countless international rugby matches but have never cheered or shouted, although I sing the one anthem along with everyone else. I've always considered myself to be an emotional person but it seems I work hard not to show it.

★★★

Year after year it's always the same. The pub goes quiet at the end of November and the beginning of December. Once New Year is over it's the same for most of January. People ask of me, 'Why is it so quiet?' and I always give the same answer. It's quiet in November and early December because they are saving up for Christmas. And it's quiet in January because they didn't save enough and their card statements are due. Me, I go the same as usual in case I should miss something. The day when I can't afford two halves of bitter and a cup of tea is not here yet, but something tells me that it is not far away.

I don't spend a lot of money (about a £1 a week) on the juke box in the pub but rather I try to influence the musical choices of those that do. It being much cheaper doing it this way. Most of those that I influence have the opportunity to choose five records and they invariably ask me to choose the 5th. I always choose 'Sweet 16' by the Furys. Not only is it a really nice song but the music played between verses is exceptional. I'm no musician but I think the haunting tune is played on a mandolin. But the more it is played the more it is liked and now it often features on people's choices without any prompting from me.

This suits me just fine, I am having an influence without having to say anything. It often seems to me that I have lived my life like a candle in the wind, whatever that means.

29 December 2018

I'm scornful of the young men at the local gym, with their grimaces and their grunts, as they lift weights repetitively, all the time looking into the mirrors to see if anyone is watching them. When I was their age I seemed to spend all summer manhandling bales or sacks of corn and all winter getting the same bales and sacks of corn back out of the barns and feeding them to livestock. But it's not their fault that most repetitive manual work is done these days by machinery and if, all those years ago, a machine had turned up in the field to lift those bales and sacks, no one would have welcomed it more than me. The modern day equivalent of manual work is to go to the gym and, fair play, they are doing that.

But it's the older ones that amuse me the most. There's men there of my age or older who turn up in pristine new gym outfits. It's all new from the tip of their trainers right up to the new sweat bands on their heads, and everything in between. They have alternate new kit to wear later in the week. But if you watch these men when they are lifting weights you can easily see that they are only lifting the weight if a couple of bags of sugar, and that not for long. When they get next to you on the exercise bikes you can see what degree of difficulty they have it set at. It goes up to 25, they have it set at 1 or 2, sometimes at 0, which as far as I can tell is free-wheeling. I set it at 12, always, and every time I try to go a bit further in the same time, which is what I assume it is all about.

And as the outfits worn by others get newer and newer, so I deliberately dress down as a sort of compensation. I go to the gym in whatever I am wearing on the farm but if I am due a change of clothes I sometimes make them last another day because it's gym tomorrow. Sometimes the family say 'You can't go to the gym dressed like that' but I can, the scruffier the better, and if I haven't shaved for a couple of days, so much the better for that. I am the same as them, they dress up deliberately, and I dress down, just as deliberately. Were ever two opposites so similar?

★★★

If you are a farmer, there is so much that can go wrong, that you have no control over, that if you are not careful, you can become very negative. Costs can go up, returns can go down, often at the same time. Disease of both animal and crops, can strike without warning, then there's the weather, which usually heads the list of things that can go wrong.

Take sheep for example, they are born with an inherent desire to die and just keeping them alive can be a life's work. In these circumstances it is very easy to see yourself as a victim, it's not helped by the fact that your efforts are largely unappreciated by society in general.

This year will be remembered as the year that livestock farming came under concerted vegan attack. It's not the best of feeling when you are working on Christmas day, to know that there is a vociferous sector of society that thinks you are some sort of lowlife.

★★★

For many years I used to have to go to Scotland a lot. I made many good friends there, lots of them still keep in touch. I soon became aware that they victimise themselves especially with regard to the weather. As a rule the weather gets worse the further you go north, it's a fact of life. I would meet someone and they would ask how the farming was going. I might say that our ground was wet and we had an inch of rain on Sunday. 'We had three inches.'

As I became aware of this I used to add a bit on in order to see what their reaction would be. 'We had six inches of rain on Sunday.' Six inches is a prodigious amount. 'We had 10!' 'It was minus ten degrees on Monday night.' 'We had minus 20.' As it was with the weather, so it was with rugby. 'What sort of team will Wales have out against us next week?' 'Not good, we've got six players injured.' 'We've got 15!'

5 JANUARY 2019

There is one theme that has dominated our conversations at home for months now: heating. For over 20 years we have had LPG central heating. We like our sitting room to be warm but we only use the heating upstairs if it's really cold and we put it on for a couple of hours to take the chill off or if we have bed and breakfast guests in.

Last April it broke down and we phoned the man who usually looks after it and he said he didn't do it anymore. He recommended someone else and this person got it going again and so I told him he could look after it in future and he could service it as soon as he liked. We get to October and he still hasn't been and the heating wouldn't work. He never answered my phone calls and so I chased him by text and email. Eventually he came and said we needed a new boiler. We said OK – he came again in two weeks' time with a colleague to measure it all up and that was the last we saw of him. We must have phoned 20 others to come, mostly they didn't, we even asked the gas suppliers to recommend someone but they never replied. Weeks and weeks went by. We only had a small electric fire so I bought a portable gas fire for our living room.

Our house has two floors upstairs so it's impossible for any heat on the ground floor to seep upstairs to where we sleep, at the top. The house is lovely and cool in the summer but freezing in winter. Getting out of the shower on a cold day is one of the bravest things I have ever done. I always have a shave as soon as I get out of the shower, I'm shivering so much I don't need to dry myself afterwards, all the water from the shower has been shaken off. It would be no surprise if the Duke of Edinburgh turned up one day and gave me a medal. All my working life has been spent out of doors and I always accepted that being cold and wet was a part of that life, but I never liked being cold in the house.

Enough is enough, I got the man who looks after our oil Rayburn to take the gas out and he put in a second-hand oil burner. That's working fine. I put it on upstairs for half an hour before I have a shower but no one else knows that. The central heating boiler shares an oil tank with the Rayburn, this tank is on the small side, so all I have to worry about now, is running out of oil, which is a new big worry. They always say that as one door closes and another opens. Wonder if that's what they mean?

★★★

I've not found it that easy driving at night, of late. Sometimes, when I have met other cars on narrow rural roads, I have flirted with the ditch. Then I discovered that one headlight wasn't working. I had wondered about the lights but there's a screen on my dashboard that tells me you everything you might need to know, it will even tell you the tyre pressures, so I had assumed it would tell me if a bulb had gone.

I found out the old fashioned way, I switched the lights on and got out to have a look. I asked Stephen, who works with us, if he would call into the garage to get a new bulb as he was going into town. On his return he says he has booked my car in for Thursday morning. 'What for?' 'To change the bulb, they have to take some panels off, it will take 3½ to 4 hours.' I mutter some unprintable adjectives. 'They say it's not such a big job on the new models.' Is that meant to make me feel better?

★★★

It has become something of a tradition around here, amongst my friends, that if one of them goes on holiday, they buy me a stick of rock. Sometimes in the summer, there is rock everywhere. I'm not crazy about rock but a present is a present. At some point I have to eat some in order to keep the tradition going, traditions are like that, you have to work at them. I break a piece off and eat it in the evening. I'm always in my favourite armchair, my wife is sitting opposite doing a crossword and my dog Gomer is always asleep next to her on the settee, on his back, with all his bits and pieces on show. At the merest rustle of the wrapping he is wide awake and at my side awaiting his pieces of rock. I didn't think he would like peppermint but he does, or anything else that I may eat during an evening.

Over the last three days I've had a cold, and when I get a cold, I usually get a sore throat as well. Best for me to clear things up are Fisherman's Friend lozenges. The dog hears the rustle of the packet and comes across as usual. My wife says, 'You can't give him one of those, they are so strong they might kill him.' But he gives me such a sorrowful look that I break one in half for him. He likes it so much he climbs on my knee for another, which he duly gets. I know a good joke about Fisherman's Friends but I don't think the editor would let me tell you it.

★★★

It's become a norm for banks in rural areas to close. My own account has been at four different branches in as many years. As banks close you are moved, like it or not, to a bigger bank in a bigger town. When we used to go to our original branch, we could go in our 'rough', in our working clothes. The girls behind the counter didn't mind if you were in wellys and dirty overalls, they were often farmer's daughters.

Now it is more of a formal sort of occasion. It's a bigger bank in a bigger town, you have to park in a proper car park where you have to pay, so it's probably best to change your boots and take your overalls off. I was in the queue at our bank and I see another farmer come in. I don't know him except by sight and I know he keeps pigs. He has clearly come straight from work and hasn't changed his clothes. He leaves a pig muck bum print on a chair and he is leaving pig muck footprints on the floor. Pig muck has a smell all of its own and the other customers don't like it. I do, it is a reminder to them that they live in a rural area.

19 JANUARY 2019

I don't go to the pub for the drink, I go for the company. Company is usually thin on the ground in the pub in January so sometimes it's a dilemma whether I should go or not. I nearly didn't go on Sunday night but went in the end, more out of habit than anticipation. What a revelation, the pub staff were having their Christmas party. It had started at 6 and when I got there at 9, it was in full swing. They were all dancing to the juke box. It was gone 12 when I went and I was the first to go!

★★★

Do you know what a 'stopper' is? I'll explain. On the land I rent is a large area of woodland, these woods taper to a point at one end. On shooting days, despite their best efforts, the activity of vehicles and personnel makes some noise and the pheasants, the day's quarry, hear them. Pheasants aren't dull so they seek to escape. They know if they fly they will be shot at, so they seek to flee on foot using the trees as cover. Because of the shape of the woods, the pheasants tend to gravitate towards the narrow end where they know they can escape under a gate. That's where the shoot put a stopper, he is one of the beaters and he is stationed at this gate and if he sees pheasants approaching he taps his stick and the pheasants should turn back. It's not only pheasants that escape this way. If there are any hares in the wood, and the shoot are not after them, they take the same route.

I tell you all this because our shoot has put the same stopper in place for 20 years and he likes to count the hares that go past him, the most he ever saw was 35. Thus far, in three months shooting, he hasn't seen one, and that's the first time in 20 years he hasn't seen a hare. Hare populations are being decimated by hare coursers but no one seems able to do anything about it. If it were badgers there would be a public outcry and police everywhere. I haven't seen a hare for three months, not a live one anyway.

★★★

The barn behind our house has been converted to two homes. They are not ours but are let out by the person that now owns them. At first it was strange having people living in the yard but it lends itself to being quite private and we have become good friends with most of the people who have lived there, which is how we prefer to live our lives. (I said *most*, we were quite glad to see one go).

At the top house they have a dog and because they are out all day they leave that dog outside in their garden. The dog, for his part, spends most of his day running up and down the fence barking at our dogs (who bark back, so it's not an issue) and barking at anything else that comes and goes on our yard. The neighbours leave their house door open all day so that their dog can go inside should it so choose. Thus far their dog hasn't worked out how to get in and out of their garden.

Our dogs being made of sterner stuff, they have worked out how to get into the garden and how to get out again. This is not an issue for the tenants who love our dogs. But there is a downside, there usually is. It took no time at all for our dogs to work out that if it is cold or wet they had only to get into the garden and then they could get into the neighbour's house and spend the day stretched out on a settee.

26 JANUARY 2019

It's the middle of January, and the land is really dry so I can drive anywhere I like in my truck. I have driven over all my grass fields, carefully crossing them at 20 yard gaps looking for hares. There is only 2-3 inches of grass on these fields so if a hare was squat down you would see it easily. I haven't seen one. We have 20 acres of kale and the shoot have about ten acres of cover crops and there could be hares in there but I doubt it. My drives around the land are not as joyful as they used to be.

★★★

I've got two really bad knees – too much milking, too much rugby and too much tug of war. The knees stumble a bit, which is not a good combination if you don't have good balance. People say I should get new knees but I haven't been given the chance. I suspect that 'they' think I will end up in a wheelchair anyway, in which case two new knees would not be a good investment for them. They haven't said as much but I can work it out for myself. My main preoccupation is to avoid a fall. I usually have one fall a month, any more than that and I consider that I've been careless. I've become an expert at falling, I soon worked out that it is better to fall on the bed or settee or even carpet than it is to fall down steps or onto concrete. I can't do heavy work on the farm but I can drive about OK and identify work for others to do.

My philosophy is one of doing what you can for as long as you can, there's plenty worse off than me. There is no treatment and one thing I have learnt in life is that there is no point in worrying about things that you can do nothing about. I have not told you all this to try to stimulate your sympathy, rather to set a scene.

One of the things I am determined to keep doing as long as I can, is to go to the pub. The car park is often dark and I don't walk well in the dark, so I park right across the door, just leaving enough room for people to walk in and out. I got to the pub on Thursday, Saturday and Sunday evenings and can get in an out unaided. Not that I always choose to do so. That is my own fault. On Saturdays there are usually two of my lady drinking companions there. When it is time to go home I get to my feet and they do also. They go on either side: each takes an arm and holds a hand firmly. I quite enjoy this. As I'm getting all this attention it is only fair that I put on a bit of a show. I enact a feeble gait and stumble a bit. If I stumble a bit they hold me tighter. All this is good!

But it brings with it problems. These two ladies are rarely there on Sundays and Thursdays, so when I get to my feet, there are men that leap forward to help me. They are not my close friends; my close friends have worked out what I am doing on Saturdays. Call me old fashioned if you will, but I'm not bothered about men holding my hand.

★★★

I'm sitting in the bathroom on our top floor. That's all the detail you need to know. The door is wide open and a mouse comes across the landing and pauses in the bathroom doorway. It is surprised to see me there. I'm surprised as well, not at seeing a mouse, you often get mice in these old farmhouses. I'm surprised because we have not recently seen any trace of mice and I can't get over how well it looks. It is a big mouse, it is sleek and fat. Whatever does it find to eat up here?

The mouse completes its scrutiny of me, comes into the bathroom and disappears under the shower tray where the waste pipe comes out. Then I remember that I had dropped a new tube of toothpaste in that corner and next day I couldn't find it!

I tell my wife about the mouse. She is a mouse-catcher of some renown and she puts a trap close to the shower. Within 24 hours she had caught three but the trap has been completely empty for two days now. All my working life I had to get up early to milk. I managed that OK but there would often be times when I thought that, 'just another ten minutes would be nice.'

As an aid to getting up, I bought one of those devices that made you a cup of tea by the bed, when the alarm went, and I used it for years. Every night I used to carry a tray upstairs with all the stuff I needed to make a cup of tea, I would fill the kettle and put the tray and all the other requisites on the floor. One night I was awoken by a strange noise. I put the light on and there were three mice lapping away at the milk. I soon stopped that by using a taller milk jug.

2 FEBRUARY 2019

I told you that I needed a new headlight bulb in my car and that I had to book the car in because they have to remove panels to get at the bulb. I've just had the bill, £40 to change a bulb! No wonder this country is in such a mess.

★★★

A while ago, I needed new glasses. I usually have three pairs, which adds to the confusion. I had new lenses in my writing and reading glasses. I had new lenses in my bi-focals; I'm not a big fan of bi-focals but they are quite handy in the evenings if you are reading and something on TV catches your interest or you want to watch the replay of a goal being scored. I had to have a pair of new every-day glasses because the frames of these were beyond repair, and I was disappointed with the new ones, in fact they were no better than the old ones. But I persevered with them, which is what I do, although my driving at night certainly wasn't good enough.

I made an appointment at the optician and she said that I should be OK because I'd just had new glasses. I said that the everyday glasses were very disappointing. I was a bit indignant by now but I tried not to show it as she is always so kind and thoughtful. I sit down in the chair and she puts a chart up and I read the letters I can. She says, 'That's not good at all, take your glasses off.' She examines the glasses and says, 'These are a pair I prescribed for you three years ago.' I had been struggling with glasses that were supplied the prescription before last! We both had a good laugh over this. All I have to do now is find the real new ones.

9 FEBRUARY 2019

I assume that our kitchen table is very much like other farmhouse kitchen tables. It's quite a big table, probably because it's quite a big kitchen. When we came here all those years ago, there was a baking oven and a big boiler to wash the clothes. We ripped all those out.

Back to the table. At one end is a pile of newspapers, magazines and other stuff. This pile grows until it either falls on the floor or until it is so big there isn't room to sit down. In either case, harsh words are exchanged and we have a bit of a sort out. But there is a new addition to the paraphernalia on the table this year, a fly swatter.

You get flies around farms in summer, and last summer was the worst I can remember, but what are they doing in winter! For about eight weeks there have been big lazy bluebottles about our kitchen. Not a lot, three or four a day, hence the fly swat. I was intrigued by their presence, where had they come from, and in winter, in a cold house? But I was even more intrigued when I went in to a bedroom we hadn't used lately. On the window sill were hundreds, (and I mean hundreds) of dead ladybirds. That's a mystery to me. I haven't seen a ladybird in the house for years. No matter how much we think we know about nature, it continues to surprise you.

★★★

We had a crime prevention officer at the Parish Council meeting last week. He was a advocating the use of smart water to prevent theft. Smart water is something (a liquid), that you use to identify an item that is stolen. Each liquid is different, it cannot be removed and it can be traced back to you. There are other liquids that do the same job but smart water is probably the best known. You can use it to identify everything from a tractor to a vase and should either item be stolen, and it is marked, the police can always identify your belongings and return them to you. It is an eminently sensible idea, and is relatively cheap. But the officer had another message. If the water was used by a community, like a village, it could reduce theft by 80%. If everyone uses it, and there are warning signs available to say you have done so, the effect can be dramatic. If everyone uses it there is the possibility of getting it cheaper through the police. One tube will mark about 50 items.

This, as we will see, brings us, rather tenuously to triathlons. My son used to do triathlons. I used to do triathlons. We have a local one, it's done on tandems. I did it several times after I finished playing rugby, I did it with a neighbouring farmer. I was in my 60s and he was in his 50s. I did the swimming, slowly, and he did the running, also slowly. But because we had both played rugby in the front row we could push those pedals down along with the best of them and we always came about 100th out of 150. Except for the year the chain came off.

My son went much further afield to do triathlons on his own. Triathlons are a bit like going to the gym. People have a variety of kit in order to compete. You get some who have streamed-lined crash helmets, an all-in-one lycra suit and a bike that doesn't have spokes on its wheels but has a solid-looking wheel that must have cost a fortune.

My son always used to amuse me; he kept his bike in the shed where the cows lie, it wasn't a posh bike. He would get it out the day before a triathlon, lean it against a wall and hose it down to knock any cow muck and cobwebs off, pump the tyres up and he was ready. His kit consisted of rugby shorts and a singlet.

I was asking him about a triathlon he had been on one day. I said do they have any security (told you we would get to security) over those expensive bikes while you are all out running and the bikes are left on their own. He said no but he had the comfort that if there was anyone there nicking bikes, his would be the last to go. Message from my son, just in case anyone fancies competing in a triathlon: the water in Lake Bala in north Wales is the coldest in the world.

Not that I need to worry about security, when I am in the house the dog Gomer is always asleep somewhere near my feet. He's gone very aggressive lately and barks and growls at the slightest noise. This isn't very handy if I'm asleep as well. He likes watching police documentaries with me. I think he thinks he's a police dog.

★★★

I've got this friend. He goes to a different pub to me and he goes two or three times a week, and he takes his wife. I don't take my wife, which is a big saving. But nowhere near the saving he makes. On her dressing table his wife has a bowl where she puts £2 coins which she is saving. If they are going to the pub he helps himself to a handful of those coins. When he buys the first round of drinks, she sees the £2 coins. 'Ooh, look at all those, I save those, don't spend them, I'll buy them off you.' And so he gives her five of the £2 coins and she gives him a tenner. So far she hasn't worked out although she has said that it's odd how he gets lots of £2 coins and there don't seem to be many in her bowl. I suspect it is only a matter of time.

16 FEBRUARY 2019

When I was at school, TB had a big impact on my life, for two reasons. Firstly this was the time in my life that I started to work on local farms and decided farming was for me. I didn't, obviously, know what form that would take but the farming bug came out and bit me and still does. I listened, avidly, to all the conversations centred on TB because this was at the time when the nation sought to clear TB from UK cattle. Most of the farms around our village were small dairy farms with about 20-30 cows. As I remember it, most of these cows lived in cowsheds with wooden stalls, they spent the night in there in winter tied by the neck. If you wanted to be clear of TB, (attested), these wooden stalls had to be ripped out and replaced with tubular steel, so there was an expense involved. Also, as I remember it, you could still buy and sell cattle that had failed the TB test. Even to me, who knew very little, this seemed ridiculous. I particularly remember one farmer coming home from market and telling us that he had just seen the highest yielding cow in the county sold for little money because she was a TB reactor and she had been bought by a producer/retailer, which is someone who milks his own cows and sells the milk on a milk round. My use of the word ridiculous is clearly appropriate.

The second impact on my life was a very real one. Just outside our village was a large country house, it was big enough to be called a stately home. It was a TB hospital. It was a part of our daily lives that we saw patients from the hospital walking the lanes, I think that fresh air and exercise was an important part of their recovery process. Even as young boys we would look at these patients and know that there was no way we would want to get TB, and we would know that the patients we saw were the better ones.

If we move on about 60 years we find that I did indeed become a farmer. My son and grandson do the farming now on the farm where I live but the irony is that TB has the biggest impact on their farming lives over all other issues. If they lose cows to TB they are understocked and don't meet their milk sales targets. At the same time they have the expense and extra work of keeping all the calves they would normally sell. All this at a time when you have no way of knowing if you will or will not get TB and as long as there is a reservoir of TB in wildlife, there is very little they can do to prevent it. And that anxiety gnaws away at you. I can see bovine TB having an impact on their lives for another 20 years, maybe more.

★★★

I know you shouldn't wish your life away but the spring is so nice you can't help looking forward to it. Already the days are lengthening. Strangely, the evenings seem to get lighter quicker than the mornings, I know that can't be right but that's how it seems. I'm quite glad to see the end of the shooting season, it will bring some normality to Saturday nights in the pub. All my friends should be there - now that there's no beating to do, they won't be missing, presumed drunk. Now we will have endless dog stories: 'My dog retrieved a bird from three parishes away, he had to cross two rivers, a main road, a railway line and a lake.'

They will move on, as the year moves on, to lambing stories but we all know about lambing, so these stories are less easy to exaggerate. There have been lambs in a field down the road for a month now and now and those of my friends who lamb at a more conventional time are starting to talk about lambing and are getting their sheds ready. Spring may be on its way but you should never think that winter is over. It will fight a sort of rearguard action and come back for a few days when you least expect it, often catching you out. If there's a more forlorn sight than a daffodil in full flower bent double with the weight of snow on it, it has to be that of a young lamb with an icicle on its chin.

The traditional time for lambing around here is in March and there are hundreds of lambs turned out into the fields, with their mothers, at this time. They can often be caught out by two or three days snow and this can cause huge losses. It happens so regularly that this phenomenon even has a name, it is called 'lamb snow'. I can remember, when the children were small, standing cold and wet at our May fair, wishing that they would come home, and all the hills around would be white over with snow! I can look forward to spring all I like but winter could last for weeks yet.

23 FEBRUARY 2019

The hare coursers have been about, I can see the tracks of their vehicles in the snow and frost. I am tempted to put a sign up 'You've already killed them all.' The keeper, at this end-of -shooting season catch up, tells me that over the whole season he has seen just one hare on my fields. What a big impact the coursers have had. My neighbour next door chained two gates together and for good measure put a tree trunk across the gates. I saw the chain he used, it came from an old muck spreader, and I know that the steel used is particularly hard. The tree trunk was moved onto the side and the chain cut. But it wasn't just cut, it was cut at every link and those links were put in a neat pile in the middle of the track. This tells me two things. It tells me that the hare coursers carry a motorised disc cutter with them so that they are able to cut their way into everything. It also tells the world, by taking the trouble to cut every link in two, that they have a sinister and threatening message. 'You can't stop us and we will do what we like!' And those dead hares would tell us that they are right.

My son had a good ride around our fields and saw one hare. He also doesn't have to keep one eye on the dog Gomer, who follows my truck so closely that when I look in the wing mirror he's so tight to the back wheel that I fear for his safety. This is not helped by the fact that both wheel and dog are black. My neighbour on one side has sheep in every field and is not troubled by the coursers. It could be that the coursers dogs hunt by sight and cannot follow a hare amongst a flock of sheep. He tells me he still has hares about so we just have to hope that one of his visits mine. Then we could be away again, it takes two, but we all knew that didn't we?

★★★

Most nights I have the most amazing dreams, the detail is often extraordinary. Last night I dreamt I was doing some tree surgery and got stuck high up and couldn't get down. I'm afraid of heights and afraid of chainsaws, so this dream was bizarre. In 2003 I walked over Sydney Harbour Bridge and after that I thought I'd tested myself enough with heights, awake or asleep. I well remember, as we approached the bridge, looking for ways to do a runner, then I saw a party of old grannys coming off the bridge and thought if they can do it, so can I. In this dream, I was so terrified up the tree that I spent about ten minutes wondering who I could phone to rescue me, then I realised that all I had to do to be safe, was to just wake up!

The night before that I dreamt I was the speaker at the House of Commons. I used to tell the family at breakfast what I had dreamt but they stopped listening long ago, so I'll tell you. The speaker dream probably came from my custom of watching Prime Minister's Questions on Wednesdays. I often hope that no one else around the world is watching, or they will be thinking, 'What a way to run a country.' All they will see is rows of people shouting at each other. MPs seem to think that their constituents judge them by how many times they see them on TV: that's why they usually sit in the same place, so their constituents will know where to look. If they get called to speak, so much the better but they don't put any emphasis on what they have to say. Some contributions make me cringe. I wasn't House of Commons speaker for long in my dream, I didn't allow members to repeat what they had already said and I didn't allow them to say what someone else had already said. This dream cut sitting times by more than half.

★★★

I need to tell you about my friend the florist. She is a florist of some renown. She has won prizes for her floral art at major shows. Every week she goes demonstrating at flower clubs all over the county, see sings as she arranges or she amuses with stories. I've been to one of her evenings and she puts on a good show. Every year she goes to other countries to compete in international competitions. It is important to note that she doesn't sell bunches of flowers but she will arrange a bouquet for you. If you just want a bunch of flowers then you need to go to a garage forecourt or a supermarket, to be honest, she is a bit scornful of these sort of flowers. She had a big birthday this week so I arranged to meet her van delivery driver at a local supermarket, where I bought her a bunch of flowers. I paid for the bunch of flowers but she paid for their delivery. She could see the funny side but I bet she kept them well out of sight.

2 MARCH 2019

A knock at my kitchen door. There's a man there, dressed like a farmer, who I don't know. He introduces himself and he says he intends to write a book and he had called to see if I would advise him. I ask him in and he tells me his life story. I shan't tell you all that, he was here 2½ hours, but I shall tell you a bit of the start and the finish.

He was born on a Welsh hill farm, one of seven children, I know roughly where it was and he tells me there was no cart track to the farm, just footpaths so you can guess that we are talking isolated. He left school at 15 and went to work on farms. His first jobs were to live in at the farmhouse as family, a common practice then, and his wages were £3 a month. This is exactly the way I started and my wages were just the same. All through his life he saved his wages. If he wanted money to live on, he did extra work in the evenings and at weekends.

As he got older he got better jobs, got married and his love for his wife shone throughout his story. By buying cottages and doing them up, they got into the property ladder and were eventually able to buy a small run-down farm. When he retired he had a large farm and a large herd of dairy cows. He and his wife had never paid into a pension but had planned to sell farm and cows and to keep 30 acres, build a house and farm buildings and breed pedigree British Blues (a beef breed). The plan was falling into place when he lost his wife to cancer.

But he carried on with the plan, he bought about 15 top quality heifers and he sold the progeny at pedigree sales at Carlisle and it is top class stock. It was easy to tell that his driver in all this is the memory of his wife. Countless times he said, 'I was so lucky to have married her.'

What makes this story different and special is that every penny he receives for stock sales he gives to charity. He gives half to RABI, an agricultural charity, and he gives the other half towards the ovarian cancer charity. If you had heard his full story, like I did, you would know it's a love story; it doesn't have happy ending but it's a love story nonetheless. His herd profile is 'Old Barn Blues', which relates to the first farm he bought and the Blues refers to the breed his wife loved so much. Sounds a bit like a song! So far he has given £30,000 to the charities. Isn't it good to know that there are such people still about?

★★★

Years ago someone gave me one of those American style post boxes. It's designed as a black and white cow and is on a post up the yard. It's about 100 yards from our house, which isn't that handy, but it's handy for the postman. Because it's not handy for us the post doesn't make it to the house every day, in fact I sometimes think it only gets emptied if the postman can't get any more in the box. The next stop for the post is the kitchen table, usually in front of me. I go through it all but rarely open anything. This infuriates my wife but I tell her that I mostly know what's inside and mostly it's a bill. When I do get around to opening it, I reckon that about 20% needs keeping and the rest, which includes empty envelopes, is to be recycled.

Last week I was opening the post properly and noted, sort of subconsciously, that it contained a card and it was addressed to me. The significance of the date completely eluded me and a valentine card dropped onto the table. It's decades since I had one. I've never sent one to my wife since we've been married and she's never sent one to me. I've always thought that sending a valentine card was part of the wooing process and that was it. But hardly a day goes by that I don't tell my wife just how lucky she is to be married to me. We have a friend who used to send valentines to people with jealous partners which caused no end of trouble. I was expecting trouble as well, I thought we'd at least have some plates banged down. But I think the valentine was sent by my granddaughter and I think my wife had worked that out as well.

★★★

I'm sitting at the kitchen table, there's three women there as well, one of these is my wife. They are all gossiping, which is fair enough; I'm pretending to read the paper but really I'm listening to them. It's surprising what you can hear from women, especially if they think you are not listening. Sometimes it's not for the faint hearted! One lady is talking about her husband, apparently he's done something best described as erratic, I don't know what he's done as I was a bit late to hear that. 'He's always the same when there's a full moon, you'd think that you could buy a tablet for it.'

I've heard this often before, how people's behaviour can be affected by a full moon. Someone who is usually perfectly rational, doing things that are completely out of character, once a month. There used to be a farmer near here who was always getting into trouble. Mostly he led a sober sort of life but he would have too much to drink once a month. Too much drink, too much noise usually leads to trouble. He would have what we used to call a 'break out.'

The important thing was that local people knew what he was about and why. They even acknowledged this in his name. They called him 'Cosmic Ken' and they used to look after him and see that he didn't come to any harm. Even the local police knew what was going on and if they should be called out to him, they usually took him home. The only time he got into trouble with the police was if he got involved with policemen from outside the area. That is one of the big pluses of rural life, most people know most other people and look out for them. If there happens to be a full moon, they just have to be more vigilant.

9 MARCH 2019

Wow! Some good news. My son has seen two hares in the same field! There's something of Noah's Ark to it. That's all it takes for nature to recover, you need just two, even where you think all is lost. I look forward to the hare-breeding season with an optimism I didn't have a month ago. We will do everything in our power to help the hare population recover. The only thing we do that might harm them, especially the leverets, is when we are mowing grass, but at present I think we will mow half a field then move on to another. If there are leverets in the first field it will give them chance to escape; it's not a perfect solution I know but we will do what we can. Leverets have more to fear from Red Kites than they have from me. If the hares are successful, and we hope they are, will they be wiped out again by the coursers? I feel they will.

One of my maxims in life is not to spend time worrying about things you can do nothing about. Experience tells me that we can't do anything about the coursers, they seem to be beyond the law, so I am more pragmatic about it than my neighbours. They have the coursers on their land as well, and seem to get really incensed by it all. But it's the actual act of trespass that winds them up, whereas with me it's the fate of the hares.

★★★

I always read the letters in newspapers. I like to know what other people see as important. Even if you don't agree with a writer, if you understand where they are coming from, you are better able to counter their arguments. There was one such letter in our daily paper this week. It received prime position on the letters page and was illustrated by a colour photograph.

It concerned the rearing of calves and its headline was 'Raising calves like this is a travesty.' It described these calves as being reared in crates but the picture didn't show crates, (which are illegal), it showed hutches which are very different. The picture showed a sea of these hutches, too many to count, so we can assume that this was a huge dairy farm.

A bit about calf hutches. They are plastic and are usually used to house just one calf at a time. The calf is free to go into the hutch and lie down on straw when it is fed. The big advantage in rearing calves in this way is that, should it need it, each calf can be given individual attention. The first sign that a calf is ailing is a loss of appetite, this can be spotted immediately if a calf is on its own but is much more difficult if it is one of a group. We don't rear calves this way, it's not a cheap option, but those that do, swear by it.

There is nothing more precious, on a dairy farm, than a heifer calf that will be a cow one day one which will join the milking herd and it is important that you make a good job of rearing it. Rearing these calves in hutches is acknowledged to be as good as it gets.

After they are weaned and eating solid food successfully, the calves are moved into groups and more traditional housing but it always helps if they have had a good start. The big advantage with hutches is that it is easy to clean them with a power washer and you can move the hutches to another clean site next year thus avoiding a build-up of disease. It's all down to perception, you can look for the worst or you can make an effort to understand why someone is doing something a particular way. On the farm concerned they have clearly invested a lot of money in doing the best that they possibly can for their calves. This is the sort of letter that vegans write, they look for the worst, even when they are wildly wrong. They are not really concerned with how calves are reared, they don't want there to be any calves.

★★★

Here's another story of calf-rearing and perception. Every year we are assessed for farm assurance, and we have to pass. Farm assurances was born on the back of the BSE, mad cow disease. BSE wasn't caused by anything farmers did but we have the cost of the legacy. It would take the whole of this book to describe farm assurance in detail. If there is one word that describes it, it's 'traceability'. Everything you do is part of a paper trail that, should it be required, it is possible to revisit and check. For example you have to record each visit by the vet, what was prescribed and to which animal, you have to have your milking equipment checked, you have to have proof that the rat catcher has called, and so it goes on. It has spawned a whole industry.

I was having a visit, which takes several hours, and so far so good. To finish we went to the calf shed. The inspector said that he couldn't pass the calf rearing because there was only one calf in the shed and that calf needed to be able to see another calf. I said that it couldn't see another calf because it was the only one we had and just as soon as another was born (a week) it would have company. I pointed to a cat that had followed us in, and suggested that the calf would come to no harm if it thought it was a cat for a week. If there was a funny side to this, he didn't see it, but he made me go into the house and fetch a mirror out of the spare bedroom. I had to hang it in the calf shed so that the lone calf could see itself. It's all a matter of perception.

16 MARCH 2019

Those of us who live in rural areas have to have a car, and there are downsides to that. I park my car near the door of the pub when I'm there. It's not a lonely place to leave the car because it's where the smokers congregate and I can tell that whilst they smoke, they often talk of my car. They tell me, one night, that when I had driven off previously, I had left a pool of oil on the floor.

I book the car into a local garage, leave it there five days, and then go to see what's wrong. 'We haven't touched it yet as we are too busy to start any big jobs, the engine needs stripping down and rebuilding.' I take the car home straightaway; I can feel a four-figure sum coming on.

I phone the man I bought the car off, he's a brilliant mechanic, his only trouble is that he lives about 60 miles away. I always think that vets and doctors and mechanics have a lot in common and the most important part of their work is to get the diagnosis correct. I meet the man half way and he lends me a car. He works as a one man band, he buys and sells cars, does a bit of repair work and over the years I have bought lots of cars off him. There are six cars he supplied in my extended family at present, he's just found my granddaughter her first car. It's 16 years old, one owner and only done 40,000 miles. He's always been straight with us, the only time you are likely to get stung is by the nettles that grow where he parks the cars for sale.

After a week, I phone him and he says that the oil was leaking through a sensor on the engine and he just had to tighten it up. So much for rebuilding the engine! He says that he is busy but will meet me tomorrow. After three days I phone him and he says he hasn't had time to come, that the MOT is nearly up and he will do that. A week slips by and he doesn't answer the phone. Eventually he does and says he has had the flu. He phones three days later and tells me he has found a big thorn in the tyre and he has sent the tyre away to be repaired professionally as the spare is one of those narrow 'get-you-home' tyres that looks as if it came off a wheelbarrow. He's had my car for over five weeks now. I made a note of the mileage before he had it, that should make interesting reading. I can't fetch it back because he's moved house and I don't know where he lives. But he's probably saved me over £1,000. You just have to be patient.

I've recently had a nice letter from a lady who used to live around here 30 years ago. She tells me that she enjoys reading what I write because she likes trying to guess who I am writing about. She said some nice things about me and I showed them to my wife, who replied that the lady clearly didn't know me. This lady reminded me of the time I went on rugby tour dressed as a vicar. When you go on rugby tour it is quite common to, shall we say, have brushes with authority. It occurred to me that it might help if the tour leader was a vicar. I didn't think that our vicar was much fun but I was chair of the school governors at the time and it is a C of E school so I knew him quite well. He surprised me by thinking it was an excellent idea and he lent me the full kit, I think it was his second best outfit.

We left the rugby club at 10ish and pubs started to open at 11 so we stopped the coach often. I did look like a vicar, it must be my nice honest face, and everyone we met took me as such. My first dilemma was what to drink. Everyone else was drinking pints of beer but I wasn't sure that a genuine vicar would drink a pint at 11 o'clock in the morning so I ordered a schooner of sweet sherry. That was big mistake but I looked the part. I stayed on the sherry until I went to bed. We were staying at a small hotel run by an ex army type. He was much taken by me. 'Another glass of sherry padre?' 'That's very kind of you.' 'It's a pleasure to have a man of the cloth staying here.' Next day I was like death warmed up, but only warmed up a bit. I think it was 4 o'clock in the afternoon before I could keep a cup of tea down. Don't think I've had a sherry since.

23 MARCH 2019

We have been what they call 'closed down' with TB since July last year. It means that we were not allowed to sell any stock unless they go for slaughter. We have to send a small percentage of cows for slaughter every year, they are cows that have come to the end of their productive lives. If that cow has been with you several years, it is usually done with a heavy heart. Years ago we used to send them to a small local abattoir that was only 20 minutes away and we knew that those cows would not have to undergo a traumatic journey. Then legislation changed and a lot of small abattoirs closed and those cows sometimes had to undergo a three hour journey. Oh the irony! We get people coming on to the farm to ensure that you care properly for your livestock and then you get legislation changes that commits an old cow, that has been a faithful servant, to three hours crammed into a lorry. Talk about double standards! Now we send them to a new slaughter house that is about an hour away, which is a lot better.

The hardest part of being closed down was what to do with some of the calves that are born. We keep all the dairy heifers, they go on to be cows in the fullness of time, but we also have the dairy bull calves that are born and we have beef cross calves. All of these we used to sell at a month old. When we were closed down we took the decision that we would have to send the dairy bulls for slaughter. They are not worth much anyway and if you spend a hundred pounds to keep them on it is doubtful if you will ever get your money back, you would need to keep them until they were 12 months old to put any value on them and we just don't have the facilities to do that. We have never had to send calves for slaughter before and seriously wish that we hadn't had to now. It's just one more negative to bovine TB that doesn't appear in the statistics.

Ironies abound. Rearing calves when you are organic is an expensive business, the dry food that they eat costs a lot more than conventional food and organic milk powder is so expensive it is best to rear them on cows' milk and so you have less to sell, and so it goes on. And there is no discernible premium for organic calves!

★★★

But it isn't all bad news. Last week we passed our TB test. This is the second clear test we have passed and so now we are free to sell calves again, we can have a bit of a clear out, we can get some much-needed money in and there will be more room in the buildings. We didn't expect to pass, we gave up expecting to pass long ago. There are several dairy herds in the locality that are also closed down and without exception they are all closed herds meaning they don't bring any animals onto the farm. This is bio-security as good as it gets. The only animals that gets on those farms that shouldn't, are badgers.

★★★

They are sort of teasing one of my friends in the pub. He was injecting ewes for foot-rot and he injected himself by accident. The teasing is only half-hearted because they all know that injecting yourself with animal medicines can be very serious, especially if it is a vaccine and it is oil based, as this one was. He went to A&E quite promptly and after waiting four hours was told to go and see a vet as they would be able to advise him better. This advice is not as irresponsible as it first appears because there is a cross-over between human and animal medicine and in this particular case the vet is more likely to know the answer.

When I played rugby and had a painful injury, I would go to the vet and he would x-ray it then I would take the x-ray to the doctors for him to have a look. My son did the same when he was playing but he also used to get cut about the head a lot. The vet always stitched him up and I used to take the stitches out. The vet didn't charge him, although I thought that I should, but it made it difficult if the vet did it free of charge. I remember he once had 18 stitches below his eye. He was in the pub, as usual, and the landlord asked him if he would mind going home as the mess below his eye was putting other customers off!

My favourite vet/human story concerns a young lad I knew. He was a shy timid boy but he was also very bright. When he went into the sixth form at school he had to start thinking about a career, and one profession he considered was to be a vet. You have to be very bright to be a vet because there is so much competition for places at vet college. He arranged to spend a week at his local vets, so he would better know what was involved. On his first day he was assigned to go around with a lady vet. Her day's work took her to see a badly injured horse, the horse was so badly injured it was decided to put it down.

The detail of what follows is how it was told to me by another vet in the practice, I think I have it right. Vets carry an injection that they use to euthanise horses but it is so lethal, should you have an accident and inject yourself, there is no time to be lost administering an antidote. In fact it is so lethal that it is best to prepare the antidote before you even get the lethal injection out of its box. The lady vet explained all this to the youth and told him that should she inadvertently inject herself, he was to instantly pull her jeans down and inject her in the backside. Lest there should be any doubt over what he was to do, she pulled her jeans down in order to show him her preferred site. He didn't become a vet; in fact I don't think he went back the next day.

30 MARCH 2019

People's attitudes to animals (and birds) continues to baffle me and defy logic. Most people I talk to don't like the way chicken is reared on an industrial scale. But they like eating them and the nation eats millions a week. They particularly like eating them because they are cheap and they are cheap because they are reared in vast flocks, in vast sheds. Now do you work that out?

I have been reading in the press about wild boar in the Forest of Dean. They say there are too many boar and propose a cull. But I also read letters from people who say that the boar should be left alone and allowed to flourish. These letters really intrigue me. They, they writers, know full well that wild boar will turn over your garden, turn over your playing field or turn granddad out of his grave. They are perfectly capable of turning a pram over and eating they baby inside. They might not do it this week, next week, hopefully never, but it could be today. It would probably take a tragedy like this for culling action to be taken seriously. Wild boar are not the most endearing of creatures. They might look OK when they are babies, (possibly I did as well), but the adult has nothing going for it in the looks department, and is nasty with it. No doubt those who would leave the boar alone are advocates of rewilding as well, I've read letters to that effect.

But I suspect if rewilding became a norm and animals like wolves were allowed to roam the land, the tone of letters would change. The rewilders would be silent, they would have

achieved their goal. The letters would then be from those that
have to live with the consequences. 'I took the dog for a walk
in the forest he didn't come back, I think he was killed by
wild boar or wolves, I don't know which, but no matter I've
still got his lead. I can get another dog.' Or, 'They couldn't
let the school children out into the playground, there's been a
pack of wolves hanging about there all week.'

Was there ever a more emotive or contentious subject
than that of badger culling? I read letters most weeks that tell
me that badgers play no part in the spread of bovine TB. But I
had a ministry vet in our kitchen two or three years ago who
said they had identified the strain of TB they had found in my
cattle as having its source in badgers. If you were me, who
would you believe? The science of the vet or the emotional
letter writers?

He went on, earnestly, to say that I should keep electric
fences around all my fields to keep badgers out. I have used the
word earnestly quite deliberately because he clearly thought it
would work. Keeping badgers out of fields has as much chance
of working as King Canute had of stopping the tide. Badgers'
main food is earthworms, they eat about 200 a day. They find
these mostly at pasture, along with all the other grubs and
beetles they find under cowpats. When you go down to fetch
the cows for early morning milking, you can often see marks
in the dew where badgers have been hunting for worms and
turning over cow dung. If you prevent them visiting pasture
presumably you will starve them, is that OK then?

I recently read a book about bovine TB (*Double
Damned* by Trevor Jones) which tells me that my cattle are
most at risk in the spring when they are turned out to grass
because badgers have built up infection on pasture over the
winter whilst the cattle were housed inside. That's something
to look forward to! If you think that badgers play no part in
the spread of TB, you should read this book. If you write

letters to the press against badger culling you should be forced
to read it. Badgers were proved to be a factor in the decline
of hedgehog populations, in the badger culling trial of 2007,
but that it never mentioned. Organised gangs roam the land
decimating hare populations, but it often seems that there
is only me banging on about it. The hare is such a lovely
inoffensive creature, there is a sort of mysticism to hares; but
if you are to use letters to the press as a yardstick of support
then you can only assume that badgers and wild boar are held
in far higher esteem. As I said to begin with, people's attitudes
to animals baffles me.

6 APRIL 2019

It's different to the normal order of things. They drift into the
pub between nine and ten. It could be five past nine, it just as
easily be five to ten. They are in their working clothes, they
are red of eye, hollow of cheek and largely unshaven. These
are the lambers. It is not difficult to guess at their evening
thus far.

They have gone to the lambing pen at about five pm.
They have seen to whatever wants seeing to there and then
they have gone for their tea. After tea, but only if things are
quiet at the lambing pen, they have slept in their armchairs.
They have roused themselves at about 8.30ish and gone back to
the sheep. If all is OK then they go to the pub for an hour, and
they go to the sheep on their way back home. They probably
don't go to bed but sleep in the armchair. Psychologically it's
a lot easier to rouse yourself to go back outside to the sheep
in the early hours if you are already dressed. They probably
haven't changed their clothes for over two weeks and it shows,
(and smells). They don't go to the pub on Saturday night
because most people get changed to go out on Saturdays and
there's no point in putting your best clothes on if you may be
on your knees in the detritus of a lambing pen at midnight.

On large farms with more staff it is possible to have a rota to share out the burden of lambing time but on family farms it is usually one person, or perhaps two, who does all this extra work. It is common enough not to see one of your neighbours for three or four weeks, unless you see them at the vets where they have taken a difficult lambing. Lambing on a family farm can be a traumatic time anyway and, if it coincides with cold wet weather or snow, it is so much worse. The lambs keep turning up regardless and you have to move some outside lest they get mixed up and mis-mothering occurs.

Many years ago I used to keep about 400 ewes and all the phenomena I have described used to be familiar to me but there is one big difference. They all seem to scan their ewes nowadays, so in 99% of cases they know exactly how many lambs each ewe is about to have and they mark them accordingly, so when someone in the pub is asked if he'll have another pint he often says 'no thanks, I'd better go now, I've got a three on!'

★★★

Once a month we have what we call the diners club in the village hall. This has split into two distinct groups. One group consists of locals, usually with farming connections, and the other group consists of retired people who have moved here in the last few years. The two groups are distinct. There's no acrimony to it, it's just that most people prefer to sit by people with similar interests. I prefer to talk about farming to a farmer.

The diners were mixed up a bit last time because some of our regulars were absent (lambing) and their absence was remarked on. 'Where's all your regulars tonight?' 'Lambing.' 'Oh' You could tell by their reaction that they didn't have a clue what that meant. In a month or so time there will be fields full of ewes and lambs soaking up the spring sunshine (with a bit of luck) and people will enjoy seeing them and remark on how lovely they look. Unless they have actually done a lambing themselves they have no idea of the work involved before you get to that stage in the sheep cycle. Perhaps I'm being unfair: if you've never done it, why would you know? But if it was me in their place living in the countryside but knowing very little about it, I'm sure I would be curious enough to want to find out.

It's my birthday today. It's not one of those big birthdays so it's no big deal. Earlier in the week she is doing a big jigsaw and *Masterchef* is on TV, and I am reading the paper. We always have to watch *Masterchef* but it's been on for 20 minutes and so far she hasn't looked up from her jigsaw. I don't point this out, that way lies trouble in a marriage. She says, 'It's your birthday on Sunday.' 'I know.' 'Do you want a present?' 'No thanks.' 'Do you want to do anything?' 'What like?' 'Go out for a meal or go out for Sunday lunch?' 'Not really.' But she won't let it rest, 'Sally,' our daughter, 'would like us to do something.' Eventually we settle for a take-away Chinese that we will eat at my daughter's. She says 'I'll fetch it and you can pay for it.' I gaze into the distance and contemplate life and how strange it can be. Here I am, just reading the paper and half watching *Masterchef*, and suddenly here I am, about £60 light. A takeaway Chinese is no longer a cheap option.

I decide to negotiate. Eventually we settle. She will buy the Chinese and fetch it and I will forgo a present. It's a victory of sorts but not much of a victory. I can't remember what I bought her last time she had a birthday. I know I had to buy her a new dishwasher and she said it would be half birthday and half a Christmas present but she'd forgotten about that by Christmas and I had to buy her a new kitchen door. She's always wanted one of these stable doors in the kitchen. I'm sure there were flowers and a meal out involved as well. You hear a lot about there being inequality of the sexes. Too right.

13 APRIL 2019

The front of our house faces the prevailing wind. We had old metal windows at the front that didn't shut very tightly. If there was a gale all the curtains would move, some doors would have to be wedged shut and the Christmas tree, well the Christmas tree just couldn't stop moving. If it was cold at the same time as the gale it was freezing, you put your arm out of the bed during the night at your peril. The answer was double glazing but I always thought it would be too expensive. Truth be told I didn't know what it would cost. I never minded being cold outside but I didn't like being cold in the house and last winter was very cold. I wondered if the cheapest option would be to fit secondary glazing so I had a price for that. But we could fit new windows for the same money so we did.

We put in eight new windows in all, that's all the front of the house done. It's a lot warmer. Thus far it has been a milder winter, so comparisons are difficult, but I do notice a big difference in sound. I don't hear the very early lorries going by. There was a car rally around here last weekend, there's a rally about every two years. I've always found the organisers decent to deal with. We have three fields that have a council road running through them and they like to use this. We always move livestock elsewhere for the night. It saves them having to shut gates and it saves me having to worry whether they've shut them. Live and let live is a good policy. But car rally drivers are noisy blighters and I used to be woken by them and once awake I would hear every flourish on an accelerator within a mile and believe me there would be plenty of flourishes. But I didn't hear them this year, in fact I'd forgotten that they were about. It was only when I went on my rounds next morning and I saw a junction on a lane covered with tyre marks where cars had gone wrong that I remembered that there had been a rally at all.

★★★

It's about seven or eight miles to where my daughter lives and there's two ways of getting there. You can drive on the main roads which take you through a small town. This is my wife's preferred choice, she prefers it because she says she likes to see who is about, as in, people she knows. The other way takes you on very narrow lanes, some too narrow for a modern articulated lorry, it climbs up to a small hamlet and it takes you through the middle of two woods. I always go this way. If it's daytime I can see what the farmers are doing and if it's dark I can see what wildlife is about.

We were driving home a few nights ago, in the dark, my wife was driving and she had chosen the rural route. This is very rare for her but I didn't ask why, it's always best not to ask a question if you haven't some idea what the answer will be. We are just approaching one of the woods and she slows down: there's a rabbit on the road. She says 'mind bunny'. I have a much different reaction. It suddenly occurs to me that I haven't seen a rabbit for weeks and I say so. 'Where have all the rabbits gone?' Sounds like a 60s pop song. Twelve months ago we would see rabbits on the road from the start to the end of the journey. They have probably succumbed to myxomatosis again, if they get plentiful they usually do.

This decline is serious stuff: it upsets nature's balance. If you are a vixen it's very serious indeed. If you have a litter of cubs, rabbits will provide most of their diet. There will new season baby rabbits about, these will be not so worldly and are easy to catch, and there will always be road kill. I'm no great lover of the fox, they've killed far too many lambs and hens of mine over the years. And my turkeys, I nearly forgot about the turkeys.

But I fully understand that if a vixen had a litter of cubs, she has to go to any lengths to feed them. What's a vixen to do when such a large proportion of her diet just disappears? What's she to feed her cubs? Lambs probably.

20 APRIL 2019

It is snowing heavily outside. I don't think it will snow for long because I saw this snow shower coming over a hill a mile away and over the same hill the sun is now shining. Thus far we have about two inches of snow out in the garden but a friend who lives only five miles away, but farms on higher land, is to subsequently tell me that he had five inches all over his farm. This is exactly the sort of weather event that I described recently. Locally it is called lamb snow because it comes suddenly and usually unexpectedly just at a time when there are a lot of young lambs turned out in the fields with their mothers. A lamb can stick a lot of cold and wet if it is able to fill its belly regularly with warm milk but if there is a deep snow, the ewe's udder may well be down in that snow and therefore inaccessible to the lamb.

Losses in a lamb snow can be catastrophic. I know of an elderly lady, well in her 90s who always says that we should expect these sort of weather events in April because this is the old March. We have asked her why she describes it in this way but she doesn't know. It could be something that she was told as a child so we could be talking of the 1920s and the person who told her might have a memory that went back as far as 1850! That's why people's memories are so precious.

In the 1960s I had a man working for me who was himself in his sixties. His memory went back to before the First World War and he had always lived around here. He never stopped talking; his nickname was 'Rattler Bill'. Some people found his incessant chatter tedious but I found it fascinating.

I once knew a man who had worked all his life with working farm horses and a man who had been to a hiring fair. It was always my intentions to sit down with both men and to hear a bit about their lives. I never got around to it and sadly they are both gone now, their memories with them.

I told you that the rabbit population has largely disappeared. I was asking a keeper about this. Not my keeper, one on another estate. He tells me that all the rabbits on his estate have died as well, that it isn't myxomatosis but a liver disease. Moving on to hares, the consensus amongst those of us who work here, is that we have two. It might be three, it might be one but we are hoping it is at least two. Two is all you need to recover the population. I've got good news and bad news. The good news is that there must be two hares because I have just seen my first leveret. The bad news is that the leveret I saw was about 30 feet in the air clutched in the talons of a buzzard! This makes me so cross. If I were to drop a plough in the ground I would expect to attract at least 20 buzzards and at least 20 Red Kites. Birds of prey are prolific around here but hares are not. I can't do anything about the birds of prey in order to protect the hares. I suppose 'nature experts' will say this is natural predation and therefore is OK. It all comes down to balance in the end. If there are no rabbits then there is more pressure on song birds and leverets.

The answer could be to leave animal carcases about the woods and fields for the birds of prey to gorge on, but you are not allowed to do that either.

★★★

The optician told me a long time ago that I had a cataract, that it would eventually need removing, but that it was not 'ready' yet. But my eyesight was getting noticeably poorer. (I nearly said visibly poorer!) since Christmas, so I got her to refer me for treatment. This first assessment said that I was nearly blind in one eye, no wonder I kept scraping the left hand side of the car on walls and fences, and marked the cataract for urgent removal. It was all done in a bit of a rush in the end. They had a cancellation and they phoned me at 1 o'clock one day said that if I could get in by three for a pre-op, they would do it next day. It wasn't a painful experience, in fact there was no pain at all. It was uncomfortable because of where it was and because you didn't know what to expect. You had to hold a nurse's hand in order to squeeze it if you were in pain. It's a bit disconcerting to have someone digging into your eye whilst the doctors and nurses discuss the progress, or otherwise, of their vegetable gardens!

They did us batches of six, we went together to a room where they prepared us. I was first to go in, which is as it should be. When I got back, the ones still waiting were asking, 'What was it like?' 'It was OK,' I said, 'but I had the last of the anaesthetic!' That quietened them down. I know that some people have bad experiences of the NHS but I have only good and I find it reassuring that I am able to access all that professional care and no one asks for any money.

27 APRIL 2019

I haven't heard it myself – and those who have, have not seen it – but they say there is a curlew about. Most of my life in summer followed a sort of ritual. I would get up early, put the kettle on for a cup of tea, then take a second mug up the yard with me. I would prepare the parlour for milking and then I would set out to fetch the cows. We live in a wide valley so that the bottom fields in the valley are low lying and wetish. There are pools about and numerous ditches. There is not a lot of fall in this valley so that the ditches are always full of water, you could probably call them water meadows. The whole area is popular with all sorts of water birds. So I would set off to fetch the cows.

Firstly I would send the dog off to gather them together and start them towards home. To spur them on and to encourage the dog I would call the cows, 'Come on!' It would be a sort of bellow that was designed to waken a sleepy cow from her slumbers. But that was not all it woke. Somewhere, in the low lying meadows, curlews would take to the wing. I never paused to watch them but I could hear their distinctive cry. If I didn't hear them, then I might pause. Because not to hear them would be exceptional. Then I would direct my next 'Come on!' towards where the curlews should be. I hoped it would rouse the curlews but it was designed to be shared with the cows as well. I don't think that nature ever devised a more beautiful sound than the plaintive cry of the curlew, especially first thing in the morning. I haven't heard one for years but it seems I might do soon.

Where have they all gone? So-called nature lovers will blame the activities of farmers but the fields I refer to are just the same as they were 40-50 years ago, and probably hundreds of years before that. They haven't been ploughed or drained, they are still as wet as they ever were! Farmers who see what goes on in the countryside every day will probably blame the activity of predators like foxes and badgers. The list of birds of prey who have a hand in this is almost endless and includes kites, buzzards, carrion crows and ravens. Left unchecked predators will wipe out ground nesting birds, don't say I didn't warn you.

My No.2 grandson goes on one of those speed awareness courses today. He was caught doing 82mph in a 70mph limit. This was quite remarkable, no one in our family has ever driven that fast before, and no one in our family thought that the car he's got could go as quick as that. I went on a course once. It was at a time when I had to do a lot of driving, I had been caught doing 35mph, three times, through sleepy villages at 2 o'clock in the morning, hardly the stuff of serious crime. But moving to nine points focuses the mind and I was glad to go on the course. The man who took the course was of an earnest disposition who clearly took life seriously. He sat us all down in a circle, about 30 of us, and asked us all to say what we thought was the most hazardous thing on the road that we were likely to encounter.

He started with the man next to me which meant I would be last. Without hesitation the man announced that the most dangerous things on the road were farmers. As we went around the circle it seemed that the majority took their cue from him, so that by the time they had got back to me, there were over 20 that had said: 'Farmers'. By now I had decided that proceedings needed livening up a bit so I got to my feet, refused to answer, said that as a farmer I thought the proceedings to be racist and this was an example of ethnic cleansing of the very worst kind. I pretended that I was going to walk out. The supervisor got himself in a fair state pacifying me, I could see he was not too concerned about any sensitivities that I might have but he didn't want to be accused of running a course that wasn't politically correct.

I know of a dairy farmer's wife in west Wales who was taking her children to school. She didn't spot that the police were having a blitz in her area with hand–held speeding devices. In one day, she was caught twice on the way to school and twice on the way back. She returned home and started to prepare her husband's breakfast oblivious to the fact that she now had 12 points and had lost her license.

★★★

Some in the family say it's 13 weeks, I say it's 11, no matter, but I've got my car back. To be fair the man who had it has been ill, twice. He didn't know but I took a note of the mileage before it went. He had done 800 miles. Once again there were those in the family who thought that this was bad, and to be fair to them, 800 is a long road test, but in about three months I was expecting 2-3,000 miles and also to be fair, he did lend us a car. We go on holiday at the end of the month with some friends and last week we were discussing which car to take. He said, 'Do you think there is more room in the back of yours than there is in mine?' I said, 'I can't remember.'

4 MAY 2019

It's not that I'm nosy, it's just that I like to know what's going on. I love to know what people are doing and what makes them tick. My brother is fascinated by just how many people we know. We have long conversations around this kitchen table about folk we know who may live miles away and if we don't know them, we know of them. My late mother-in-law was an expert at this and I really miss her input into those conversations. She always knew if people had baggage in their family history, especially if they were a bit pretentious. She reckoned that when she went to school only a few progressed to the secondary school in the town and others stayed in the local village schools. You only progressed in the town school on merit and she could name several high profile locals of her age who had spent all their time at school without moving up from the first class.

But right now my circle of information is frustratingly incomplete. At the parish council we get a local police report that covers incidents in several local parishes. We only get the briefest of details like date and location and nature of the offence, but if it should say there has been an assault in our parish, how come I don't already know about it? It's annoying that after the event, I still can't find out who was involved. I don't think it could have been in the village or I would have heard about it but our parish is over six miles from end to end so it could have been anyone.

Police recently reported that two men had knocked on a door and offered to do maintenance on all garden equipment. They had been directed to the garden shed and taken the lawn mower, strimmer and all the hand tools away, never to be seen again. In this case of naivety a little anonymity is to be welcomed! There have been reports of a terrier in another parish that is always biting ramblers and joggers. I asked the parish clerk if there were any contact details as it sounded like the sort of dog I would like. This remark didn't go down very well with various of my colleagues. I'm not a gossip, but I find that if you are discreet, which I am, then you get told lots of secrets. This just suits me.

★★★

We went for a meal with four farming friends recently and the conversation drifted towards how commonplace it is to go out for a meal these days but for our parents it wasn't. Fifty years ago there was a farmer's bus trip to an experimental farm about three hours away. We had a lunch booked at a hotel and on our table there was a farmer from about six miles away. In no way do I intend this story to be derogatory. He was farming about 1000 acres then which is a big farm even today, he as a very hard worker and his sheep and cattle were as good as anyone's for miles around. The first course we had for lunch was melon. He hadn't seen melon before, he watched how everyone ate it and then he asked my father-in-law what it was. My father-in-law, who had a sense of humour, told him it was swede. This farmer was familiar with swedes so he tucked in with relish. 'Our swedes aren't as sweet as this.'

But that wasn't the end of his confusion. The next course included sweet corn which he hadn't seen before either. Once again he asked my father-in-law who told him that they were yellow peas. How things have changed! On the bus I sat behind my father-in-law and an uncle. When they got on the bus they each had 40 cigarettes. They had smoked all those by lunch time and each bought 40 more for the return journey. That's changed as well! How much passive smoking I did on that journey I prefer not to know. They weren't boy's cigarettes either, they were untipped Players and Senior Service. Eighty a day was a bit excessive but smoking was more of a norm then and I knew plenty that regularly smoked 60, my wife included.

★★★

We have a small local hospital. It used to be called a cottage hospital but now is called a community hospital. Various clinics are held there which saves people a lot of travelling. There is a residential section for people no longer able to care for themselves and there is a hospital section for people who have been in the regional hospital but are not yet fit enough yet to return home. In this section you also find patients that are there because they are in the last of their days. This is particularly important because they are largely cared for by people they know which is a great comfort to them.

I know a man who was there recently. He must have had a premonition that he was about to die so he asked one of the nurses to go out and buy him the best bottle of champagne they could find. He drank it all himself and died in his sleep that night. That's style.

11 MAY 2019

There's this council single track lane goes through the middle of our yard. It goes eventually to the next village which is about two miles away. There's two cottages half way down the lane, one is lived in, the other is a holiday cottage and rarely so. The council keep the lane quite well from the cottages on but the mile or so from our farm as far as the cottages is largely impassable unless you are walking or on a motorbike, neither of which form of transport I ever use if I can help it. The lane is too narrow for modern tractors and is overgrown so you would damage the cab and you would soon say goodbye to your wing mirrors. Years ago I used to take the cows down it but they used to walk in single file and take ages, these days I take them to the same place but down a wide track we have built across the fields.

When we moved here the lane was maintained by two local council employees that we called lengthmen, they only had wheel barrows and shovels but used to keep local lanes in good order, they used to keep ditches clear and culverts flowing. Most of the pot holes around here are caused not by vehicle but by water being allowed to run on the roads. They used to cut the grass on this lane, for its entire length, by hand, twice a year. I think that this was a legacy of the man who lived here before me who apparently thought himself to be more important than ordinary people. I always thought that cutting the grass on both sides of a track for two miles by hand was a waste of time and effort. The lengthmen soon worked out that I liked it left and only did it for about three years. The first mile of the lane is largely abandoned by the council and I don't think it's ever seen a high-vis yellow jacket. This suits me just fine because if there should be a thief about they could use this lane to get onto our yard and into our buildings largely unnoticed, and now they can't.

And so we move on to the present day. We have neighbours who live at the far end of our lane. She's a lot brighter than me but so are a lot of people. Meanwhile some wildlife-lovers in the village are conscious of what a natural resource verges on the side of lanes and roads can be. They have persuaded the council to cut them later in the year so that flowers can go to seed and they are hand pulling the plants that could take root if left unchecked, like hogweed, cow parsley and ragwort. I'm with them on this. But people like Chris Packham really annoy me. They are always pointing a finger at farmers for the decline in hay meadows yet we live in a small country and allow thousands and thousands of acres of verges and margins on dual carriageways and at the edge of motorways to be wasted as a natural resource.

I can get good money from the government if I plant a field down to what they call a 'bird and bee' mix. It is a grass mix full of native species and wild flowers and they subsequently provide food for insects and thus birds. Why these mixes are not planted on the sides of roads is a mystery to me. They are in public ownership and farmers are repeatedly told that the public want nature to be enhanced, so why not!

But the story just gets better. My neighbour goes to a meeting in the village hall where these plantlife people explain exactly how they want to enhance these verges. Their aim is to achieve a diverse and complete mix of plants so that the food chain will be complete for birds and insects. These plants are thus called food plants and a verge can be categorised from 1-5, five being good and meaning the variety that is present is sufficiently diverse for all species to benefit. At the end of the evening my friend has to walk home about 200 yards, some of which is down 'our' lane. She counts 12 of these food plants during her journey. She tells her friend who is driving all this, who comes to have a look. She brings with her a man who is an expert and he declares that if there were such a thing our lane would be a five plus and as far as he knows this was the best lane of its type for 200 miles. Quite how he knew that is beyond me, the countryside is full of abandoned lanes like ours. What can we learn from this? That if nature is left alone and doesn't get human pressure and interference it is well able to look after itself. But we knew that anyway, didn't we?

25 MAY 2019

It's a Sunday afternoon. I am idly picking my way through the Sunday newspapers and she is watching yet another football match. I say, 'Why are we watching this, you don't support either of these teams?' She says, 'But I want to see Chelsea lose.' Fair enough. Best not to say too much, it's the Rugby World Cup later in the year and I will need to dominate the remote control.

I turn back to the papers and read my horoscope, which is good. I decide, in the circumstances, that rather than watch the football I will read the newspaper from cover to cover. Towards the middle, there is an article by an organic farmer who is well known for criticising other farmers. I own an organic farm as well but I don't see it as my role to criticise other farmers, who in my experience do the best that they can in their own individual circumstances.

Turns out his article isn't about farming at all, it's about the plight of migratory birds. They are being trapped all across the north coast of Africa, the Nile Delta is a particularly popular site. Apparently the delta is full of insects so the birds fly low to catch them and go into nets. This has probably gone on since man was about but the difference today is that they are able to buy cheap nylon nets from places like China, which are deadly efficient. If they escape these nets they are shot.

Years ago I used to go, on behalf of a friend who was into commercial shooting in a big way, to fetch a car load of clients from Heathrow. They were mostly wealthy Americans and they didn't talk much to me but as far as I could tell they were constantly circling the globe as they followed the hunting and fishing seasons. I remember one man telling his companions about shooting parrots in South America. They used to way-lay these parrots as they flew from forests to feed on fruit in orchards, and have another go as they flew back. I'm sure he said they shot about 3,000 a day! Another said he had had a good time shooting migrating doves in the sand dunes of Morocco. Why would you feel the need to shoot migrating doves? So how do we evaluate the damage that netting and shooting do?

Fortunately, I can bring some scientific detail to all this. Here is the detail. Our house is about 50 feet wide at the front. About 35 yards in front of our house, in the field, is a pond about the size of a tennis court. Here, in close proximity, you have everything a house martin could wish for. There is ample mud in the pond with which to build a nest and there is the house where you can build that nest. And after the chicks are hatched, there are lots of insects flying over the pond with which you can feed them. And build the Martins did. The eaves of the house were full of house martin nests: 50 feet, 50 or 60 nests?

They weren't always popular, mind. They would waken you at dawn feeding their chicks and as our bedroom windows are usually open, birds would miss their nests and fly around the bedroom. They weren't popular with the ladies of the house. I could never work out if it was on the way to the nest or on the way out but your house martin likes to poo whilst on the wing. Most of this poo ended up on the windows. This also made them unpopular with the window cleaners.

One day I found the window cleaner climbing his ladder with a big stick, intent on knocking down the nests. There followed an animated conversation, in fact so animated, we had to find another window cleaner.

Anyway, back to the science. I go outside to see how many nests there were this year. I'm not as observant as I thought I was. The house hasn't changed and if anything there is more mud in the pond than there ever was, but as far as I can tell there were just three nests last year and this year, so far, none. Obviously what goes on elsewhere in the world has an impact on wildlife here. Just like global warming, it's an international problem.

That's why people like Chris Packham make farmers so cross. He tries to stop us protecting our crops and livestock from bird pests in this country but if he really wanted to make a difference to a global problem he and the other eco-warriors would picket coal fired power stations in China. But I suspect that these professionals would get short shrift from overseas locals if they took their agenda elsewhere in the world.

1 JUNE 2019

When I first started to milk my own cows, for the first three years we sold the milk in churns. There was a downside to this. The milk was adequately cooled between cow and churn, as we had what was called a surface cooler. The warm milk was run down the outside of a stainless steel piece of kit, and refrigerated water was run on the inside. The evening milk was always vulnerable in hot, humid weather in the summer nights, which could turn it sour as it stood overnight in the churns. We moved to a bulk tank then. This was a big step forward for milk. It meant that milk was kept refrigerated all night and therefore was a much better product for a farmer to sell and for people to consume.

But the old churn milk wasn't all negatives. For three years my routine was to set off from the kitchen, mug of tea clutched in one hand and in the other a milk jug, to do morning milking. When I returned to the house after milking, I would bring with me a jug of milk containing sufficient for the family's requirements for the next 24 hours. I can remember that when we had churns I would always fill the jug from churns where the cream had settled, so if I was lucky in my choice of churn I would be returning to the house with a jug full of what would be close to single cream. Yum yum! What better could you have to tip on your cornflakes or porridge?

But the advantages of churn didn't stop there. People used to pencil messages inside the churn lids. Inside the lid you could buy or sell things. A dog or van or a tractor, get a job or even make a date. Mostly it was filth. It's surprising what people will write if they think that they can remain anonymous. That's why the churn lids of yesteryear can be compared with the social media of today. The social media of today gets to a wider audience than churn lids ever did but I remain convinced that social media was invented by dairy farmers, and churn lids. The reason that dairy farmers always had a pencil close at hand was because each churn had to carry a label to say where it came from and what it contained.

It didn't make any difference really because they used to tip all your milk into a vat and weigh it at the dairy, but it made a big difference if you had one of those churn stands on the side of the road, because your neighbours would stop and read your labels to see how much milk you had sold. These days the volume of your milk is determined by flowmeter on the tanker but there was a time that, when a milk tanker was fitted, it was calibrated with water, seals were fitted on the legs, and the volume of your milk was assessed by the tanker driver, who used a dipstick that was fitted to your tank. The amount of milk you had was determined by the tanker driver. This made the tanker driver the most important person who ever came onto your farm, you upset him at your peril. But he didn't have margin for error, the tickets that he issued at each farm had to be somewhere near the quantity in his lorry when he got back to the dairy.

Lots of farmers had a theory that milk would 'settle' so if they were due for a midday collection they would return to their dairy, say, half an hour before the lorry was due, switch the paddle on and give it a good stir to 'unsettle' it. This practice was part of their daily routine and they would stop whatever they were doing, wherever they might be, to do it. If they were off for the day, someone else was delegated to do it, and woe betide them if they forgot. I'm not sure about the science of liquids being able to settle, but I have never let such practices be a part of my life; that's why most farmers have more money than me!

But keeping on the right side of the tanker driver remained important and if he liked a cup of tea, then he had one. If he had made a special effort to get to you in the snow, then a bacon sandwich was always a good investment. When we first went to bulk milk, the tanker came at around 9am, and it was routine for the driver to come into the house for his breakfast. It was before we had mains water and we really struggled in the summer. His big lorry had two compartments in the tank and once a week, in the summer, he would bring us a load of water and run it in to our well whilst he ate his breakfast.

But it wasn't all pluses. I knew one of the relief drivers quite well. He came one Saturday morning, and called to me as I went about my work. 'I've just given you 50 litres more than you actually had.' Immediately my suspicions were aroused. 'How did you do that?' He named farmer a few miles away 'He had about 300 tons of swedes tipped on his yard, and asked him for one for our Sunday dinner and he said no, so I knocked 50 litres off his milk and gave it to you.' This wasn't as good as it sounded. The relief drivers daughter had a pony — what if he asked me for some hay? Besides we were short of hay. 'I'd rather you didn't do that again.' He didn't like it but once you condone cheating you are on dangerous ground and you don't know where it will end. Besides, he had already written he ticket for the extra 50 litres, so I quit whilst I was ahead.

8 JUNE 2019

I'm driving around the fields, as I do most days. I go into a field of grass that we have previously grazed but is now six inches high. About 150 yards away I can see four birds' heads sticking up above the grass. At first I take them to be the heads of cock pheasants but they are not behaving like cock pheasants so I drive across for a closer look. They are two carrion crows and two lapwings. The lapwings are distressed and are flying short distances, landing again, and trying to lead the crows away. The crows are working the area and are so purposeful in what they are doing that they don't fly away at my approach. The combined behaviour of the four birds tells me that the lapwings have eggs or young close at hand and that the crows are intent on finding them.

The crows need shooting but I never carry a gun which would soon put matters right, that's what gamekeepers have always done. I could go home and fetch my gun, which would take, what, half an hour? Finding the key to my gun cabinet and some cartridges could take longer. I haven't used the gun for years. Or I could do it the Chris Packham way. I could go home and apply for a licence to shoot these two carrion crows. What would that take: three days, a week? What chance would you give for the lapwing eggs and or chicks, with that timescale? That is the reality of how he and his supporters would have you do it. I just hope that he is still around in 20 or 30 years' time so that society can see how much damage he and his like have done and hold them to account for it. Do you want your grandchildren to see a world dominated by carrion crows and other winged predators or would you like to be able to show them skylarks and lapwings or let them hear the cry of a curlew? It's a very simple choice.

★★★

There's a lot of walkers about lately, some of them are on what they call walking festivals. I'm fine with that, the countryside is beautiful around here at this time of year, so why not share it? I like to see footpaths used: what irritates me is if I have to spray a footpath off within a crop, and then no one uses it. I had one such field, I sprayed it off for ten years, never saw anyone use it, haven't sprayed it for five years, and no one has said a word. The only downside that I can see to walking festivals is their practice of descending on a small town or village, filling it with parked cars and then going off for the day. Our small local town is often thus afflicted, the car parks are full, the on-road parking is all taken and for the rest of the day there is nowhere for anyone else to park. The walkers are within their rights, I know, but it does seem a little inconsiderate. It doesn't affect me, I don't do shopping, but the shopkeepers are not best pleased. Why don't they approach a local farmer and park in his field and give him £1 a car to give to the air ambulance?

There is another issue: dogs. No one loves the company of a dog more than me. I do most of my writing in the mornings and he, the dog Gomer, is asleep with his head on my feet as I write. This is good from two points. It says we are good friends, which is important to me, and I mostly go about the house barefoot, and he is keeping my feet warm.

Most walkers keep their dogs on a lead but some don't. There is a big issue, nationally, with livestock being attacked by dogs. I only have cattle running in this high land by the footpaths and they are well able to look after themselves. We have a longhorn bull with them and he sports a fearsome set of horns. They are probably the bovine equivalent of having a Kalashnikov rifle. But my immediate neighbours have ewes and young lambs in their fields. I gave up any hope of some of the public respecting a farmer and his stock long ago, but I see these dogs loose on my fields and I am appalled. Sometimes the dogs are a field in front of their owners, there is no control at all. If we assume that these dog owners have little regard for livestock, what about the wildlife? Within these fields there are the eggs and young of skylarks and lapwings, and there is a nice crop of leverets as well. These wildlife young have enough predators to contend with to stay alive without marauding dogs. These are not isolated incidents, they happen most days.

★★★

Someone has dumped a mobile home alongside the road where my son-in-law farms. This sort of thing is just one more blight that some in society inflict on farmers, because farmers are expected to pay the cost of removal, which seems so unfair. But there is an urgency to all this. The mobile home is close to a public footpath that is part of a walk that the council promote as a tourist attraction, so they are not best pleased. They have tried to get my son-in-law and his landlord to move it but they have refused to take responsibility. I wonder who will blink first.

15 June 2019

The two lapwings that I told you about last week are still there. I've spent time watching them and I can tell that they don't have chicks or eggs at the moment. The carrion crows have done their worst, presumably, but the lapwings might lay again. Thus far there aren't any house martins nesting across the front of our house. There are swallows nesting in our farm buildings but I haven't heard any swifts about. Perhaps there is still time for the house martins to come but they are surely cutting it a bit fine. There's a cuckoo about, I haven't heard it but lots of folk have. To a man (or woman) they have all said, 'I heard the cuckoo yesterday, haven't heard one for years.'

Freshly cleared silage fields are like a magnet to birds of prey. It gives them access to worms and grubs and any small mammals that might have been killed by harvest machines. I counted over 25 kites and over 25 buzzards on one field alone. I didn't bother to count the carrion crows, there were too many. It's interesting that the carrion crows don't seem too bothered by buzzards but if there are kites present they keep well in the background. I think that if I can see over 50 buzzards and kites about, and dozens of carrion crows, but only two lapwings, that surely tells a story. We used to have lots of skylarks as well but I am sure there are less this year. I've seen the occasional hare but two weeks ago I saw three together in the same field. Two weeks ago, I saw several tiny leverets, one was 30 feet in the air being carried off by a buzzard. I haven't seen a leveret for some time, either they have grown big enough to hide in the woods, or predators have taken them all.

★★★

Spring is an important time for farmers as well. Most of the year's growing is done in the spring. We put a tractor and driver into a local contractors silage gang, which at this time of year takes him away for days on end. He reports that grass crops are a lot heavier than they were last year. If you remember we had a late spring in 2018 and as a consequence, crops were light. Then we had a drought so second crops of grass were almost non-existent. We went into the winter with the nation's silage clamps and barns carrying their lowest stocks of fodder for years. If it had been a late spring this year I suspect that the national fodder situation would have been critical. My late father-in-law kept a lot of cattle and at the end of a winter he always liked to have two bays of hay left to carry over for the next winter. He called it being on the safe side because you never knew what challenges nature would throw at you.

★★★

It's Saturday night in the pub and, as usual for a Saturday night, there are a lot of women about. I'm sitting with about six of them around a table. Their husbands and partners are all in a tight group by the bar talking loudly about tractors and shearing. I am not sure what the ladies are talking about, because, like their men folk, they are all talking at the same time so even to a practised eavesdropper like me, it's difficult to follow all the conversations. I decide to liven things up a bit. I say, very quietly, to the lady sitting next to me, 'I'm on telly on Monday night.' 'Ooh that's nice,' and she passes the message on, 'Roger's on TV on Monday night.' The message makes its way around the circle. No one seems a bit surprised that I might be on TV, which is sort of flattering. Eventually one of them asks the question, 'What programme are you on?' 'I'm a contestant on Love Island.' I've never seen *Love Island*, don't intend to, but I've read that there is concern about ongoing welfare of the contestants. It is heartening to hear the laughter around the table at my revelation. The laughter is so unrestrained that their partners pause in their farming conversations and wonder what they've missed out on.

23 JUNE 2019

I am not sure if it is driven by environmental concern or cost cutting, but so far, as I write, none of the verges at the sides of roads have yet been cut. I'm not sure if they were cut because they always had been but we need to know if this wholesale cutting was ever necessary. Most of my driving is done around narrow lanes and the view at junctions is often obscured by the profusion of cow parsley, so why not just cut the verges about 20 yards back from the junctions and leave the other flowers, like campions, alone. It will be interesting to see if non-cutting has an effect on the composition of these verges.

★★★

This is a true story for Spring-time, I saw it, it only happened a mile away. Just before the young rooks fly, the boldest may leave an overcrowded nest and venture out onto an adjacent branch. They cling to this branch and are fed there by their parents. Their aim is that they will be the first offspring that the parent sees when returning with food, and their fluttering and hopping for that food can easily be seen. Sometimes, their fluttering will cause them to lose their balance and they will end up on the ground before they can fly, but their parents will still feed them there.

Not for long though: they will soon be hoovered up by a passing fox. Foxes know that a stroll under a rookery is always worthwhile. Anyway it seems that a local nature lover sees a young rook perched on this branch, notes that it is there for 24 hours, and takes its fluttering, begging for food, as a sign of distress and phones 999 for the fire brigade. The fire brigade turns up, parks under the tree for three hours and block a B-road in the process, so diversions have to be put in place. I don't know quite what the fire brigade were doing for three hours: augmenting the money they receive for turning out I shouldn't wonder, but I am surprised that they answered the call in the first place. But the fact that a local animal lover is stupid enough to dial 999 because a young rook is out on a branch comes as no surprise at all.

★★★

There is the usual crowd in the pub on Sunday night. The only difference to normal Sunday nights is that four of them have been shearing all day and they have stopped for a pint on the way home. Stopping for a pint is one of the biggest understatements of the age. In my experience it never means one pint, invariably it means several, and in this particular case it looks as if it means eight, that's two rounds each they have bought, and it is starting to show. There is another, more subtle, difference. The bar smells of sheep. There is the sheep smell on their clothes and every time they go outside for a cigarette, the muck trapped in the cleats of their boots is starting to dry out and they leave a trail of it on the floor. That smells of sheep as well. Some of those present don't like the smell of sheep and it shows. I think it's only natural for shearers to seek refreshment in a village pub and I wonder for just how many generations they have done that. The smell doesn't bother me and for those that find it distasteful, it's a reminder that they live in a rural area.

I learnt to shear when I was in my 50s, which was over 30 years too late, but I've always liked a challenge, and as challenges go, this was a big one. I went on to shear most of my own sheep and I also shore the sheep of others, if they didn't have too many. My sheep were kept in fields I rented which were, unfortunately, only 30 yards from the pub. We used to shear in the open and I used to get two friends who worked on local farms to help me. We used a petrol engine that drove two machines, so we caught our own sheep, sheared it, wrapped our own wool and one of the others would shear whilst you were attending to the bale. None of us was very quick and it used to take us all of a weekend, a weekend of hard work. The biggest trouble was our proximity to the pub. We used to go there at lunch time and have a bowl of chips and carry bottles of drink with us for the afternoon.

At close of shearing we would call in the pub again, 'We'll have one on the way home.' (which, you remember, was where this story started). The landlady always used to say, 'I bet you lot could eat sausage and chips.' All this refreshment was paid for by the person who owned the sheep, me. To do otherwise would have appeared churlish. One year the friends couldn't help me and I got a gang of professional shearers in. They had finished by 3 o'clock in the afternoon. They cost about half of what I had previously spent on wages and food and drink and all I had done was put an 'E' on each sheep as it was shorn!

29 June 2019

A deal is a deal. Most buying and selling in farming is done on trust, it is confirmed mostly by word of mouth, occasionally by a handshake but it's an important principal of farming that your word is your bond and should be good enough for anyone. Occasionally, and with hindsight, a deal may not be as good as you first thought but if you have given your word you still honour your part of the deal and put the incident down to experience.

There was a time when I had to secure annual grass lets every year to keep sheep, young cattle and make extra silage. I never knew, some years, where we would end up renting so I was pleased and surprised when a man called in and offered me fields and the use of some buildings close at hand. It wasn't cheap but it was just affordable. Two months later, before the due date, he turned up and wanted more money. I refused to negotiate further and as there was no written proof involved, I didn't get the ground, but folk knew and it didn't do him any good.

I once met a man whose nickname was Diesel. I asked a friend why he was called thus and he said that the man's grandfather had a scam going with a fuel delivery driver, whereby the driver would short-change his customers all day and the grandfather would buy the fuel at half price at the end of the day. All this happened before the man I met was born but the stigma and the bad name lasted generations.

Very rarely I have been ripped off and I have accepted that with a pragmatic shrug of the shoulders. But I have always told the offending party. 'I know you ripped me off and want you to know that I know, so don't think that you got away with it.' Having said that, and not meaning to cast slurs on a profession, I always feel ripped off when I go to the dentist. Because of the nature of their work, you are hardly likely to tell them so.

For years and years I went to a good friend of ours, she was one of our bridesmaids, she moved around to three different practices, and I followed her each time. She didn't rip me off in the surgery but she always made sure my appointment was at midday so that I could take her for lunch. You are hardly going to begrudge a friend the price of a salad or a jacket potato if, the next time you meet her, she will fill your mouth with weapons. I once spoke at a local dinner and I teased the doctor. For years afterwards, whenever he approached me with a needle he would say, 'You took the mickey out of me at a dinner!' Our dentist friend retired and I didn't give it much thought until I realised it was three years since I had seen a dentist. I located a new one and when I first saw him he said, 'What can do for you?' I told him a filling had come out and I needed some plaque removing,

I asked if he was going to do it now and he said I'd have to make an appointment! Five minutes later I was outside on the pavement and they had charged me £50 quid to tell me what I knew when I went in there!

★★★

Two years ago I was having a routine check up and he told me that a tooth at the back was loose and did I want him to take it out? My mind worked quickly, it can do sometimes, and I thought that I no longer have a full number of teeth and it wasn't hurting so we would leave it alone and on top of that he would charge me to take it out anyway. About two weeks ago this tooth decided it had had enough and took up a sort of half in half out position and I could move it in and out of its socket with my tongue. It seemed that I could move it a mile, any difference in your mouth feels like that, but it was probably a millimetre. (Note how effortlessly I switch from imperial to metric.) It was agony and I had horrendous toothache. It was painful to eat, I had warm milk on my cornflakes, makes them softer, and bread and butter instead of toast. I had two painkillers to go to bed with so I could sleep, which is not like me at all. It felt as if a good pull would remove it but I'm not brave enough for that. At the back of my mind was the thought that, if I went to the dentist, he would charge me to remove it and I was determined to let nature take its course. No one is as stubborn as me.

But after about ten days of this I had to ask myself if I really wanted toothache to be a perpetual part of my life. The answer was no, so I decided to give it one more weekend and then I would go to the dentist. Then on Sunday morning when I as having a cup of tea at breakfast, it came out. I put it on the kitchen table and all the pain and discomfort was gone as well. I asked my wife, if I put it under my pillow, whether I would I get some money off the tooth-fairy. Why can't people just say no if that's what they mean, why go on and on about

it? Much to the unconcealed disgust of my family, I have put
the tooth in my drawer in the kitchen. My daughter goes to
silversmith classes. Perhaps she'll make a keyring of it for me.

6 JULY 2019

Compared with some gardens, ours is not pristine. It worries
my wife but I have been telling her for years that it doesn't
matter. Our garden may be lacking in terms of neatness but
I am yet to see a garden on TV that enjoys such spectacular
views. All the farm buildings are 'up the yard' behind us, so
from our garden we have 180° degree views of the surrounding
countryside. I keep the lawns tidy, even my wife says that I
keep them tidy. At this time of year I cut them twice a week.

The only blemish on the lawns is the mole that has
recently turned up, but I have plans for him. A neighbour
made the mistake of telling me just how good a mole catcher
he was and I feel he owes me a favour anyway. The only
success I have had eliminating moles involved sitting in the
garden for ages with the Sunday paper and a shotgun on my
knee. I've never been given to planting flowers or weeding
but that doesn't matter as your eyes are always drawn to the
rolling hills, valleys and woods.

When I am sitting indoors in my armchair I can see
about 20% of this view. I can see across the valley and fields
to the horizon which is a big hill, planted with trees and is
about two miles away. If you look at the skyline of trees,
and you know where to look, there is the slightest of dips in
the outline. This marks a field of about ten acres within the
large wood. I know where to look because for years this field
belonged to a neighbour who used to grow barley there and
I used to buy the straw. In the corner of the field there was
the remains of a cottage and even today I wonder what sort of
life it was for those who lived there. It's at over 1,000 feet so it
would be cold in winter, no electric, no water close at hand,

(not that I could see anyway), and an hour's brisk walk from the village. It's quite steep to get up there and even steeper to get down with a load of bales behind.

We didn't have such good kit in those days, we had a two-wheel drive tractor and a four wheel dray to carry the bales, which means there is no weight of the load transferred to the tractor to aid wheel grip. The only way we could get down was by zig-zagging down through the rides in the wood and I can still see those same rides today. I don't think we used the word 'scary' in those days but I'm sure we used the word 'hairy'. It's only two miles away but it used to take over an hour to get a load home.

Through my window over the last two years I get glimpses of a pair of red kites that have been hunting the valley in front of me, remorselessly. I don't know where they nest, a pine tree somewhere in the woods probably. Some of the wildlife I can see is less wild. In the foreground of my view is our pond and two swans can be seen. They are slow and sedate. It's not difficult to be slow and sedate if you are made of plastic and are held in place by a length of baler twine tied to a piece of metal. My wife has always wanted swans on the pond and several times I have sourced some from animal rescue centres, but they have never stopped long and have legged it to a nearby lake where there are about 70 other swans. These plastic ones will have to suffice and first time visitors often mistake them for the real thing. 'Those swans look nice.' I don't see it as my job to disappoint them.

Stephen, who works with us, has been tidying up the field in front of the house, cutting the thistles and nettles. That's all you can really do, when you are organic, give the grassland weeds a hard time. He calls in on his way for his dinner. 'I've got good news for you.' This is a change, he usually has bad news. It's usually that a machine has broken down and new parts are going to cost a fortune. In order that

I can tell just how good the news is, I need to put some detail on it. Immediately in front of our house there is a roadway that is used for access, then there is about ten yards of lawn, then there is a fence, then a dry ditch. I suspect that the ditch was once a haha but it had fallen into disrepair long before we came here. A haha is a combination of a ditch and a stone wall that was designed to keep livestock out of your garden. Wonder why they called them hahas?

Stephen continues, 'There are twin leverets in the ditch next to your lawn, they are tiny, I bet they have just been born.' This is very good news, we don't see many hares here at home. After dinner I go to the gym. When I return I always spend an hour in my armchair, I give my legs a bit of stick at the gym and they usually need an hour to recover. In the background is the view as I have previously described it. In the foreground are six red kites fighting and squabbling over something in the ditch. Aren't I lucky to be able to see all this from my armchair? I fear that the leverets are not so lucky.

13 July 2019

Thirty years ago, about once a year, someone would say that they had seen a deer. It was a rare occurrence and those that hadn't seen it would be envious and keep an eye out for it. Now it is a rare occurrence for us nor to see deer every day. They seem to come out of the woods at night in ever increasing numbers. I'm not sure if that is because there are more deer or if they have moved. I suspect the former, there are probably more of them and if there are more, that will make them move on to fresh ground. That's the thing with deer, they can jump so well, they can go anywhere they like. I remember a friend was taking me around his farm in his Land Rover, we went around a corner and came across two red deer that had not heard us coming. They were standing next to a traditional sort of fence, netting topped with two strands of barbed wire. They just jumped it, they didn't take a run at it, they just sprang over it, with ease.

For us the presence of deer can be a negative. They come into the field where we graze the cows. This is quite strictly controlled with electric fences and we monitor grass growth with what we call a plate meter. We know how much grass is there and we ration it with the electric fences so that the herd has enough grass every day and when the grass it at its most nutritious. The deer don't jump the electric fences, they seem to stroll through them. This probably gives them an electric shock, so they crash through the next one as well.

Sometimes, when the cows are fetched for morning milking, there are fences down and cows everywhere. It has become such an issue that it is threatening to compromise our grazing system and we may have to devise another, which is a shame as we had it working well. There's a fallow deer that seems to have formed a relationship with one of our cows and is to be seen with the herd most days. It comes home with the milking cows at milking time and even goes into the yard where we gather the cows as they wait to be milked. It hasn't entered the milking parlour yet, but I can see it is thinking about it.

★★★

Dotted about regularly in the countryside, always forlorn, often neglected, are hundreds of red phone boxes. These are monuments, if you will, to the relentless march into our lives of the mobile phone. I suspect that these phone boxes are so little needed that they are largely redundant. All sorts of uses can be found for them but a few generations ago the presence of a phone box in a village could have been a life saver and it is appropriate that they are life savers once again as they are often used today to house the local defibrillator.

We use our landline less and less and if the mobile signal around here didn't ebb and flow like the tide, I suspect that it would go the way of the phone boxes. But there is a difference, we don't use our mobiles as a preference, but because we are being driven away from the landline.

We get so many nuisance calls that we don't always answer it. Some are predictable, there's always one at 8.45 in the morning and another at 12.45 midday. We just let them ring. I don't answer the phone very often, only if I recognise the number that is calling, and if I don't recognise it they can find out my mobile number or send me an email. I know there are steps you can take to reduce these sorts of calls but we've tried that and they seem to work for a couple of weeks and then you are back to normal. The trouble is that I have some sympathy with the person making the call. They are only trying to make a living. It must be one of the worst ways to make a living that I can imagine. The more so because I know lots of people that seem to enjoy being abusive to these callers. That's not for me: I just don't pick up in the first place. About once a week there is one of those calls that says that if you don't send some money this morning you will be arrested this afternoon. If you are looking for a reason not to answer the phone, what better reason could there be?

★★★

We went to a 60th birthday party the other night. It was one of those surprise parties and I think the surprise almost worked. The man whose birthday it was, was sent to the pub on some pretext but he recognised some of his friends' vehicles outside.

I once did a surprise party here at home for my wife when she was 70. She said there were three things she didn't want for her birthday: she didn't want a party; she didn't want a corgi puppy; and she didn't want to be 70 anyway. In the end she got all three. The party was due to start at 2.30 on a Sunday afternoon and at 2.15 she hadn't a clue and she only realised when two people turned up early.

At this recent party, they did a *This is Your Life* format, and very good it was too. My favourite story was when the main character was young and he used to take a tractor a mile at night to where a stream ran alongside a lane. There he used to shine the headlights into the stream and try to catch the trout that were attracted. Someone reported him and the local policeman investigated. The policeman said he had no issues as the individual was driving on the road for recreation and not for reward. He was 12 at the time. Oh, for policing like that today.

20 July 2019

If there is one thing I can't be doing with, it's tennis. Wimbledon fortnight, is to me, the worst two weeks of the year. If I were to be writing the bible today, tennis would be on a par with a plague of frogs and other pestilences. To make matter worse it dominates our televisions and household. As the 'excitement' builds up to the finals, so the standard of catering in this house take a nosedive. 'I thought we would have salad tonight for tea.' Salad means a table laden with a multitude of plastic containers containing various salad options. I've no problem with that, some are good, some are very good. The trouble starts when try to open them. (Have you tried to open a new toothbrush lately without some secateurs at hand?) I watch in awe as my wife passes these containers from the fridge to the table without once taking her eyes away from the television that is perched on top of the filing cabinet. The skill level surpasses any at Wimbledon.

The trouble is you can't escape the tennis. Before it started my eye caught a headline that said spectators could now have vegan cream on their strawberries, a cruelty-free treat was how it was described. Of course there is no such thing as vegan cream, cream is a word that belongs to the dairy industry. Just as there is no such thing as vegan chicken or sausage. If vegans find livestock farming and meat eating so abhorrent why do they insist in describing the things they eat with traditional livestock names? I am sure I read somewhere that the EU were going to ban vegan food producers from using traditional words like milk, cream, cheese and sausage, and good for them. I am sometimes told that I am not politically correct when I criticise vegans, not that being politically correct has ever bothered me. But I actually respect their right to do what they want and the lifestyle choice they make, but respect is a mutual thing, and they don't respect me and other livestock farmers. The 'cruelty' jibe is one that particularly annoys me because it simply is not true. Any TV news bulletin will show you that there is untold cruelty to humans all over the world.

★★★

Yesterday I was going for my daily ride around and I happened on my son and grandson moving cattle. There were about 30 dry cows and in-calf heifers in a field and some of them had to be brought home to calve. They had to be taken half a mile to some buildings to be sorted out so that the nine could be brought home in the trailer. There were junctions on the way which unruly cattle could take and one of these was blocked with a loader, but it couldn't be blocked for long, just in case a car came along. It was a hot mid-morning and the cattle were under the trees but just one call was all it took to bring them out onto the road. They went leisurely to the sheds, filed in as required and within ten minutes those that were left were making their way back to the field. At no time had there been any stress. There had been no shouting, not even a raised voice, no sticks, no dogs, just placid people who care for them. None of this would be possible if cruelty were involved. Stock that are scared of you take a lot more handling.

★★★

Anyway, back to the tennis, which is where all this started, if you remember. So I've eaten endless salad with good humour. I always got to watch the evening news afterwards, only for the TV to be switched on to tennis as soon as 'she' has cleared away. I have gritted my teeth in response to the squeals and cries of exertion from some of the female tennis players and as for when someone challenges a line call… All this has been tolerated with a smile, without argument, and she's starting to get suspicious, she knows I'm up to something, but she hasn't worked out what. Too right I'm up to something, it's the rugby world cup later in the year. The remote control will be mine; I think I've earned it.

★★★

The tractor drivers and farmers are in a group by the bar, talking about their progress with silage or otherwise. Otherwise usually involves spectacular breakdowns. One young driver says he has to go to a neighbour to bale some silage in big round bales. The neighbour farms high up on a hill at a farm that in surrounded by woods. The field in question is steepish but nothing that he needs to worry too much about. The consensus of advice is that he needs to take care on the corners as they are awkward and tight-ish. Then a voice calls out, 'That's not all you need to take care of, there's lots of snakes up there and they come out to sun themselves if it's warm.' This is true as I've seen them myself. The young man in question is aghast, there is usually an element of bravado goes with these tractor driving stories but he makes no pretence other than that he his terrified. That's how snakes affect some people. 'I shall stay in the cab, I don't care what goes wrong, I shan't open the doors.' My only contribution to the discussion is to say that I would take the steps off his tractor as snakes can climb steps.

When I go home he is on his own having a cigarette in the car park. 'Snakes can't really climb steps, can they?'

27 July 2019

Because I don't have good balance, the biggest danger is a fall. Touch wood, I haven't fallen for a long time, but if I do, it's important where I fall: onto the bed or settee is fine, concrete is to be avoided. That's why I always try to avoid being the one who has to fill up the car, as garages are all kerbs and hoses which could trip you up.

Anyway we are going to my daughter's for tea one Sunday evening and I stop for fuel, so that my wife can put it in. Halfway through the operation she stops the pump and calls out, 'Is this car petrol or diesel?' I look in the wing mirror and see that she has the green nozzle in her hand. Angry words are exchanged. I drive the car off the pumps, we have to abandon it and phone for a lift. Next morning I decide to call the breakdown service I'm a member of. The recorded message tells me I have to join a queue but I decide to wait for my call to be answered as I would like to shift the car. I time it, it takes half an hour before I speak to anyone. The person wants to know the registration number of the car. Of course I don't have a clue but they won't go any further until they get it. I have to put the phone down and phone the garage where the car is, they say will have a look and phone me back. This may seem a long-winded way of doing things but it's quicker than me finding any documentation, believe me.

I phone the breakdown organisation again, of course I am at the back of the queue again. I time it, it takes another half an hour. I explain the problem and give them the registration number. The man says, 'You have misfuelled your car.' This is a new verb to me. I used to use trains a bit, and they used to talk of 'platforming the train.' 'We have a service that will pump out the tank, put in clean fuel, and put in an additive to make sure all is OK.' I say we'll do that, and he says it will cost me £220. I say, 'I'll pass on that,' and ring off. I got a local mechanic to do it for £30. I've subscribed to that organisation for 40 years, they have got me out of some tight spots and I've never begrudged a penny I have paid them. I don't know now, but an hour on the phone wasn't good. And it took three bars of the battery on my mobile.

★★★

The cedar tree is one of my favourite trees. Ours is not very pretty because it lost its main limb in a storm years ago but for as long as I can remember there has been fungi growing under it at this time of year. This year there is the most fungi I've ever seen and it is this that has caught my eye. 'What will you do with it?' asks my neighbour. 'Same as I always do, I'll chomp them up with the lawnmower.' 'You can't do that, they are mushrooms.' 'No they are not, they are toadstools.' He won't have it. From above they look like mushrooms, but if you turn them over they are very pink, mushrooms are dark brown. If you are unsure, why take a chance? 'If you don't want them I'll have them for my tea.' I try to stop him but he gathers two arms full and carries them off to his car. When I go back into the house later he has put some on our draining board. Ann takes one look and puts them into the dustbin. That morning I had been to a funeral; looks like I'll soon be going to another.

★★★

As usual I go to the pub at 9 o'clock on Sunday nights. There are about ten in there but they slowly start drifting away, 'It's work tomorrow.' I expect that there will be the usual four or five of us for the last hour.

I often wonder why I bother on Sunday nights but the maxim, 'Use it or lose it,' applies to rural pubs in small villages. But at 10 past 10 the door bursts open and about a dozen come in. They are all regulars but you rarely see them on Sunday nights. They are in high spirits, they have been, since 5 o'clock, at a pub two miles away where an Elvis Presley tribute act was appearing. They are telling us all about it, apparently he was very good. Then they name a near neighbour of mine, 'He went home halfway through the performance and fetched a Suffolk tup.' 'Why did he fetch that?' I ask. 'Because he said the tup likes Elvis music.' It seems the tup was very well behaved. I suspect it was one he reared on the bottle, it was in the pub an hour, it was house-trained and it ate three packets of crisps. Not one of them thought it was in the least unusual for a full grown tup to be wandering about in a pub for an hour on a Sunday night.

3 August 2019

At this time of year I always watch the Tour de France. I don't pretend to understand the tactics of the riders, they are much too complicated for a simple farmer, but I just love the helicopter shots of the French countryside. I like to see the crops in the fields and how their harvest is progressing. As the riders go further south so too does the harvest activity increase. Some of the buildings you see, be they castles, churches, monasteries or stately homes are quite spectacular, often built on precarious rocky promontories.

There was a time when I used to go to France quite a lot, I used to sell game there, we used to go there on holiday most years. I always liked the French and France, lots of people don't, but I like the way they stick up for doing things their way. I don't go now but you never used to see a French policeman driving a Japanese car and I don't think that the French would have sold the mini or Land Rover concepts elsewhere in the world. And I like the little courtesies, like when someone enters a small bar, he shakes the hand of everyone there.

If you were travelling you could stop at a wayside inn and get the *plat du jour*, no choice, but always very good and usually very cheap.

One year we went for a week with some friends to Carcassonne. I was always the driver, we had a hire car, but I didn't ever get any help from my passengers. If you were driving on quiet rural roads and you got distracted you could quite easily find yourself on the on the wrong side of the road, and by the end of the week you rarely had any wing mirrors. One day, one of our companions said that she had always wanted to visit the Camargue. I had a look at the map and it was miles away (or should I say kilometres) but I said it would be fine, that's the sort of nice person I am. It took quite a while to get there but I love travelling in France so it was no hardship. We saw flamingos, wild horses, rice and wild bulls and until then I didn't think rice grew in Europe!

Then it gets time to stop for lunch and we stop in a village. We are just going into an inn when wife indicates another one, just up the street: 'All the cars are outside that one.' We walked up there. What a memorable time we had! I think we were there three hours, we still talk about it, we had pork steaks in a tomato sauce, a really good cheese board and lots of carafes of rose wine. Our meal was presided over by the patron's jovial wife who didn't speak any English so all the conversation was between me and her. There was a lot of banter, in an ungrammatical sort of way, and much laughter as we struggled to understand each other. 'What did she say?' my companions would ask. 'She wants to have my mobile phone number.' I think my wife still believes that. I later did business there for ten years and when I started, the man I dealt with only knew one word of English: 'OK,' but with a good French accent. Ten years later he could still only say, 'OK.'

10 AUGUST 2019

Years ago I was off for a few days and as I drove up the yard the first thing I saw was a peahen and one chick. (I'll tell you more about the pea fowl later). She sees me and sets off at speed down the lane that runs through our yard. I know that the only way the chick will survive is if I shut them in for a month until the chick gets stronger. I set off in pursuit. It soon becomes clear that there is no way that I will overtake her so I decide to run down one of the adjoining fields so that I can get in front that way. I vault over a gate — told you it was years ago — and come down on a rock that is hidden in the long grass. Three days later I find out I have broken my ankle.

Next week it is the Royal Welsh Show and I go on crutches. I have a terrible day, my ankle hurts, the crutches rub and so my arms and armpits hurt. This pain must have left a lasting legacy because I hadn't been to the show for three years, since my mobility had deteriorated. But things have changed. About six months ago I was given an 'as new' mobility scooter. These are not as stable as they look — the second time I took it up the yard I rolled it and had to wait until someone happened by to lift it off me. Humiliating! Then some good friends got me a ticket for the disabled car park (which is close to the main entrance) and armed with two grandsons I went to the show. I'd always thought that navigating a mobility scooter through a crowd would be a doddle, but not a bit of it. You have to drive a foot behind the person you are following. If they stop without warning, which they do frequently, you could take the skin off their heels. Why a foot? You leave more than that and people will see that as an opportunity to cross in front of you. Driving through a crowd is all about concentration, emergency stops and skilful steering. Even my grandsons were impressed with my driving, and they were probably hoping I would fall off.

★★★

We had some good friends came to stay for the weekend and we took them one night to a nearby pub that does a good value for money, steak night. It's not the pub that I go to regularly, it's about four miles away. We get there just before

7 and the car park, like the pub, is full. The only seats we can find are those that we have booked in the dining room. We have our meal and then move back to the bar which is now much less busy. I don't know many that are in there, just a few by sight, but there are a couple of caravan parks close at hand and most of the people could be on holiday. Normally I would try to eavesdrop on conversations but I don't need to tonight as those that are by the bar are talking very loudly so it's not eavesdropping at all really.

Two couples are in conversation, I would age them at around 40ish. They haven't met before and introduce themselves. One says, 'Are you local?' The other couple say, yes, that they have been living here a year. 'We are local as well but we have been here two years now.' As the conversation progresses I find out that the four of them all work about 50 miles away. Whilst all this is going on, in ones and twos, about 15 people come in. I know them all, they get a drink and move to the far end of the bar where there are plenty of tables and chairs empty. They are also locals but there is a difference, they are all in their 60s and 70s, they were all born and bred around here, as were their parents and grandparents before them. They had a range of occupations but mostly connected with the land. They are here, as they are every Friday night, to play in a dominos match. The question I ask is this: are they the last generation of real locals?

★★★

Our TV in the kitchen is not working since the thunderstorms. I think that's a good thing but I daren't say so, so I just keep my head down and don't say anything. Breakfast in our house can be a long affair. I have my breakfast and Ann and Gomer have their toast, butter and marmite. But then people and family members call in and they have a cup of tea and so we have another, and the whole process can easily take an hour. There was a time, before the TV broke, when Jeremy Kyle would be on in the background and when that programme stopped we moved to Judge Rinder, which isn't much better. Hence I am in no rush to see the TV fixed. I think the grandsons could easily fix it, but I don't say so. Yesterday an old friend called in, had the compulsory cup of tea, and Ann told him about the problem with the TV. He tells us that when he last moved house he wanted to get the TV working so he fixed the satellite dish to an old ladder, moved the ladder about until he got a good picture, and then leaned the ladder against the house in the appropriate place. This was to be a temporary solution. He's been in that house for 20 years now and that ladder and dish are still leaning onto the side of the house.

17 AUGUST 2019

Sometimes people say to me that they miss stories of wayward poultry. Most famous of these was Neville, our aggressive cockerel, who would run 50 yards to attack you. He went into a fox about five years ago but people still come onto our yard, wind their car window down, and check if that cockerel is still about. Then we had a small flock of turkeys who were so aggressive that they wouldn't let our neighbours out of their houses, and if they got out they wouldn't let them back in again. They got so big and nasty that I had to put them in a pen in a wood. They too went into a fox. All I've got now is my dog Gomer but he is not without his funnier moments.

Earlier this week I was driving around a freshly mown field, I let Gomer out for his exercise and I was following him with the truck on tickover. He finds two hares in the bottom of a hedge and sets off in pursuit of them. I think that the hares were involved in a lovemaking agenda and they seem both to part company. It's a biggish, 25 acres square field and the hares run around 50 yards and then stop to look at the progress of the dog, who is in feverish pursuit. They wait until the dog if about ten yards away and then they lope off another

50. He is going as fast as his fat little legs will carry him but the hares are in no danger. If he aspires to catch a hare, he needs to cut down on the marmite, butter and toast and grow his legs about a foot longer. He's not dull, he soon works out that he is wasting his time and I let him back in, I can feel his heart pounding as he climbs over my legs.

The sole reason I don't have pet poultry roaming the yard is because of our pullet rearing enterprise. We rear pullets that go on into free range egg laying units. They are not our pullets; the owners pay us to rear them. If we had free range poultry wandering the yard they could compromise the pullets' biosecurity. The pullet owners are such decent people to work with, there is no way we would wish to do that. But goats or donkeys wouldn't be a bio-security threat, would they?

★★★

I've always had this weakness for buying things. When we first started to do bed and breakfast we used to often get families here for a week's holiday on a farm. In spring time I would scour the auctions for unusual poultry or sheep. When I got home, Ann would say, 'Whatever did you buy that for?' and I would say that I thought the children would like it. It wasn't for the children at all, it was for me, but it was an excuse I used to get away with. I'd always wanted some peacocks and one day I saw a cock and two hens in the paper. I bought them. It took several years to get them going, they can be the most stupid things. One hen soon found her way into a fox so I only had one hen to build my flock. She bred chicks most years but they are not good mothers. The hen would make her way at some speed across the yard, her chicks would be about 20 yards behind doing their best to keep up but a yard behind the chicks would be a feral cat.

Eventually they got themselves sorted; I think we had about ten peacocks in the end. They used to roost high in a sycamore tree close to the house. Who would ever think that such a beautiful bird could make such an awful noise? If someone went to the bathroom during the night and switched the light on, away they would go and they would go on for some time. It was a high tree and they used to roost in the very top of it. The cocks used to have to sleep facing the wind so that their long tails would be downwind, if they got it wrong they could be blown off.

Now here's a strange thing, about 30 yards away from the tree, over a wall, we had a nondescript hen house where we kept about 12 nondescript hens. About three times a year, when I went to shut the hens up for the night, the peacocks would all be in there, on the perches, amongst the hens. That night it would snow. They would stay there just as long as the snow lasted. Then one night, the snow would still be on the ground but the peacocks would be back in the tree. Next morning a thaw would have set in. How did they know that?

When my son was a little boy, we went one Sunday to have lunch with some friends. I well remember these friends had some bantam chickens and I also remember the man saying, 'Would your little lad like a cock and two hens?' I also remember the little lad in question not looking too bothered but his father was enthused 'Yes please.' When we got home I just loosed them onto the yard, to make their own arrangements. I know that poultry running free are vulnerable to foxes but that's how I like to see them. Bantam hens are prolific layers and they used to lay in the bales in the barns. You would only find a nest once. If you found a nest and took the eggs the hen would lay somewhere else. Next time you saw her she could have ten or 12 chicks. After 12 months I counted the bantams, there were 75! They used to live in different areas in identifiable groups. Each group had a different territory and should one group stray into another's territory, terrific fights would break out in gateways, there would be blood and feathers everywhere. A modern day analogy would be gangs of youths straying into another postcode area. One day a visitor was admiring the bantams, 'I would like some of them,' 'Help yourself.' 'How many can I have?' 'All you can catch.' Thankfully he caught the lot. I think he wanted the hens to hatch and rear pheasants. Which used to be the traditional way of rearing pheasants. I didn't ask him what he was to do with the cockerels.

24 August 2019

There's a friend calls. She has a grandson with her. I'm doing my emails and he comes to watch. He asks if I'm on Facebook and I say no. 'I am, do you want me to put you on?' 'Go on then.' We spend about an hour on it, so now I am on it as well. I hope he calls again shortly because I haven't a clue how to access it. He's six. The ladies that go into the pub have their phones out all the time. They are making conversation but they are also looking at Facebook all the time as well, lest they should miss something. It caused a bit of a stir at first, 'Did you see, Roger's on Facebook!' They waited for a week to see if I would put something on it. Now they have been waiting three weeks, still nothing, and so the excitement has died down.

★★★

The man our family has been buying cars off for 30 or 40 years phones up for a chat. He says 'I've got a Bentley in.' This is way beyond his usual remit. He tells me that he had sold it before he had bought it. I don't know how that works, probably best not to ask. He thought he would try it whilst he had it. He went to see his son in it. The fuel gauge is a quarter full so he puts £60 in it. He has to put more in to get back home and the computer tells him that the car is doing 8mpg. I've just been reading of an exclusive conference for the very rich and famous that was held in Sicily, to discuss the environment. Goodness knows how many private jets and luxury yachts it took to get them all there. I bet they've all got cars at home that only do 8mpg. And I bet they discussed the damage cows do to the environment when they belch.

★★★

Last time I ordered my tea in the pub, the landlady disappeared around the corner of the bar and when she reappeared she was sniffing at a carton of milk, (not a good sign), she can't decide whether it's OK or not so she passed it to the men who are sitting on the stools along the bar. They pass it along the line, all have a sniff, but can't decide on its suitability. She then tips some in to a beer glass for them all to have taste. This gives a sort of mixed result. 'We can't decide on this milk if it's sour or not, will you have some soya milk instead.' She says this as if I had not witnessed the whole selections process. I say that I'll take a chance on the cow's milk. The tea is fine and I try to forget the various noses that have been sniffing at it. Soya milk indeed! The landlady didn't know I was a dairy farmer. She knows now.

31 AUGUST 2019

Those adverts you see everywhere for pre-paid funerals: where do they get the costs from? The costs they quote for a funeral wouldn't pay for a farmer's funeral, wouldn't even pay for the sandwiches. Farmers just love funerals. Their first port of call when the local paper arrives, is the obituary column. They will go miles to a funeral even when the deceased is only known to them by sight. 'I'm going to such and such funeral on Friday.' 'I didn't know you knew him.' 'I said good morning to him in the market 20 years ago.' With a funeral to go to, a farmer has a smile on his face and spring in his step. Why? Because of the prospect of a free tea.

★★★

As a species, farmers are mostly miserable. I'm not having a go, they don't come much more miserable than me, and I've dedicated a lifetime to perfecting it. Why are we farmers so miserable? It could be by nature, or it could be the diseases, plant or animal, that can afflict us, and then there's always the weather, the list is endless in theory but should you get to the end of the list, you go back to the beginning and start all over again: it's remorseless.

Then on top of that there is all the blame that goes with being a farmer, the public in general and pressure groups in particular, who blame you for everything you can think of.

The latest is climate change and keeping livestock. Never mind that rain forests are cut down every day as people seek alternatives to replace animal protein. I often get blamed for that and we haven't even got a chainsaw. We are at the mercy of political change. Farmers put cattle, sheep, pigs and poultry into a breeding cycle and they, the progeny, will come out at a time decided by nature, regardless of trade deals.

We personally don't produce beef but the beef trade affects the value of the beef cross calves we sell. I've noticed for some time that the beef trade is down considerably on last year. I was recently in the company of one of the West Country's leading beef farmers and I asked him why. He said that there is a combination of factors, one which is that the Irish presently export more beef than they produce.

How do they do that? I hear you ask. Well some of the Irish beef that finds its way to your table might have passed through Ireland on its journey but where it came from originally is anybody's guess. So when politicians talk of trade deals around the world, just be wary. Food, plant or animal, could be from anywhere, the politicians certainly don't know. Personally I wouldn't be too worried about eating chicken washed in chlorinated water: all mains water is chlorinated to a degree. But I don't want to eat beef treated with hormones. I've recently bought a new electric shaver, and I won't need that if my beard stops growing.

★★★

It seems no time at all that I could go to the pub at 9 o'clock and I didn't need to put my car lights on. As the year continues its relentless progress towards winter it seemed appropriate to introduce the next topic of conversation. 'How's my Christmas turkey doing?' 'They have all arrived but you might not get one this year.' 'Why not?' 'Because if one dies it will be yours.'

He's been telling me this for years but the turkey has always turned up. 'This could be your last year to supply it, I'm going to give you one last chance to supply a tidy one.' There is nothing wrong with the turkey we have received thus far, in fact they have been perfection, the only problems we have had, we have had to cut them up to get them in the oven, but I am not going to tell him that they have all been beauties.

7 SEPTEMBER 2019

I just hate this sort of unsettled weather at harvest time. We don't grow any corn but we buy about 80 acres of straw in the swath. The combines venture out for a few hours between the periods of rain and do what they can. I don't blame them for that, I would do the same.

But the straw is not always good enough to bale behind the combine or you can't get the contractor there. Then it rains and the straw gets wet. It might be there a day or it might be there a week. You might have to move it to dry it out and this in itself becomes more difficult as combine cutter bars get wider. If you have to move it, you always lose some if the straw is brittle and you might get some soil in it.

★★★

On August bank holiday Monday, there is what is called locally, 'a sports'. It's an unpretentious, uncomplicated, day out for local people. It's been going for years and years and it is as well supported as it's ever been. I don't go anymore but my children take their children just as I took them. There are all sorts of things going on: cookery competitions, produce, handicrafts, children's races, adults' races, archery and gymkhana, almost too many activities to mention.

I have a friend who is a renowned gardener and he entered fruit and vegetables every year. He used to do well but he could never win the cup for the most points overall. He always came second and the same man always came first. But his son moved to live in a town some 20 miles away and one August bank holiday, the son paid an early visit to a local national supermarket. They were just putting out fresh fruit and veg and the son sees the man who always won the cup, and his family, sorting out the best specimens to take to the show. Once again the man wins the cup but the story spreads around the showground like wild fire and he never enters a show again. It's strange how people can delude themselves. People around here who grow vegetables take great pride in what they produce and to cheat in this way was considered very low indeed.

All of this goes back to people living in cottages and working on farms. Your ability to grow a good crop of vegetables had a direct bearing on the standard of living of your family. I sometimes used to go into a pub some miles away, now like so many others, sadly closed. They had a collection of photographs on the wall, which by some photographic wizardry depicted local characters with laughably gigantic vegetables. I particularly remember a picture of two local men trying to cut up a single potato with a six-foot two-man hand saw; one man with an onion that filled his wheelbarrow; and six men carrying a single runner bean on their shoulders. Very much as you would carry a coffin.

I also remember a new family of high achievers moving to the area. They had three daughters aged between 10 and 15. They entered all the races they could but turned up to the sports all wearing matching tracksuits. Tracksuits had never been seen there before and created a lot of interest, as did the warming up that took place. When the races began the tracksuits were removed to reveal matching running outfits. The 'best in show' trainers were removed and spikes were put on. Not only was it the first time for spikes to make an appearance but it was the first time for a lot of people to see them. What did the local girls do? Girls down from the hills kicked off their shoes and ran barefoot and gathered up their skirts and tucked them into the legs of their knickers. Needless to say, local girls won every race.

You don't usually get many ladies in the pub on Sunday nights but if it's a bank holiday next day you get more and they discuss the sports next day. 'You done all your cooking for tomorrow?' 'Yes, I finished this afternoon.' 'How's your Swiss roll looking?' 'Not very good.' 'Why is that?' 'Because I've eaten most of it.'

14 SEPTEMBER 2019

Rugby has always been a big part of my life, both on and off the field. I played until the day before I was 50. We won that game, which is just as well because I well remember lying on the floor and someone deliberately stamping on my ankle and I couldn't have played for a month anyway, and I remember thinking during that month, I don't need that in my life, at my age.

I played for the county for one season which wasn't easy if you were a dairy farmer. It must have been when I was in my sort of prime. I had the unexpected first call one morning to play that afternoon. There was no way I was going to say no. The game was over three hours away and the call came when it was too late to get someone to do the afternoon milking. I remember doing my best but I also remember that with ten minutes to go we were well beaten and there was a ruck with boots and bodies flying everywhere and thinking, do I need to be in there if I've got to milk when I get home? It's a long way up the yard to milk on a wet November evening, especially if you've got a dead leg.

The close rugby season is a sort of vacuum in my life but this year the rugby has come back with a bang, with the start of the World Cup and I've already seen my local team play twice in pre-season friendlies and we are still in August. On the dresser behind me is a picture of me holding the rugby world cup. When it was in Wales the cup went on tour so folk could see it and I was asked to speak at a dinner where they had the cup.

I've seen quite a lot of world cup rugby in Wales and England. I went to the world cup in Sydney in 2003. I had a ticket for the final but I sold it because I couldn't take the chance of watching England win. My reasoning was simple, if they win I'll hear about it for the rest of my life anyway. I was right about that. That's the big difference between English and Welsh supporters. Welsh supporters hope to do well. This Welsh supporter thought that with a bit of luck we might get to the world cup semi-finals. Now, with two key players already out injured and still two warm-up matches to play, I'm not so sure. England supporters, and I know lots and lots, take it for granted that they will get to the final and probably win that.

We went, two carloads of us, to see England play Wales in 2015, half of us English supporters and half Welsh. The English supporters assumed that, as the host country, they would win the whole thing. The Welsh supporters, although they weren't admitting it, thought they were probably right.

As it happened Wales famously won and England didn't get out of the group stages. Some of our England friends were stunned by the result. One was in such emotional turmoil that he didn't speak for four hours, and even then it was only to order a pizza.

I can't remember which year it was but four of us went to Marseille, when the world cup was in France. It was one of the best trips ever. We flew to Lyon and stayed there two nights and then took the train to Marseille where we stayed three nights. We went in order to support Wales in the quarter finals. We got there OK but Wales didn't, they didn't qualify for the quarter finals, so we had to support someone else. One morning we thought we'd do some sight-seeing. High on the hill, overlooking the old port of Marseille is a sort of church, I don't know why but I think it was called a citadel. It's made of white marble and with the sun on it, even at a distance, is quite spectacular.

We decided to go by taxi. There was a long queue of people waiting outside the hotel but not to worry, there was also a long queue of taxis waiting for customers. My friends were talking about what they had done the day before but as usual I was watching what was going on. The filling of taxis was very slow and a group of drivers had got out for a chat whilst they waited. I interrupted my companion's conversations, 'Look at this!' One of the taxi drivers was in full Elvis Presley kit. He had a white one-piece suit on, a black wig and all the trimmings. Sometimes fate takes a hand in your life and sometimes fate is good, so good that we ended up in the taxi driven by Elvis Presley. He takes us up to the citadel and suggests that he waits for us and takes us for a ride around. Whilst he is waiting he lounges on the bonnet of his big Citroen and I think that more tourists took a photo of him that day than ever they did of the citadel. After that he takes us for a ride around and there can't be many people who can say they have been driven along the Marseille waterfront, on a beautiful sunny day in a taxi with all its window down and with five occupants singing *Love me Tender* at the top of their voices, being driven by Elvis Presley. Most of my best friends, I have met through rugby, and rugby has provided most of the best fun as well.

21 SEPTEMBER 2019

For various unrelated reasons, there has been quite a lot of land sold around here in the last few years. Some of it has been parcels of land, some if it whole farms. I can think of about ten lots within about six miles. If just one area changes hands it's a big talking point locally so ten in a relatively short space of time is a big deal. The conjecture about who has bought what is endless. Some people are seen viewing this land and are therefore seen a prospective buyers. Some people view the land so that they can be seen and so that other people think they can afford it, but they have no intention of buying it.

It's quite common now for land to be sold by private offer but at one time it was usually sold by public auction. A public auction of a farm could pull big crowds and a village hall or the function room at a pub would be crammed with people who had come to watch the drama unfold. I don't know why they have moved to private offer. All the wheeling and dealing is done behind the scenes so presumably they can get more money out of people. If it is private it also gives more scope for liars. 'Did you hear how much that farm made?' 'I know because I was the under-bidder and just missed it.' The reality would probably be that they hadn't bid at all. At least with a public auction everyone would know who had bid and who had kept their hands in their pockets.

Now here's the thing. Most of the land I mentioned has been bought by people who are not farmers. They might live locally but it is not farming money that they are spending.

They seem to have access to funds elsewhere. Perhaps in these turbulent times land is seen as a safe place to put some capital and with interest rates so low the yield is not so important. For as long as I remember people have been justifying buying land by saying, 'They don't make it anymore.' This was as true now as it has ever been.

★★★

We've lived here over 50 years now and every year a pair of Canada geese have set up home on the pond in front of our house. I doubt if it's the same pair but every spring a pair have arrived, built a nest, and raised a brood of youngsters. The family has always stayed until the young ones could fly and then they have all flown back to the lakes where the parents come from originally. The size of the brood has varied, the biggest we have had is ten, this year there were five. This is the first year in over 50 years where they haven't reared any of those young successfully. By the time the goslings were two weeks old, red kites had had the lot. It's all part of the pattern of life and death in the countryside and there are plenty of Canada geese about anyway. I've been saying for a long time that there were too many red kites about. Most people don't agree with me but I would ask of them this. If a red kite can carry off the young of a robust bird like a Canada goose, what else is it eating?

★★★

It's my wife's birthday today. I order a bunch of flowers but Jane the florist, who delivers them, calls it a bouquet. She stays two hours drinking tea, and entertains us. There was a time when she used to sell poppies locally. She used to call here at about 6.30–7pm. Between us we would drink about three bottles of wine and she would leave between 10 and 11 and she only had sold one poppy! After she's gone I tell Ann that I've also bought her a big present but it won't be here for a week. I tell her that it has cost more than I usually spend so I've bought her something we can share. I can see that she is thinking about this and I can also see that she likes the idea of buying something we can share. I don't have to wait long, 'What have you bought?' A load of heating oil.

I was watching the Prime Minister on the news last night. I wonder why his mother didn't teach him to tuck his shirt in properly when he was a little boy.

28 SEPTEMBER 2019

There are hundreds of acres of cereals grown in this locality. In fact it is quite easy to forget how much until it starts changing colour as it ripens. There is a bi-product to all this, the straw. Those that grow the cereals are mostly large-scale farmers who also keep livestock and they keep some of the straw for their own use. It provides comfortable bedding and eventually it is returned to the fields whence it came for it is now mixed with manure and enriches the soil.

You have to only travel a few miles, west, and there are very few cereals grown. These are livestock farms and any spare straw is much sought-after. It is again used for bedding but if it is barley straw, it is often fed as well. So harvest time not only sees combines and loads of grain on the road, it also sees lots and lots of straw bales making their way to where it is needed. You would have thought that carting bales of straw on the road would be a benign operation, after all it has probably been moved on the road for just as long as man has been growing cereals, but it has become quite contentious.

If you should drive through our village there are bits of straw everywhere. It fills the gutters, it covers the pavements and most of the people in the village don't like it. Those that are real locals don't mind, they see it as just one more indicator that the season and the year is moving on. But they are in a small minority, most of the people in the village are retired and are not real country people. They don't like their village to be littered with straw and they show it.

We don't grow any cereals but we buy 80 acres of straw and we take three loads through the village every year to be used in some buildings we rent a couple of miles away. When you drive through, the villagers show their displeasure. They don't wave their fists, because the tractor drivers are mostly younger and bigger than they are, but boy do they scowl. And why is the village littered with bits of straw? Because the hedges, bushes and trees in their gardens overhang the road. It's OK of there are no other vehicles about, you can miss the overhanging branches, but if there is something coming the other way, you have no alternative other than to scrape your load of bales against all these branches.

It has the same effect as taking a rake to the bales, all these bits of straw get dislodged and end up on the floor. I think it's all quite funny, it is a reminder that these people now live in a rural area. When they moved here, what did they think grew in those fields anyway? Besides, it's the stuff that is growing in their gardens that is the cause of the problem, but they haven't worked that out yet.

★★★

Talking of straw, and we were, it is an easy step to talk about mobile phones, as we shall see. I've had my phone for years and it's very basic but for some time I have had trouble charging it. The connection between, phone and charger had become worn and the only way I can charge it is if I sit there for hours holding the charger lead in place. The slightest movement and you would lose connection and have to start again. I often sat in my chair in the evening for three hours and only put one bar on the battery. I'd much prefer to be reading but can't because both hands were busy holding phone and charger together. Enough is enough so I take myself down to the local mobile phone shop.

I've been dreading this. All I want of a mobile phone is that I can make and receive calls, the same with texts. I was dreading having a phone with a touch screen. It has been explained to me, by patient grandchildren, what an app is but I'm still not sure, and if I have no intention of ever using one, what does it matter?

I show my phone to the young man in the shop and explain the problem. I don't expect it can be fixed, very little is made today that anyone can mend. He says I will need a new phone and I ask if he has anything similar. He finds a very basic phone, the layout is very similar to mine and it is not touch screen. It has a lid on it, which I don't have, but looks simple to use. He takes the battery off in order to retrieve the sim card and a piece of straw falls out. I like this, it's a nice rural touch.

Many years ago I was involved in an organisation that gave me what they called a Blackberry to use. I've not heard of a blackberry for years, I expect they have been superseded by some new piece of kit. If I had trouble with the blackberry I sometimes used to take it into what was called the IT department. This was in the corner of an office peopled by two or three earnest young men with beards. I remember they all used to look at each other and roll their eyes if they saw me coming.

They only had one solution to a blackberry that wasn't working. They used to take the battery out, wait for two or three minutes, and put it back in. Annoyingly this mostly used to work. But I always had the last laugh. Whenever they took the battery off a piece of straw would fall out. Because of the rarefied technological world they lived in I don't think they had ever seen straw before and they would all gather around and try to work out how it had got in there. But as the people in our village could tell them, straw can get everywhere.

5 October 2019

My life has just gone through one of its greatest upheavals ever. Our house has two floors upstairs. We have slept on the top floor for years and years and we have let the rooms on the middle floor to our bed and breakfast guests. We don't do B&B anymore, for various unrelated reasons, so I decided to move down to sleep on the middle floor. There were several advantages to this. I wouldn't have to climb two flights of stairs when I went to bed. (There were 28). They are highly polished oak stairs and my wife has been hoping I would slip on them for years and years. I always go up and down barefoot, to avoid this. There is a nice bedroom on the middle floor and I always fancied that anyway. But the main motivation is that I thought it would be warmer in winter.

You would think it would be a simple matter to move bedrooms but it isn't. My wife gets two of her friends to help her. Why do we need help? Because I'm a clothes hoarder. The last time we had a bit of a sort out these ladies reckoned I had 72 shirts. I only wear about five regularly because they are always top of the pile. Some of the shirts I've never worn although I've probably thought it was a good idea to buy them at the time, some shirts are souvenirs of occasions or trips I have been on.

I made a plan: I would take charge and I would supervise these ladies as they emptied drawers and wardrobes, refolded shirts and carried them down to my next bedroom. I should have known that three ladies would soon get the better of me.

Various black bin bags appeared, as if from nowhere. All these bags had names, one was called 'chuck', one was called 'charity shop' and two were called 'this will fit my husband.' Soon there were clothes flying everywhere. 'Do you want to keep this?' 'Yes please.' It didn't make any difference, it got stuffed in a black bag anyway.

There were trousers and suits that I haven't worn for 30 years. The reason I haven't worn them is that I haven't been able to get in them for 30 years. But that's not a reason to get rid of them. And then there are memories, as well, and memories get more precious as you get older. Soon it is all over and the ladies go down for coffee, carrying their black bin bags like trophies before them, some of my memories are in those bags. I am left mentally battered and bruised by the experience and sit there on the bed, sort of licking my wounds.

But they haven't got all my memories, some of them are on the bedroom wall. I've been lucky enough to have done a fair bit of foreign travel and developed a sort of ritual. I would always have a haircut in a country I was visiting for the first time. You wouldn't believe some of the places I've had my hair cut. But a haircut doesn't last long, they reckon a bad haircut only lasts two weeks. A part of my ritual was to always buy a hat as a souvenir. Most of these hats are now hanging on nails on my bedroom wall. I've got a Stetson and a Davy Crocket hat that I bought in Canada, a pith helmet I bought in Africa, a crocodile Dundee hat I bought in Sydney. There are lots of French berets from my various trips to France and all sorts of hats from Europe.

Most resplendent of all is a Mexican sombrero that takes pride of place. It took some imaginative packing to get it home undamaged. Mexico is a bit different to everywhere else. One day I ran out of cash. I couldn't understand why there were no cash points about, but I worked that bit out when I visited a bank. I called into this bank to see if I could get some cash on my card. They asked me to call back in the afternoon whilst they made some phone calls. I called back, I was a bit early but that's just me. They asked me to wait for ten minutes. Whilst I was waiting this armoured vehicle arrives outside. Six guards get out. Three stay outside and three come inside. They are delivering cash. All the guards are wearing sunglasses, they all are smoking cigars, but the most disconcerting of all, they are all nonchalantly carrying shot guns. There are about four of us who are customers and they tell us to stand against the wall. The shotguns are not pointing at us, but they nearly are. Some bags are carried in and they exit just as quickly as they came. No wonder they don't have cash points.

12 OCTOBER 2019

A journalist who I don't know asked a friend of mine to ask me if it is true that a herd of cows lying down is a sign of impending rain or whether that was a myth. My mother used to ask me that same question quite often. I always used to say that they were lying down because their legs were tired. This wasn't necessarily the informed intelligent answer, she was looking for. She also used to ask me if swallows flying low were a sign of rain. I used to say that the swallows were flying low because the flies were flying low. But she never used to ask me if the flies were flying low because they knew it was about to rain, which I always thought was the logical, next question.

Lying down is a very important part of a cow's life. A cow likes to eat as quickly and efficiently as she can and then she likes to lie down and digest what she has eaten. In her case it means lying down and ruminating (chewing the cud). A cow's favourite place to lie down is out at grass in warm sunshine (not hot, just nice and warm). This is not possible in winter when cows have to be housed to keep them out of mud and cold rain.

Dairy farmers spend a lot of time and effort making sure that their cows have somewhere dry and comfortable to lie down when they are housed. Most cows lie in what are called cubicles, an individual space to lie down. In Canada they are called 'free stalls', which is a better name but are just the same thing. Our cows lie on beds of soft sand but some farmers invest in mattresses for the cows to lie on. The cows eat lots of food every day and lots of food means lots of poo. To produce nice clean milk you need a nice clean cow. These cubicles are carefully designed so that when the cows is lying down her poo doesn't get in her bed but goes into a concrete dung channel which can be kept clean. I always reckoned that when cows are out at grass, and can lie anywhere, they search out a pile of poo to lie in. Except that on this farm we don't call it poo. I think therefore that cows lying down and rain is a myth and should that myth prove on occasions to be true, then it is probably coincidence.

I quite like myths and sayings. My favourite one is that you rarely see a dead donkey and a poor farmer in the same field. I don't know if the future shape of farming's international trade will have any effect on the mortality of donkeys but my instincts tell me that there will be no shortage of poor farmers. A lot of family farms will cease to exist. And the trouble with farmers is that they will go out of business one or two at a time, so no one will notice. If they all failed the same day it would make headlines.

★★★

One thing in my life that I have never been very good at is selling raffle tickets. I don't want to sell them and in my experience, folk generally don't want to buy them. Sometimes, organisations that I have been associated with have held raffles and I have made half-hearted attempts to sell some. Then I went through a phase when I filled in the counterfoils with family names and paid for them with my own money. Now I decline to sell raffle tickets. Over the years I have raised a lot of money for charity and good causes but much prefer to organise a 'do' where everyone has a good time and gets something for their money. Throughout my life, I have bought my share of raffle tickets and accordingly I've probably won my share of cheap bottle of wine and 'stuff', that's how it works. But only one raffle prize sticks in my memory. I once won 200 cigarettes. This prize was misplaced because I've only smoked five in my life. When I was about 15, a friend and I bought a packet of ten and we smoked five each in the cinema. At the time I was working on farms, evenings and weekends, for my pocket money and I remember thinking, 'What a waste of money that was,' a sentiment I have thought ever since. I also remember scrubbing my fingers carefully for days after lest they carried nicotine stains and my father saw them. Therefore my experience of winning anything and my experience of smoking is very limited.

But all that is changed now. Last week there was a Michaelmas Fair in our local town and Jane, my florist friend, had a sort of raffle for the local hospice. I call it a sort of raffle because she puts 100 numbered squares on a piece of cardboard and you have to buy a square for £1. She gets the prizes given, she gives lots herself, and she makes £100 for her charity. The important thing to note is that I won a prize. Now there is a spring in my step and the occasional smile on my face. I won a teddy bear. 'They' all tell me it is a pooh bear but I don't remember ever having a teddy bear as a child so to me, that's what it is. There was some discussion as to what to do with it. Someone suggested that I give it the dog Gomer to play with but he would only destroy it, so now it is safe on a chair in the bedroom. At last I've got a teddy bear. Better late than never.

19 October 2019

It's a big event in any child's life, when they leave home for the first time and go out into the wide world. For lots of children this is when they go off to university. For rural children it is particularly challenging, they have lived their lives thus far in what most urban dwellers would consider an isolated situation and they are suddenly put into a new life in the centre of a city. My eldest granddaughter has just made the same journey. She has been brought up on a farm just outside a village, we don't think of it as being isolated, but most people would think it is. She is a bit of a family favourite having been challenged by dyslexia, a challenge she has taken in her stride, so much so that she won a prestigious prize at sixth form college. My advice to her, as she made this big step in her life. Don't let the b_s beat you. It's always stood me in good stead.

★★★

I go to the pub on Sunday evenings at around 9pm. I was just about to go yesterday when my son called in. We spent a quarter of an hour chatting and then I said, 'I shan't go to the pub now, it's too late, it's hardly worth it.' My son says, 'You've got to go, I've just come from there and the girl behind the bar told me she has brought some cakes for you to have with your tea.' I went and had my customary two halves of bitter. When I ordered my cup of tea, four cupcakes turned up as well. I had to feign surprise. The others there are quite envious and say that they are considering drinking tea as well. It's not the tea they want, it's the cakes. I only eat two, I gave two away.

★★★

I have only watched the Rugby World Cup sparingly thus far. The first rounds often include mismatches and I get no pleasure from watching a team beaten by a large score and possibly humiliated. It's a good yardstick for life itself: why would you want or get pleasure from seeing someone getting a hard time. There are several options available to watch the world cup. Most of the local pubs put these early games on with a bacon bap available as a breakfast. They say they are not allowed to serve beer before 10 am, but most of them do. This sort of scenario is not really for me though I do remember on my last three visits to Ireland that we took early morning flights and found that a full Irish breakfast, washed down with a pint of Guinness at 9.30 in the morning was not without its merits. The rugby club do a similar offering to try to do extra business but it's half an hour away. I prefer to watch the games that matter to me, the Welsh games, in the privacy of my own home with like-minded supporters, that way we can share our emotions at winning or losing, whatever they may be.

My two eldest grandsons got up early on the day of the Wales v Australia match, did their work, and went to a local pub. They so enjoyed the victory that the day turned into a pub crawl. It's not for me to critical, I've done the same thing myself when I was younger, but I think their day lasted over 12 hours. We used to call an unplanned day of drinking a 'breakout'. Local builders, who are driven off site by heavy rain or other adverse weather and inadvertently spend an unplanned day in the pub call it a 'pig day.'

I asked my eldest grandson where he had been all day and he said, 'Supporting local businesses!' Which is a new way of putting it.

26 OCTOBER 2019

When I was 20, I worked for a farm relief agency for a year. Most of the work was to provide cover in times of holiday or illness. The downside was that in some cases you ended up working for employers who were so bad that their regular employees had just walked out or you could end up doing jobs that regular employees refused to do and the employers had no intention of doing themselves.

I particularly remember working for a week on a farm where they had a deep litter laying unit built into eaves of a Dutch barn. The idea was that you heaped all the litter in a big pile and it heated up and produced ammonia which would purify all the litter so that it could be use again for the next crop of layers. That part was hard work but it was OK.

The element that wasn't OK was that in order to ensure the litter was purified thoroughly, the whole heap had to be moved to the other side of the shed where it could reheat and produce even more ammonia. Every time you put your shovel into the heap it released a cloud of steam and ammonia. You could do about ten shovelfuls, holding your breath as best you could, then you had to run to the door in order to get some fresh air and wipe the tears from your eyes. I should have refused to do it but I didn't much like the farmer and I wasn't about to let him beat me. Some people call this stubbornness. It's a lesson that has always stayed with me because when I had employees of my own I never ever asked them to do a job that I wasn't prepared to do myself. It wasn't all bad experiences though, you usually lived in the farmhouse, as family, and you were made very welcome.

★★★

I spent a month working on a dairy farm in west Wales. They treated me very well. Most of the work was to catch up on maintenance, fencing and building repair and the like, and to give the boss a lie in whilst I did the morning milkings. I'll always remember that they had the most beautiful three-year-old blonde daughter, she was a delight. She used to spend a lot of time with me, as I worked. I remember thinking at the time that if ever I have a daughter I would like her to be just like that. And in the fullness of time I did have a blonde daughter, a bit more feisty, but a delight nonetheless. And she had a blonde daughter as well, who is even more feisty. I wanted a blonde little girl in my life and ended up with two. Just how lucky is that?

2 NOVEMBER 2019

I've got a friend who keeps horses and she asks me if I will sell her some small bales of straw. We haven't had small bales of anything for years but I know of a friend who always makes some small bales of straw. We went from small bales to big round bales and then big square bales. The advantage with big bales is that you use machines to load and stack them. I arrange for her to buy some small bales. It's only two miles away but she doesn't know where it is. She says she will call and pick me up so that I can show her where to go. She as one of those big 4x4 trucks, which she keeps in pristine condition. When she collects me the dog Gomer joins us. 'You needn't think he's coming with us, I've never allowed a dog in my truck.' I find this strange because I know she's got four dogs. 'If he doesn't come you don't get any straw.' We hear some bad language then but she can see that I mean it so she opens the door at the very back, the door that opens the pickup part of things. 'That's no good, he likes to ride in the front.' We hear more bad language but she makes the mistake of opening the driver's door, and the dog is in.

We are going down the lane to the farm and Gomer's making whimpering noises of excitement. He likes to stand with his head between the front seats so he can see where he is going. He knows where we are and, as we go there quite often, he knows that there are five dogs there and he loves to see them. He is a very sociable dog and gets on well with all other dogs. This is unusual in a terrier; terriers usually want to fight the world and that includes any dog that is bigger than they are.

We arrive at the farm and back up to the bays. It is very muddy and I fear the worst. The five dogs that live there are in barking attendance and Gomer can hardly contain himself. She opens her door and Gomer tries to do his usual exit. His usual exit is to wait for me to open the door, to run across my lap and dive out. This time he runs across her lap and dives out. With a dexterity that amazes me she catches him halfway between lap and mud and unceremoniously bundles him back inside. She loads a couple of bales and is soon driving us home. I say, 'Gomer likes to get out here.' 'Did you see all that mud? I wasn't having that all over my seats!' I don't say anything, if she was in a girl band they would call her 'scary'. Gomer has a puzzled look on his face, he can't understand why he wasn't let out to meet his friends.

★★★

We had a promise auction at the rugby club. No matter what happens I usually end up irritated at promise auctions. I usually end up irritated by other people and more often than not I end up irritated with myself, which is much more serious. I think that if you go to a promise auction you should enter into the spirit of it all, otherwise you shouldn't go. You shouldn't go there looking for bargains for example. If you support the cause, and why else would you be there, you should pay somewhere near what an item is worth.

I try not to buy much but I usually do a lot of bidding. If something is worth say £50, I can't do with someone buying it for £20, so I run them up until it's into the 40s. But I'm not that clever, few of us are, and over the years I have been stuck with lots of things that I didn't need and certainly didn't intend to buy. That's when I get irritated with myself, it doesn't help when my wife says, 'Whatever did you buy that for?' Some of the things I've bought I've never even collected. Last time I went to an auction I bought an MOT that was 50 miles away and forgot all about it.

This auction was conducted in good spirit, the good spirit owed a lot to the wine bottles that were dotted about the tables so I didn't have to do much tactical bidding. I bought a nice picture print of the rugby club and I bought six mugs. We already have plenty of mugs. Our mugs are supposed to live in the kitchen but spend most of their time in the milking parlour and only make their way back, en masse, if someone wants to take a mug of tea to milk but there are no mugs in the kitchen. If you need an example of a promise auction being run in good spirit you need look no further than the two players who ran each other up when competing to buy a plastic one litre coke bottle that was filled with indifferent cloudy cider. They paid £45 for it. We raised just under ten grand which was really good.

9 November 2019

This business of changing the clocks always confuses me. I wanted to watch Wales play in the World Cup semi final but couldn't work out when it would start so I left the clocks alone and got up an hour earlier than I needed to. Somehow that hour is gone, it's gone forever, and I feel as if I've been cheated in some way. Wales lost, but all I had hoped was that they would get as far as the semi-final and besides, I'm no stranger to heartbreak.

I remember once I got the clock change completely wrong and put my clocks on an hour when they should have gone back an hour. This put me two hours in front of everyone else. We milk at 3 o'clock in the morning so that we can give the cows a 12 hour interval between milkings and we don't have to work too late ourselves. The cows were in at night and to do the jobs tidily, we needed two of us present, one to milk and the other to do what we call scrape out (get all the concrete clean) and put out feed for the day.

It was my job to do all this later, so I put all the cows in the yard where they waited to be milked and got on with my jobs. All the time I was glancing towards the parlour expecting someone to turn up. I started off thinking, 'They're late this morning,' but as time went on, I was thinking 'Where is everyone?' I'd finished all my work and was just going to start milking when the milker turned up. 'You're late, where the hell have you been till now?' 'I'm not late at all, the clocks went back an hour last night.' I didn't admit what I'd done but slunk off to a warm kitchen for a cup of tea. Just because you made a mistake there's no need to tell everyone.

In the afternoon, before milking. I dropped off to sleep in my armchair. My wife says, 'You shouldn't get tired, you had an extra hour in bed last night.' I didn't tell her. I didn't tell her I was in the pub till 1am either.

★★★

I'm lying in bed in the dark half asleep, waiting for the alarm to go. For some reason I'm thinking about mice. A harvest mouse has set up residence under the filing cabinet in our kitchen. This is hardly a new phenomenon. Mice find their way into these old farm houses most autumns, in fact if you don't get a mouse in the house you almost feel rejected. The reason this mouse was on my mind is that we have a good friend who helps Ann with the housework one morning a week. If I had to categorise all the ladies I know into various sections, this lady would head the list of the fiercest and she would head it by some distance. I'm really scared of her.

But here's the strange thing, she is scared of mice. She mops the kitchen floor in record time and the mop doesn't go anywhere near the filing cabinet. When my old sheepdog Mert was alive she was scared of him as well although she always has about four dogs of her own, mostly German Shepherds.

I'm thinking about her and the mouse when, just faintly, I hear footsteps on the bedroom carpet. Hell, that sounds bigger than a mouse. Let's be honest here, sometimes, very rarely, you get a mouse's bigger cousin in your farmhouse. These are called rats. We've had the occasional rat. You have to be careful with rats. You mustn't put poison down for them, you have to catch them. If you put poison down and it kills them, they will die in some inaccessible place, like within a stone wall. Boy, do they stink, and they will stink for weeks.

Years ago we had a rat in an old attic we never use, we couldn't catch it so we got two cats from the Cat Protection

League and we put them into the attic at night. We had plenty of cats up the yard but we couldn't catch them either. Those two cats lived in our attic for years and we never had trouble with rats whilst they were there.

Anyway, I can hear this movement in my bedroom and decide it's too noisy for a mouse therefore it must be a rat. I'm not scared of rats but to hear one that close and whilst you are still in bed, makes you feel just a little bit vulnerable. This faint noise gets closer and then the 'rat' stands on its hind legs and licks my face. It's my dog Gomer. I don't think he's ever been upstairs before. He's in love with my son's cattle dog and wants me to let him out because he can hear them getting the cows in. I send him on his way with a few well-chosen words. Bet he won't climb the stairs in a hurry for a while.

16 NOVEMBER 2019

I can't understand why everyone seems to make such a fuss over Halloween. It used to be OK, people used to buy pumpkins, hollow them out and put a candle inside, and that would be it. Now it is promoted endlessly and it is fast turning into a big commercial opportunity. The media, especially the soaps and in particular *Strictly Come Dancing*, try to make out that it is a big part of our lives. They equip themselves with lavish costumes as if everyone else does the same. I suspect that it came across the Atlantic, and like a lot of things, that's where it should have stayed. As for Trick or Treat, children don't venture out of the comfort of village street lighting to visit dark farmyards, which is just as well. We've got cobwebs in most rooms but we don't make a fuss over it.

★★★

I go to the pub three times a week; I think this makes me a regular. Not as regular as some, but a regular nonetheless. There's a change of management at the pub, two local girls, who we know quite well, have taken it on. One of these girls is the daughter of Stephen, who works with us. He is sitting in our kitchen having a cup of tea one Thursday and he says, 'You two coming to the pub tomorrow?' I say that I don't usually go on Friday's but he says, 'You should come tomorrow, there's a do on to mark the changeover.' We go, at about 7 o'clock, and he has saved us a seat. You need a seat saving because the place is packed, there must be over 100 there. Everyone gets a free glass of prosecco and there is a free buffet as well.

Now I've lived here for 55 years, my wife has lived here all her life, (which is much longer), Stephen was born around here and always lived here, but at least 50 of these present are complete strangers to us. If I were uncharitable I would think they are only here for the free food. Who are they and where do they come from?

There's a few people from the village there, stuffing themselves with food, who go to the pub about twice a year. We are sitting by the door that leads to the room where the food is and some of these strangers go three times to replenish their plates. I like to think that I would never have the cheek to do what they are doing. I ask Stephen's daughter if she is giving a prize for the one who has come the farthest. One of what I call a 'newcomer' comes over and says how nice it is to see the pub so full and I tell him that 40 years ago it was always this full on Fridays. The pub then has three darts teams, three domino teams, two tug of war teams and an airgun team. But then the village was a working village and not a retirement home. He moves on, suitably crestfallen, to get another plate of food.

Life has moved on and I know that I should move on with it. As if to prove one of my points the food runs out and within ten minutes half the people are gone. Working on the principal of, use it or lose it, before we go we book in for Sunday lunch. On Saturday night things are back to normal, there's never more than 12 of us in there. Someone asks, 'Where are all those people that were here last night?' Someone else, (who is on the right track), 'They all ate so much last night, they've probably got indigestion.' We went for Sunday lunch; it was our way of saying thank you for a free night on the Friday. We were the only two there.

★★★

I just had to tell you this, it's quite made my week. I went to have a cataract removed from my eye. I had the other eye done in the spring, it's a most remarkable operation, its benefits are almost immediately apparent. The biggest difference for me is that driving at night is so much easier, and safer. The hospital where I go seems to do patients in batches of six. Preparation consists of eye drops that dilate the pupils and some of the eye drops are anaesthetic. It takes about an hour to get you ready and the procedure itself takes 20 to 30 minutes, and then you return to the pre op room to recover and they give you a cup of tea and a biscuit. Before the operation they offer you a pill to relax you, they call it a 'happy pill'. Everyone else had one except me, I still cling to the idea that I'm hard.

There's three of us that have been 'done' and the nurse is telling us what we can and can't do as we recover. She is quite nice and friendly but is also quite serious. She says, 'You can't drive for three weeks.' And I say to myself that won't drive until tomorrow. She says, 'You mustn't do any housework, hoovering or gardening.' And I promise myself not to do any of that.

Then the man sitting next to me, puts his hand up and asks, 'Will I be able to play the piano?' The nurse says, 'Yes you will.' And he says, 'Great, I've never played before but always wished I could.'

23 November 2019

It interests me how much climate change has crept up people's wish list. I used to be a sceptic, not so much about the issue, but about some of the remedies on offer. For example, there used to be council lorries going about here collecting grass and fallen leaves. I've not seen them lately but I couldn't see anything green about that. To my mind if you have a garden big enough to house a tree or a lawn you surely have a corner somewhere where you could pile up garden waste and compost it.

I often think some of the problems of the western world are half the population's high expectations. When I was a child we lived in a bungalow. It had a solid fuel boiler in the kitchen and an open fire in the living room, all fairly conventional for the time. The bedrooms all had electric fires but on no account were we to switch these on. After he retired my father moved house and had central heating, which he thought was wonderful. He thought it OK to sit in the evening, watching television, in his shirt sleeves in January.

The two warmest place I've been in lately are the foyer to the gym and the hospital where I had my eye done last week. I understand that sick people need to be kept warm but an extra blanket would do that. There's no excuse at the gym. It isn't warm, it's hot. I could turn our central heating up to keep our house as hot, but I can't afford to. And neither can they. It's owned by the council but run by a private company. Two years ago they ran out of money and needed help. Our parish council sent £2,000 as did lots of others. I wonder how much they would save if they turned their thermostat down two or three degrees?

A couple of weeks ago I ran out of heating oil for 24 hours. Apart from oil fired central heating, we only have a small stand-by electric fire in our living room. I put a fleece on one evening, it was no big deal, and I was warm enough.

As yet we are still to turn the heating on upstairs. It's sort of OK. We are warm enough in bed, plenty of blankets, the worst bit is getting dry after a shower before you get some clothes on! I wonder how much difference it would make if we all turned our aspirations down a couple of degrees. My feet are cold at the moment, probably because I'm barefoot. The dog is usually lying on them to keep them warm but he is asleep by the window where a patch of sunlight is on the carpet. Guess I'll have to go and fetch my socks.

★★★

It's Saturday morning. I get up and take my usual place at the kitchen table. I look out at the lawn and decide it needs one more cut before winter sets in. It's covered with leaves as well and I always find that if they are munched up by the lawnmower and left to rot, they rot much quicker. My thoughts turn to the lawnmower. I bought it second hand two years ago and it has been a good buy. It has always started when I needed it, an admirable quality in a lawnmower, it uses less petrol than its predecessor and the biggest obstacle to its longevity is when my grandsons borrow it to cut the grass around their mobile home. One thing I have learnt in life is not to push my luck and so I decide that I will mow the lawn on the next dry day, and then I will send it for a service. I make a cup of tea and turn my attention to yesterday's paper. Next time I look out of the window it is snowing heavily. The lawn has disappeared but then so have the leaves. It snows for about an hour and there is about an inch everywhere. So much for waiting for winter to set in.

30 November 2019

It's 2 o'clock in the afternoon, it's lashing down with rain and it's windy and cold. I decide to go for a ride around the farm in my truck. There are three advantages to this.

It's dry in there, it's warm and it also looks as if I am doing something. It's 3.5 degrees when I get into the truck but when I get to the land I rent it's 2.5. it's always a degree cooler up there, even when it's hot. 2.5 degrees and raining is not good for stock that are still outside, it's cold and wet and there's nowhere dry to lie.

On my journey I have driven through flooded roads and I've seen pools in my fields where I've never seen pools before. Years ago I had an old man working for me who said this sort of weather was bad for farm workers eyes because they spent the day hiding in the buildings but they had to keep peeping out in case the boss was about.

At our other buildings, my son is putting some yearling heifers inside, they don't need any calling, they head for their sheds with purpose in their stride. I have my ride around but have to keep to the tracks, the fields are much too wet to drive on. We've got plenty of grass and usually keep heifers out until after Christmas, doesn't look as if we will this year.

Against this background it seems strange to be thinking of spring grass, but I am. February is only three months away and we usually have a bit of grass available then. We can cut some and bring it back fresh for the cows to eat without actually turning them out on the wet fields, so it's a pre-Spring bonus for them.

We've got 43 acres of rye grass that should grow over the winter, it's not particularly an early field, it's at over 900 feet, but it's dry and we should be able to get a tractor on there. The rest of the farm is full of water and the only thing that usually dries it up is a cold east wind in March, the last thing you want if you want early grass. About a mile away I can hear the sporadic gunfire from an expensive shoot. Why are they happy to spend over £1000 to stand out in weather like this? They wouldn't dream of working in it would they?

★★★

Sometime, between 8am and 9.30am one morning we received an early Christmas present. 133 tyres were fly tipped just inside one of our roadside field gates. We needed to move them in order to shut the gate. Whoever had dumped them had had to open the gate to tip them. Anyway we moved them back out towards the road, they reckon that if they are on the side of the road, the council will collect them. The police weren't much interested, only if we knew who did it. I can understand that but if we had seen them being tipped I suspect we would have been in more trouble with the police than the fly tippers, if you follow me. It's the first bit of fly tipping we've had for about 20 years. Then we had a mattress. I folded it up and pushed it in the hedge bottom and as far as I know it's still there. These tyres are more of an issue. In theory they will last forever.

They cause great amusement in the pub. I told the friend who organises our Christmas turkey that this year I would pay for it with tyres. If the tyres are still there in the spring I might plant a clematis amongst them and turn them in to a feature.

7 December 2019

We spend hours around our kitchen table talking about other people. It's what country people do. My brother, who was a teacher, can't believe that we know so many people. We've had friends who have never been here before, who have stopped in pubs ten miles away to ask directions, they have given the address and someone has said, 'Oh you want Roger.' I suspect that those people probably knew the state of my overdraft as well!

We were talking about a local lady who has just passed away. Until she retired, she had been the local 'first responder'. She had done that sort of work for as long as any of us can remember. She was very highly thought-of. Over many years she had saved many people's lives. Because of the nature of her work she had met people at times of adversity and when they were most vulnerable. Because of the skill she brought to what she did and the empathy and understanding she brought with it, she was a pillar of the community. So far, so good. I expect that thus far many of you know a similar person. But this one was a bit different.

She lived in a terraced house on the main street of our local town. Her 4x4 vehicle could be seen parked outside, with all its markings on that said that it was an emergency vehicle. But she couldn't drive, and never could. She used to rely on friends and neighbours to drive her to emergencies. I've seen her rush out of her house, and wave somebody down she knew that happened to be driving past, they would park their cars and jump into her work car and off they would go. I don't think things were always that haphazard. There was a time when most people around here knew most people, so that there was a group of local people who knew how it all worked and made sure that one of them was always available.

I've watched TV documentaries about the emergency services and they have told of the 'golden hour', that first hour when prompt treatment is so important, especially in cases that are to do with the patient's heart. This emergency response lady was never late and unable to provide excellent assistance. It reminded me of a someone I knew years ago, who made his own sort of contribution and it must have worked because it went on for years.

When I first came to live here there was a dairy farmer who lived in the next village whose extra job it was to keep all the narrow lanes clear of snow. The council provided him with a snow plough to fit on the front of his tractor, he used to do the morning milking and leave his wife to look after things and off he would go. He went out of milk about 20 years ago and then the snow plough service improved still further. He would be out before it got light and he would be out after it got dark. I would be out in the dark as well. The buildings we rent are at 1,000 feet so I would go up there early to feed the cattle just in case it snowed all day and I couldn't get up there later. I always used to put out enough food for two days but if I got up there OK, getting back was even more scary, because whichever road you chose was a steep one. It didn't matter what time you went, you could always see that the snow plough had been before you, thanks to its driver, the retired dairy farmer.

The worst snow we get around here is when there is a wind blowing the snow off the fields and onto the roads. You can drive a mile in moderate snow and you are OK if you are In a 4x4 vehicle. Then you can come across a gateway, the wind has blown snow through the gate and you are confronted by a drift that might be four feet high and as long as the gate is wide. That is why the farmer with the snow plough had to keep going all day. The drifts would soon reappear and the same road would require clearing several times.

One day, one summer, our farmer was called in by the council for snow ploughing lessons and an update on health and safety. The first question they asked him? 'How old are you?' '88' He'd slipped through their Health and Safety net! They took the plough off him and gave it to a younger man with a newer tractor. But I'm not sure the job is done any better.

14 DECEMBER 2019

I usually apologise if I mention a TV programme. I don't intend to today because the programme I refer to could have far reaching consequences. I am referring to *Meat: A threat to our planet*. It was a programme full of messages, and it is my hope to put some perspective on it.

Let's start with cattle and the feed lot in the States. I've never seen so many cattle in one group, 50,000! We are told that they put two batches a year through, that they have ten similar yards altogether, that's a throughput of a million cattle a year. As a farmer I could tell that the cattle looked well and that they were placid and content. I was also told that they received antibiotics as routine and I bet they received hormones as well. Just whether their docility was due to what feed additives they received is anybody's guess. My guess is that to see so many big cattle on one site so content, they must have been feeding them something.

If you have as many cattle as that altogether you will inevitably get sick and injured animals as well. If you had a town with 50,000 inhabitants, they would need a medical centre wouldn't they? Before I could make a judgement on just how good the welfare was on this unit, I would need to seek out the sick bay just to see any sick or injured animals. Only a farmer would find this, it's probably out of sight around a corner somewhere. And it is my guess that any cattle that couldn't cope with that sort of system would be slaughtered on a daily basis.

The presenter implied that feed lots like this are rarely seen in the UK. I am confident that there aren't any. You can only keep cattle in outdoor feed lots like this in a very dry, desert type climate. It would need to be so hot and dry that all the poo would quickly dry up just as fast as the cattle produced it. If you tried to copy that here with all our rainfall, they would soon be up to their bellies in it. If you were led to believe that is how beef will be produced in this country in future, it won't.

More worrying is the felling of the rainforests in the Amazon in order to ranch cattle. In my experience if you want to effect change, money will do it quicker than anything. If the world is saying that the Amazon rainforest is the lungs of the world, and we want to share it with you, then all you have to do is to pay to preserve trees. If you are prepared to pay more for the trees to be left alone than they earn by burning them down and rearing cattle, those fires would soon go out. I don't know anything about rainforests but I wouldn't mind betting the areas that have been cleared could reinstate themselves as forest in due course.

Then we turned to pigs and standards. Apparently there are three pigs to every human in Carolina. These seem to be kept in units of 7,000 and they could count 40 such units from their plane. All the effluent from the pigs flowed into storage lagoons and the overflow from these went into watercourses and this had gone on for years. If I did anything like this for just a few days I would find myself in prison. The only hope for me would be if they thought I was low risk and put me in an open prison, such is the difference in standards.

Then they turned to soya production. There wasn't much about this but apparently land is being cleared faster for this than for cattle. There's no mention of the fact that much of this demand is driven by vegans and vegetarians. I'll skip the bit about synthetic meat production and the bit about insects, although I think that the lack of variety of insects when there is monoculture is probably as important an issue as any other.

We were presented with a possible way forward when we were introduced to a retired vet who was living a sort of hippy lifestyle with 50 hens in west Wales. Ridiculous! Almost as annoying was the presenter shedding a tear as she looked at cleared rainforest, out of the window of a plane!

As a British livestock farmer, I feel no connection to huge feed lots in the States. I don't think that felling rainforests to graze or polluting watercourses in Carolina is my fault so I refuse to share the blame or the stigma. Everyone hopes for international trade deals that will involve food. Never mind food miles, never mind welfare, never mind feed additives like antibiotics and hormones. Never mind the rainforest, never mind the future. Ironic isn't it?

21 December 2019

I'm not really a liar but I've got a fault in my nature that gets some perverse pleasure out of winding people up. I tell people things that I have completely made up but I must have such a nice honest face that they believe me. Here's a for instance.

My next-door neighbour's partner called just before Christmas, a few years ago. I made her a cup of tea and I gave her a mince pie. The mince pie had been living in a packet and sitting in a foil container. She asked if we ever had homemade mince pies. I said never, which wasn't strictly true, and as far as I knew, a man in the village, called Mr Kipling, made ours, 'I haven't had a homemade mince pie for years,' I added wistfully. Next year she dropped off two dozen and that continued for a couple of years. Last year she dropped off 48. I only share them with special friends and woe betide anyone who helps themselves. Two days ago she came with six dozen, riches beyond belief. I eat about two a day but I think my grandsons are at them as well. If someone asks me what I'm having for Christmas I say I've already had my big present.

For the last 50 years I've been very consistent about Christmas. I haven't liked it. I don't like it starting in early November for one thing and it has always meant extra work, a lot of extra work. If we have had anyone working here, we have always given them all the bank holidays off. Stephen who works here is very good at popping across for a couple of hours to help, especially if there's snow or a hard frost, but I think that's more to do with him staying too long in the pub and running out of Brownie points at home.

The milk lorry used to come an hour early at Christmas, so that the driver could get home in reasonable time. I never minded milking early for them, but we were first pick-up for years and it made my Christmas day even longer. Then I had a Road to Damascus moment. I was trudging up the yard to milk one Christmas day afternoon

and I thought about one of my best friends who had had
the latest of a series of cancer operations the previous day. I
wondered how he was and remembered thinking, 'I bet he
wishes he could milk today.' After that I didn't mind. I can't
do outside work anymore, but dearly wish I could, so you
should never take things for granted.

I don't feel at all guilty about not being able to work
outside anymore. I never had a Christmas day off for over 50
years, and most livestock farmers are the same, but every day
I wish I still could work. Anyway, as I've been grumpy at
Christmas time for so long, I thought it was time for a change,
and a bit of winding up as well. In mid October I told my
wife I was really looking forward to Christmas this year. You
could almost hear her jaw dropping but she didn't say much.
At the start of November I suggested that it was time to put
the Christmas tree up. She usually puts it up on the first day of
December anyway. Today we are a week into December and
still no tree, so I've put it up myself all she has to do now is
decorate it. If she returns (she's gone for coffee with a friend),
sees the tree and says she hasn't time to decorate it, I shall say
that I never thought she would spoil my Christmas.

It's much the same at the gym. Music is playing all
the time. At the beginning of November I suggested it was
time to start the Christmas music. The instructor announced
to those there that Roger wanted to start on the Christmas
songs. In no time at all my exercise bike was surrounded by
five older ladies who earnestly told me that it was much too
soon. We go for drinks at my florist's house on Christmas
morning, which is always fun, and we'll have a good meal in
the evening at my daughter's. Merry Christmas to you all.

28 December 2019

There's been a lot about rugby lately in the news. First there
was the World Cup and then there was fall out about the

salary cap. Here's another rugby story. I started watching Wales play rugby when I was at school. It wasn't always a good experience. Two stadia ago, most of the accommodation was in terraces so even if you went early and got a good place, tall men would stand in front of you and you couldn't see much. But that wasn't the worst of it, not by a long way. Much of the terracing was under the main stand and at half time most of those in the stand would go to the loo. The loos must have been badly designed because they always overflowed and the wee cascaded onto the unfortunates beneath. This was my first experience of class distinction.

At the age of 17 we decided it was time to spread our wings and we decided it was time to go to see Wales play at Twickenham. We went by train, my first visit to London. I fully expected to see the stands at Twickenham, from Paddington station, I had no idea that it was still another train ride, and a long walk away. Two things stick in my mind from that first visit. Firstly, it wasn't a very handy place to get to, it still isn't. It's so far from the motorway network and railway mainlines. It's built in a suburb, what's convenient about that? The second thing that struck me was just how lavish were the picnics, clearly a tradition that took place at the rear of cars in the car park. I wasn't to know then that in a few years later my car, or cars of my friends, would be in the very same car parks. Car park tickets were much sought-after and difficult to get in the normal scheme of things but I had a good friend who was a printer and he used to produce two or three for us. One year we went down, two carloads of us, we pitched camp in the car park and put our food and drink on show.

I particularly remember that the Welsh team were going through a bad patch at the time. I wasn't admitting it but I fully expected to lose by a big margin. If you expect pain it's always best to prepare with anaesthetic. There was plenty of anaesthetic about, it was in bottles with corks in. I had quite a lot of wine, certainly too much. I had enough to drink that I was able to overcome my natural shyness and wander about amongst the other cars and make new friends. About three or four cars away there as a family. There was dad, his very attractive wife, and his equally attractive daughter. I joined them at their picnic. I could tell that the ladies were pleased to meet me just as I could tell Dad wasn't so pleased. I think that all the drink had made my personality sparkle, I don't think that the ladies had met a rough farmer before, certainly not a Welsh one, and our friendship flourished.

Before we go any further I need to describe how their picnic was laid out, I need to describe in particular their table. Their table is the hero of our story. They had their food, drink, plates and glasses laid out neatly on a table at the rear of their car. You know those tables that they put out on the grass outside pubs, where there is a bench seat that is bolted to the rest of it? Well their table was just the same except that it was half the size, it was made of plastic and it folded up and you could put it in a car boot.

It's time for kick off and we make our separate ways. I think Wales lost by over 30 points. I wasn't upset at all, but disappointed naturally. Sport is like that, you have bad times but you have to have the bad times to enjoy the good, very much like life itself. I returned to my new friends who thought I would be distraught because of the result. I wasn't, but pretended I was. They gave me more food, even more drink and showered me with enthusiastic, consolatory kisses. Dad just scowled but I was bigger than him and his wife was clearly the boss.

There comes a times in a man's life when fate takes a hand. I took two or three involuntary steps backwards, just enough to gain some momentum, the back of my knees hit the tabletop, and I fell full length backwards on to it. The table smashed, all the glasses smashed and the food was no good because it had bits of glass and plastic embedded in it. I've had a hard life; I've been in tight spots before. I thought the best thing you can do now is stay down here for a bit, and close your eyes. 'Look, look, he smashed our table!' This from Dad. 'I told you it was naff when you bought it.' This from the wife, which did nothing to mollify him. My friends, who had seen this story unfold, came to rescue me. When we drove home I could see the bigger pieces of the table, rammed into a litter bin. Smaller pieces could be seen sticking forlornly out of the mud. My friends stopped for a meal on the way home and I stopped in the car for a bit of a sleep.

4 JANUARY 2020

When you enter our kitchen, we've got one of those stable door arrangements in which the outside door splits into two. It means that in the summer you can leave the top half open, for fresh air, and the bottom half closed so that the kitchen doesn't get full of cats and dogs. My wife has always wanted one of these doors so last Christmas we bought her one. That was the theory anyway but the reality is that it was me that bought it. 'Let's buy Ann one of those stable doors,' they say, 'she's always wanted one.' 'You buy it on your card and we'll pay you.' I've not received any contributions, and don't expect to now; the only upside was that I didn't buy her anything else.

Central to our kitchen is quite a long table. My sister gave it to us about ten years ago. I had to hire a van to fetch it, it's so long. She'd done some alterations to her house since she had bought it and we couldn't get it out, so we had to put it over her garden wall and carry it out through her neighbour's house. At the far end of the table is an accumulation of circulars, magazines, post and stuff that is piled higher and higher until falls off. I get daily admonishments to sort this pile out, which I usually ignore. My seat at the table is next to this pile so when it falls off, it is my fault, naturally.

Our kitchen looks cosy because, like most farmhouse kitchens we've got a Rayburn, (or Aga) in it. But as we shall see later, it's not cosy at all. We bought the Rayburn second-hand, about 30 years ago. It was white then but the white is starting to peel off and we can now see that in a previous life it was cream. But that's not really a problem because there is rarely much of the Rayburn on view, it is usually piled high with drying clothes. There's usually a pile three feet deep stacked on top and all the rails are full as well. In fact, anywhere you can stack an item of clothing, there is an item of clothing. This is because my two eldest grandsons live up the yard in a mobile home and Ann doe their washing. As far as I can make out they change their clothes three times a day. They shower and change their clothes even when they go to the building suppliers to fetch a piece of plumbing for the chicken sheds. Their favourite trick is to present Ann with muddy rugby kit on Friday midday and when she says when do you want this for they say, 'Tomorrow.'

I could take you further into our house but it's too cold. I noticed, when I was down at the rugby club on Saturday that the radiators were so hot you couldn't touch them. We have never had that trouble. We'll go back into the kitchen. Being cold in this house is a way of life.

★★★

Years ago, we were told that butter wasn't good for you. Like most people we used the sort of spreads that you can buy in yellow tubs. Then we found out that the research that told us that butter wasn't good for us was largely commissioned by the people that put those spreads in yellow tubs. And more than that, butter might be better for you than spreads. Butter is more wholesome and natural; spreads could contain E numbers and chemicals that you would possibly prefer not to consume. I put the family back on butter right away, I don't remember anyone complaining, after all, we are dairy farmers!

But there is a downside. Butter doesn't spread as well, especially not from the fridge. We stopped putting the butter dish in the fridge and it would be OK for six months of the year. But our butter won't even spread from the kitchen, especially in the winter. We put it on a shelf about six inches from the Rayburn, but that didn't help. Then we tried putting it on the Rayburn but that was no good because it all melted and ran everywhere. Hard butter is taken off in lumps. If you try to spread it on bread, it tears great holes in it. If you put it on toast it is better but you end up eating more than you should and probably more than is good for you. We have given up on butter until it gets warmer in the spring and we are currently back to spreads. We could turn the Rayburn up, it lives on its lowest setting, but we don't want to spend more on oil, we just want to butter some bread. Living in a cold house has its drawbacks. Hibernation has much to commend it.

11 JANUARY 2020

There have always been stories about urban foxes that are causing a nuisance, being caught live, and dumped in the countryside. I've never seen it myself but I've come close. One day I was driving down a lonely lane alongside a big wood, when suddenly a van shot out of the wood causing me to swerve and brake sharply. I was so angry I tailgated him for a while. Through the rear windows I could see rows of animal cages, all fox size. Some of the fox stories are much exaggerated as they pass from person to person but some I believe, because the teller is telling you of his own experiences.

I remember the artificial inseminator calling one morning and whilst I helped him with the cows he told me that that morning he had come across a van stuck on a grass verge. He had got out to give it a push and there were foxes in cages in the back. I know a farmer who keeps a lot of sheep on a hill. He has got these yellow lights on his yard and he leaves them on all night in order to deter quad bike thieves. One night he goes to bed, looks out of the window and there are three foxes on his yard. He goes back downstairs, fetches his rifle, and shoots all three. In the next four days he shoots a total of 22. He reckoned that they had been dumped on his hill and they had been drawn to his yellow lights because they reminded them of road lights in a town. And I believe him. Where else could that number of foxes suddenly have come from?

I know of some local men who look after a small local family shoot. They rear the pheasants and do the beating and in return they get paid for the beating and get some shooting in for the rearing and feeding they do. Obviously the well-being of the shoot is important to them, both from a financial and recreational point of view. They go out one night a week with lamps and rifles to keep the fox numbers down. They are not much bothered by the odd fox taking the odd pheasant but should a fox corner 50 pheasants in a pen, it will kill the lot, that's what foxes do. they had not seen a fox for a month but last week they saw nine. Where did they all come from?

★★★

By coincidence a story comes in from a friend who lives close by. He is a renowned gardener, few ever grow better vegetables consistently. One wet morning he is in his garden shed, sorting out some shallots. About five yards from the shed is his hen run. He has about six hens and one duck. Lest you should think that this is an intensive, factory farming operation, I should point out that all these hens have names. The duck has a name as well. He is sorting through these onions and he can hear the hens clucking. Good, he thinks to himself, the hens are laying well this morning.

There are only so many eggs a hen can lay so when they are still making a noise half an hour later, he decides to take a look. Inside the hen runs is a big grey dog fox. It has already killed three hens and is started on the fourth. The fox is totally undeterred by his presence although he is only five or so yards away. He decides to fetch his gun. His gun is in the house, in the gun cabinet in his bedroom. I should explain that he is well in his 70s so we are not talking quick here, and he had to take his boots off before he went upstairs.

When he eventually gets back to the hen run the fox is still there. It has killed all the hens and is currently swinging the duck around by the neck. The duck is called Stumpy because he lost a foot to a previous visit by a fox about three years ago. The fox was shot, or as people prefer to say, euthanized. I'm sure it made no difference to the fox. It is my contention that this was a dumped urban fox. A wild fox would have run off as soon as it saw my friend come out of his shed. I doubt if a wild fox would have entered the garden whilst someone was in the shed, it would prefer the cover of darkness. Last I heard, Stumpy was very lonely and doing his best to survive the wounds to his neck. I bet this fox was one of the nine seen by the men with lamps; it was only three fields away.

I often wonder what would happen if it were the other way around. What if we country dwellers caught live foxes, which we could easily do, and dumped them in towns? I suspect there would be an outcry. They would turn over your wheelie bins and kill your pets. There's nothing like the cry of a vixen to chill the blood. Especially if it comes from the bottom of your garden. This is fly tipping of the worst sort.

18 JANUARY 2020

Ever since my two eldest grandsons were little boys, I have seen it as important to keep one step ahead of them. Both intellectually and physically. Now that they are both young men, keeping in front of them physically fell by the wayside long ago but I still manage to stretch them occasionally, intellectually. In fact if it was not for technology I could manage quite well. But every couple of days I have to ask them stuff like, 'Why won't this email go?' or 'Why can't I open this?' The trouble is that they always know the answer so they turn my laptop towards them, press a few keys at speed and it is done. One of the troubles is that they do it all so quickly that I can't follow them, so that next time I have the same problem it is back to square one because I have to ask them again and I never learn how to fix the problem myself. But I have found one way where I can beat them every time. Pretend you are stuck on a difficult word and ask them how to spell it. If they don't have immediate access to an electronic device, they haven't got a clue.

★★★

In those funny days between Christmas and New Year, my daughter gets a rare Monday off work. I go down to see her. I think she was planning to watch a film in the afternoon. 'Any chance of a hair cut?' She cuts my hair. I can see that she is not keen and I should have withdrawn the request. But I leave it hanging in the air and eventually she says she will. She's snipping away, I can tell she isn't best pleased, and I fear for the safety of my ears.

Then things take two turns for the worse. She goes to her cloakroom, to get a different pair of scissors, and discovers that my dog Gomer has done a number two on the carpet in her hallway. I won't go into the detail of what happened next, only to say that the dog was soon out on the yard and I heard language I hadn't heard from my daughter before. After she's cleared up the mess we had some animated haircutting. It was so animated that she cut her finger. 'Good job I'd just finished,' she says. I haven't looked in the mirror yet...

Things have not been that good on the domestic front. My wife and I decided to cut back on the cost of Christmas. Part of that cost cutting exercise was that we wouldn't buy each other presents. But I was suspicious, she loves Christmas so much that there could be a catch in this. She could buy me something and I wouldn't buy her anything and she would tell everybody and I would end up feeling guilty. Just to be on the safe side I bought her two nice potted plants. I haven't a clue what they are called but they look good and cost me £40. Then her washing machine died over Christmas, we bought it about 15 years ago, it was reconditioned, so we bought another reconditioned one and I ended up paying for it. Thus Christmas cost me over £200. I'm still licking my wounds over that. I was right about one thing, though, she did buy me a Christmas present: a packet of Rennies.

★★★

There's been a couple from London staying in the village for two weeks over Christmas. One Saturday morning they decide that it would be nice to go into our local town that evening, have a meal, a few drinks and return later on. To put this into perspective the town is only five miles away. They phone the local taxi.

To also put this into perspective, we are only talking of a one man band here and this man only has the one taxi. They phone him on Saturday morning to make the arrangement, let's be fair, what they want is not a big deal. They can hear the man turning the pages of his diary. 'The first time I can do a taxi for you is next Tuesday afternoon.' For a Londoner who could hail a black cab or phone Uber whenever you wanted, this must have been a fair shock to the system.

25 JANUARY 2020

I don't worry about things that I have no control over. This sets me apart as some sort of smart arse, but it isn't strictly true. I don't worry about things like the weather; farmers just have to try to do their best whatever the weather may throw at them. But even I am just a bit worried by the remorseless attacks on livestock farmers by the media in general and by people like vegans and extinction rebellion. I don't for one second doubt that the media is being manipulated by these latter two groups, because if you are in the media you are always looking for a story. What concerns me is that it is not all thought through. If someone wants to declare himself to be an ethical vegan I have no problem with that, each to his own. But the man who recently won the right to call himself that is also quoted as saying that he wouldn't travel on a bus in case it killed an insect. What are vegans saying, that they don't believe in public transport? Yet better public transport is supposed to be one of the main saviours of the planet. And saving the planet is one of the main arguments they use against eating meat. They need to get real or they will just look ridiculous.

Then there's Extinction Rebellion. Is it only me that has noticed that they don't demonstrate in the winter? It's almost as if they are saying that they have a cause that they hold so dear that they will demonstrate and disrupt to further it, just as long as they don't get wet and cold doing it. One of the most heart-warming sights of 2019 was those demonstrators being pulled off the roof of a train by ordinary people who simply wanted to get to work.

★★★

Here's what I think. I think that too many people in society think that if a field is presently growing grass, it could grow trees. This is true. They also think that grassy fields could be ploughed and crops grown for human consumption. This is not true. The UK is not self sufficient in food, so for every tree you plant, someone elsewhere in the world will probably fell a tree to satisfy that extra demand for food. Never mind about the negative impact of food miles. I recently watched a travel film about Australia. They showed an open cast coal mine which had an output similar to that of the entire UK, when at its peak. And they said that was only tiny compared with what was going on in China. The clue is in the title. 'Global warming.' What's the point of bringing the UK livestock sector to its knees if that sort of stuff is going on elsewhere in the world? I've read that they used to do controlled burning in Australia, every year. Conservationists stopped that three years ago. Now the whole lot has burned in wildfires, in one go. The world is blighted by enthusiastic ignorance.

★★★

It's about 10pm and the two eldest grandsons call in. They've been rugby training. I tell them that I needed to see them. I tell them that I've been watching them closely for 12 months and scoring them on things like kindness, thoughtfulness and hard work. They hear rubbish like this most days from me, the quality of rubbish can vary. But they listen and when I say that I have finished the evaluation and there is a prize for the winner, there is a flicker of interest. 'What's the prize?' 'The winner can join me to see that they get away safely.' 'Who gets away safely?' 'That nice Von Trapp family in the *Sound of Music*.' They groan and say their goodbyes. Ann says it is nice that they call to see us. I hear the fridge door closing quietly but I don't say anything.

1 FEBRUARY 2020

I've been thinking about dogs. You will shortly see why. I've always loved dogs and over the years I've had lots. When I first started farming I had a dog that would work sheep and cattle and a black Labrador bitch that I used to shoot with and breed from. And we always had a corgi. Then things got out of hand, but it was all down to vets. I was very friendly with the one young vet but he decided to leave his practice and go to work for the ministry. He had to go to London for three years, but he had a black lab dog. 'I can't take him to live in London so I wondered if you could have him?'

Of course I said yes, so now I've got two labs. It turned out to be a ferocious guard dog, so much so that he was a danger to anyone who called. Over the next 12 months, twice, the vets who remained in the practise turned up on the yard, unannounced. I was trying to work out what they wanted, you can't be too careful, if a vet calls on your yard it usually costs you. Each time it was the same pattern, different vet, but the same pattern. They would exchange small talk and then they would lean over to the back doors of their cars. 'Mind if I give this dog a run?' In the back of their cars would be a yellow Labrador bitch and they would let it out. They would explain that this bitch belonged to a client, that the client no longer wanted it, and had taken it to the vet to be put down. 'I didn't become a vet in order to euthanise healthy animals on people's whims, so I thought of you, will you have it?'

In 12 months, I went from having one Labrador to having four, courtesy of my vets. I bred each bitch once a year so I suppose in effect I became a puppy farmer. The trouble with Labradors is that they can have quite large litters, 8-10 is common. You could sell about six quite easily but you would always be left with some. These soon grew into exuberant half grown dogs but if someone brought small children to see them, they would knock the children down and sometimes it would be quite difficult just to give them away. I stopped breeding labs for that reason and the bitches lived out their lives, so they had a happy ending. We had to have the dog put down because he got so nasty and was a danger to everyone who came here, especially to children.

Then we move on a few years. I can't remember why but we needed a new corgi. I located a litter and we went to see them. I took my mother for a ride. It turned out that the pups were on a hill farm in mid Wales. They were cowering in a box under the kitchen table. The reason they were cowering was that when we entered the kitchen a large sow had followed us in there. As the farmer's wife, nor the sow seemed to think this event to be at all remarkable, I can only assume that a sow in the kitchen was a regular occurrence. I wanted a bitch puppy and all the pups were bitches. My mother said, 'However will you choose one?' I said that I would choose the one that had enough bottle to be first out of the box. And that's how we chose one. Ann called her Lucy but I always called her Foxy. We bred two litters out of Lucy but the trouble was that each time, we kept a bitch puppy. I still miss them, they always used to sleep in front of the television, on their backs, in a row. When I went out to milk in the morning they got so excited and made such a clamour that it was a job to get the kitchen door open.

I'll always remember, one day I was making a cup of tea prior to afternoon milking when I heard the local foxhounds about. I went out into the garden to see what was going on, and the three corgis came with me. I didn't have to wait long before a fox crossed the field in front of the house. The corgis set off in hot pursuit. After about three minutes the hounds appeared. Thus there was a sort of procession, fox, then three corgis, then hounds. I must confess to being more than a bit concerned. If you look like a corgi looks it's not a smart idea to place yourself in front of a pack of foxhounds. Then the whole procession came past again, the fox must have gone around the buildings. By now the corgis had had enough and they rejoined me on the lawn.

What's brought all this on, all this reminiscing about dogs? Well we have a friend who was at her vets the other day and someone came in with a box of corgi pups that were due to have their first injections. She knew that we loved corgi so she took a photo of them. They were adorable. I love my terrier Gomer but that doesn't mean that there isn't room in my heart for a corgi. Ann went to answer the phone so I said to the lady who had took the photograph, 'find out how much they want for them.' I knew that corgi pups were dear but there's no harm in asking is there. She pressed ass on some buttons on her phone. 'The dog pups are £1500 and the bitches £1750.' Think I'll pass on that.

8 FEBRUARY 2020

One thing is for sure, there's certainly been a lot of rain about over recent months. I don't have a rain gauge. But I know plenty of people who do have one and they tell me. The trouble is that they tell me in millimetres and that means nothing to me. I'm very much still a feet and inches man, and acres and hectares. Years ago I went to Vancouver, (very popular now with celeb royals), and one night we went to watch whatever the Vancouver team call themselves, play ice hockey. In the car park I found a broken ice hockey stick and kept it as a souvenir. Six months or so later I bought a rain gauge. I thought: I need to put this out of harm's way, somewhere where it won't get damaged but is easy to read.

I found that the rain gauge fitted exactly over the handle of the ice hockey stick. I nailed the stick to a fence on the yard and the gauge sat neatly on top. This put the gauge conveniently at eye level and the hockey stick was all set to be a daily reminder of a good holiday, which is what souvenirs should do.

Next day the young lad who worked here at the time was turning a loader on the yard. I wish I had a pound for every time I had told him to travel with the loader up in the air, out of harm's way, and another pound for every time he ignored this advice and knocked down a fence or gate post when the loader was about 3 or 4 feet in the air. The day after I had installed the rain gauge, he wiped it out with the loader. The gauge was smashed into lots of pieces and the hockey stick was no more. I've always been a pragmatic sort of person. Perhaps I wasn't meant to have a rain gauge. I've never bought another.

★★★

The wetness of the land is a great talking point in the pub. They are all starting to get twitchy, after all, it isn't long before they will look to be doing some spring field work: I know we have a lot to do. 'Our land is so wet that if you put a tractor wheel on it, water will squirt up out of the worm holes.' Inevitably there is some competition as to who has the wettest land. I notice that those who claim to have the wettest farms also had the driest farms when we had a drought a couple of years ago. It would be churlish of me to point out that this is a contradiction, so I don't.

With the late maize harvests and the late potato harvests and people trying to cart some muck around on the few dry days, the roads around here have been filthy for some time. The fields and farm tracks have all been muddy as well. Most of this mud is on my car. That's never bothered me too much before. But it doesn't stop there. The inside of the car is almost as muddy. I take the dog for exercise most days. He's getting a bit of a lump. Too much toast and marmite for breakfast, if you ask me. I take him up to our top field, I loose him out of the truck so if he follows me twice around the field, that is just over a mile. I open the door at the finish and when he gets back in he jumps into my footwell. He scrabbles under my legs and climbs onto the central console. From there he gets onto the back seat. There's mud everywhere.

This is a big bonus. When we go to rugby matches away, no one wants to go in my car. Yesterday, I took my car to be washed. I confess to having mixed feelings about this. I only wash the car about twice a year so it's not a big issue. The men in the car wash are obviously Eastern European, dubbed illegal immigrants or slave labour, according to which TV programme you have just watched. Either way I admire them, they always do a good job and I always give them a good tip.

There were two reasons why I washed my car. I always park it close to the door of the pub, and the smokers had started writing on it in the mud. I would have liked a Banksy mural, but that was a long shot. The other reason was that we went to a funeral in it. I got mud all over my suit trousers and as for my overcoat, that was in a terrible mess.

About five years ago I went to a funeral in January. It was a nice sunny day but there had been a hard frost. It was a big country funeral in a small country church. I only had my suit on and was standing outside for an hour, in the shade. I knew a lady who worked in a charity shop and I asked her to keep an eye out for a big old-fashioned overcoat, preferably grey or black. She found me a beauty in two weeks for £15. I looked it up online and it would have cost £500 new.

I took cash to the funeral for the collection plate and gave it all there. I assumed that we would go to the village hall afterwards, but we didn't, we went to the pub and I couldn't buy a drink. But my wife bought me one. This is the first time I can ever remember her buying me a drink. Wonder what she's up to…

15 FEBRUARY 2020

I return to the subject of dogs. I don't offer any excuses for this, because dogs have always been a big part of my life. I have a theory that if you have a really good working dog, whether to shoot with or to tend sheep and or cattle, it will come to an untimely end. But if you acquire a completely useless 'working' dog, it will be about your yard for years and years and will die of natural causes. I remember once, hanging about in a market. Some people love going to market, some of us find it very time-consuming. To pass the time, whilst I waited to have my stock sold, I went to have a look around the sheep pens. In one pen there was a big box of sheepdog pups. But they weren't just any sheepdog pups, they were what I called Blue Merle pups. They were all beautifully marked and they all had a characteristic blue eye. One of my neighbours was also admiring these pups and we spent about ten minutes saying what nice pups they were and how unusual.

Eventually I went on my way and thought no more about them. At about 3 o'clock the aforementioned neighbour turned up on our yard. 'Those blue pups only made £10 apiece so I bought you one.' I remember not being best pleased, I had plenty of dogs at the time but I liked the neighbour and he obviously thought he had done me a favour and I didn't want to hurt his feelings. As far as I can remember, that blue dog died from natural causes when it was 15 years old. It was mostly to be found asleep on our yard. The only time it showed animation was when it barked at birds perched on the electric wires.

I can't remember the exact circumstances, but I once lost a really good working dog. It was at a busy time; the cows were out at grass and there was a lot of sheep work to do. When you lose a good working dog, you miss it more than you do a mediocre dog, you tend to rely on its impact. I went immediately to the man where I bought the dog I had lost. He was a sheep farmer who also trained dogs. He told me that he didn't have any dogs for sale at the time but when he could see how disappointed I was, he relented, 'I've got a bearded collie bitch that's nearly ready.' I'd never seen a bearded collie bitch before and truth be told, I wasn't seeing one now. I've since seen bearded collies and they are quite small. I don't know what this one was crossed with but she was a very big bitch and looked a bit like a lurcher. Anyway I bought her and she turned out to be the best dog I ever had, she was on a par with Mert, my famous border collie. Her name was Poppy (what a stupid name to give a big dog).

After she had settled in, I never shut her in at night and she always slept on the yard just outside out kitchen window. She slept there in the rain and only sought cover if it snowed for two or three days consecutively. I've got up for morning milking several times and she has been in a snowy heap outside the window. When she heard me filling the kettle she would go, of her own accord, to fetch the cows for milking. In the winter she would get them out of their sheds and in the summer she would fetch them from the fields. She never gave them a hard time, it was almost as if the cows saw her and said to themselves, 'Here she is, time to make our way home.' If a cow wouldn't come home, perhaps it was sick or calving, she would stay with it. If Poppy wasn't with the cows, you knew that you needed to go and look for one of them. Just how clever was that?

There used to be a group of players from the rugby club who formed a shearing gang. They did my shearing and the first time they saw Poppy; they had never seen a dog like it and I remember them laughing at her. We had over four hundred ewes at the time and we used to shear them in some pens we had made, next to a wood. After an hour, their dogs were all lying in the shade but my dog worked in the pens all day. At the end of the day they made serious attempts to buy her.

I had Poppy at the same time as we had the three corgis. These corgis only had one ambition in life, to catch a rabbit. We used to go, the three corgis, the bearded collie and I, to fetch the cows for afternoon milking. Most days we would put up a rabbit. The corgis would set off in hot pursuit but never came anywhere near catching one. Poppy mostly used to watch all this going on and stay by my side, with her head cocked in a doggy expression of amused indulgence. But now and then she would also give chase. If the rabbit ran on down the cow track or across the field, she would catch it with ease. Poppy used to stand there, with the rabbit unharmed in her mouth, until the corgis were just a yard away. They would run up, probably thinking they were about to fulfil their dream, and she would drop the rabbit about six inches in front of them and the rabbit would run off. Six inches start is all a rabbit needs on a corgi and as far as I know they never caught one.

29 FEBRUARY 2020

We are still licking our wounds, metaphorically, in the aftermath of last week's storm. Most obvious of the damage we suffered was the large horse chestnut tree that came down in my son's garden. It came down at 8 o'clock in the morning whilst he was having breakfast after he had done the milking. We had witnessed a similar phenomenon before: a gust of violent wind approaches, you can hear it coming, it's moving like an express train, (is it too soon to use HS2 as a simile?) then it arrives and it takes something with it. Last time it was the roof of our straw barn, this time it was the tree. My son had walked past there just a quarter of an hour previously.

I remember when I kept sheep, I had a ewe with two lambs in the field in front of our house. She didn't have enough milk for both lambs so I used to go, at bedtime, with a bottle of milk to 'top them up.' There's a lot of trees in that field and one night it was blowing a gale. I easily found the lambs; they were out of the wind behind a big tree. Whilst I was feeding them three trees came down quite close. I'd only used half of the milk and thought, 'You two will have to take your chances, I'm not taking mine,' and I legged it back to the house. I can't remember what happened to the lambs but I was OK.

The tree that came down in David's garden, came down neatly between fences, house and cars. They couldn't get a car out until next day until someone cut a path through the branches with a chainsaw. The only damage we can find thus far is that my granddaughter's trampoline was picked up and re-erected on the roof of a neighbour's car. Elsewhere a bough has taken out the telephone wires. We have reported it and it could take a week to mend. I don't doubt they have plenty to do.

Meanwhile we live in splendid isolation. There's no broadband so I do wonder what emails are piling up. Most of our important communications come that way. But it has been a pleasure not having a telephone landline. We get about ten nuisance calls a day. It had got so bad that I had stopped answering the phone in the daytime and only answered it after tea, out of office hours, when it might have been friends or family. If we could persuade my wife to use a mobile we could have it taken out.

★★★

Because the ground is so wet, my daily excursions in the truck are limited to visits to our top field. There's a track that takes you all the way and it's at 1,000 feet, so it's our driest. When I drive around it I'm looking for signs of life. There's life at the far end. Six of my neighbour's sheep have been there three months now and as far as I know he has made no attempt to get them back. The grass is just starting to grow up here so you can see how much they have eaten. I think it's time to send him a bill and one of my sarcastic letters. I don't expect him to pay the bill, we get on very well, but it will focus his mind. No, the life I'm looking for is hares. Yesterday I saw one in this field and today I saw two.

But the hares' behaviour has changed. As far as I know there have not been any hare coursers about. The police have been more active, mainly because of the other crime that coursers bring with them. And we locals have been more vigilant, taking vehicle numbers and generally looking to see who is about. When the coursers were about regularly, you couldn't get within 200 yards of a hare: they would just dash off. The hares I have just seen were cwtched down in the grass, you could drive right up to them, and then they would just lope off to the nearest hedge, turn and watch you. Nature has an amazing capacity to replenish itself.

★★★

Change is inevitable, but whether it is for the better remains to be seen. About 12 months ago the traditional ironmongers in our local town closed down. It had been in the same family for over 100 years. The shop was sold and it was bought by someone who dispenses poetry. I don't fully understand how it works but I think that if you have a problem they will compose you a poem that will make you feel better.

Now a village grocery shop is closed. It had been in the same family for well over 100 years as well. It is to become a yoga studio. I can't see me ever going to either establishment but most of the people around here have nothing to do all day and they will be tempted. Some years ago there was a crystal shop. I didn't understand what it was about and was told it was all earth, wind and fire. I wasn't any wiser.

There was also a shop at about the same time that was kept by a lady who called herself a White Witch. She had a sideline in alternative funerals. I've no idea what a White Witch is about but I do know that I always crossed the road to avoid passing her shop.

We seem to get these obscure start-up businesses around here and often I wonder, 'How does that work?' The answer, invariably, is that it doesn't. After about three years they seem to close and move one. I wonder if they get some sort of start-up grant and when that is all used up they move somewhere else and get another?

7 MARCH 2020

The days are getting discernibly longer, and as we all look forward to them lengthening yet more, we inadvertently wish our lives away. Besides, the dark nights of winter are not without their merit. There is an order, a routine to them. Like most families we spend our evenings with the TV on. We used to argue about the use of the remote control, but rarely do now. I have a habit, a bad habit apparently, of flicking through the channels whilst the adverts are on. My wife spends the evening doing crosswords or jigsaws and I am usually reading.

But we can divert from both recreations to watching the TV should it be of interest. I pay more attention to the cooking programmes; after all they are about food and I produce food. It has always intrigued me that although there are food or cookery programmes two or three times a day, every day, the food sector that sees consistent growth is that of ready meals. What's all that about? All those celebrity chefs, teaching people how to cook, while to all intents and people are cooking less and less. If you add ready meals to the food that is eaten in pubs and restaurants, it is probably a huge percentage of the total. I've got some friends whose son lived in California for several years. They reckoned that all that he ever had in his fridge was bottled water and orange juice. Every meal that his family ate was eaten out. Is that the way we will end up? Possibly so. Food has its fashions and fads.

I think all the publicity over veganism is much exaggerated. I think there are a lot of people who have an occasional vegan day; I have a vegetarian day most week, not deliberately but because I like baked beans for breakfast and we usually have fish for tea once a week. Talking of fads, my brother says he has never touched a baked bean, he doesn't like the look of them. I tell him that should he go first, I will fill his coffin with them. I can remember another food habit that I've not come across lately: supper. I've stayed at farms where the whole family would sit down at about 9 o'clock to eat a fulsome supper before they went to bed. There would always be plenty of bread and cheese, sometimes cold meat. Always pickled onions, raw onions and homemade chutney. The thought now of eating all that, at that time of night, has me reaching for the Rennies.

When I left school, I lived in on a farm for two years and it was a custom that they had, that anyone who worked there, contractors for baling and the like, were fed as well. We used to have supper every night but if there was someone else there, we had a veritable feast. All sorts of fresh salad, choice of meats along with all the usual cheese and pickles.

I've got friends who are still on New Year resolution diets. They are doing better than my grandsons who gave up alcohol for January but who only lasted six days! The ladies go to what they call 'fat club', where if they eat something that is not approved they call it a 'sin'. I noticed that I was not allowed to buy a packet of crisps when it was my round on Saturday: thus far this year I haven't been allowed to!

Part of most diets is to eat a hearty breakfast. I knew a farmer who always ate a good breakfast but it hasn't featured on any diet sheet I have ever seen. Its main constituent was fat bacon. He used to rear three pigs a year and as far as I know he used to eat all three himself. His criteria for these pigs being ready for slaughter was that they should be so fat that they couldn't see out of their eyes. What it really means is that they were so fat, even their faces were fat. I'm sure they could see OK. His breakfast, every day, was plenty of bread and cheese, a large onion, a cut down the side of fat bacon, (this could be a foot long, an inch thick and with no lean meat apparent). All the cutting and eating was done with his penknife. All washed down with cider. He didn't carry an ounce of fat, was as hard as nails and I thought he was surely indestructible. You could meet him on a cold wet day in January and he would have his coat and shirt undone to his waist, bare down to the navel, no pullover, or vest! He suffered an accident on the farm, never seemed the same again and only lived another two years.

14 MARCH 2020

It is not my intention to trivialise the flood damage to people's homes. We have all seen the rows and rows of peoples' possessions that they have had to dump out in the street. It must be heart-breaking and testing to your resolve. Especially after repeated flooding. Our backyard slopes down to the house and once there was a violent thunderstorm one afternoon. The water blocked the drain and came under the door into the kitchen. It went down the steps out of the kitchen and into the living room. It was of no depth, it just made the carpet wet and 'squelchy'. It was relatively clean water and did not contain anything nasty. We hired heaters and kit to suck up the water and thought we had done a good job. After about three days the carpet started to stink. After four days the whole house stank. We had to throw the carpet out and the insurance bought a new one.

This time we have got off very lightly. Our landline telephone was out of order for a week after the first storm but we didn't really mind. Our lives are plagued by nuisance calls, so it was nice not to have them. Then our line was reconnected, we could make calls out OK but didn't get any calls back. That was quite good as well. Then we find out that when we were reconnected, they had inadvertently given us someone else's phone number. They had given us the number of some neighbours who are in America for a month. The engineer phoned us to say that we were now reconnected with the right number and in the next hour we had three nuisance calls. So much for progress!

★★★

We have suffered floods at the local rugby club. When we bought the ground we had been using the pitches belonging to the school and getting changed in the cricket club pavilion. There is not much choice of flat ground around here. We knew it was on a flood plain so we took advice from the Environment Agency.

They said we could expect to be flooded once every 12 years. We thought we could live with that so we went ahead with the purchase. It flooded three times the following winter. We tried to track down the person who gave this advice but he had gone to ground and his colleagues closed ranks around him. Since then the pitches are flooded most years but this has been the worst. When we finally built a new clubhouse and changing rooms, we built them on a raised area thank goodness, which put them above the recent flood level, but only just. Usually the water comes and goes, but this time it left a lot of debris, stones and wood. This had to be cleared by hand, as the ground was too wet to take tractors and loaders.

★★★

Crime has never been a big issue around here, until recently. It was a big thing when we started taking our keys out of our cars at night. We never lock our back door, so that early morning milkers can make a cup of tea. In fact it's only because we have a new kitchen door that I know where the key is. With the previous door, we didn't have a clue where the key was!

All that has changed. There were nine break-ins within three miles of here on one night. We didn't get visited and I can only assume that the thieves didn't think we had anything worth taking. And that is usually the key, because they send out 'spotters' in the daytime whose role it is to identify theft opportunities. Quad bikes and power tools were the targets and there is nothing hit and miss about it. They know just where to go and what they will find when they get there. Years ago, they would have to dispose of stolen goods via a 'fence'. Today they have the internet and car boot sales. If you were a thief, you can't easily think of anything better.

★★★

At the farm where my daughter lives, they keep sheep. One of the problems they have is when they turn ewes and lambs out to grass, the lambs pop under a stile on a public footpath and get run over on the road. It happens when the lambs are about a month old, and they form inquisitive packs and spend most of their time gambolling their time away. They can easily get through the rails of the stile. To stop this, my son-in-law nailed some wire netting to the lower rails to block the lambs getting through. The trouble with this is that walkers' dogs can't get through the rail either. Some dog walkers kick the wire netting off. My son-in-law comes across a walker who was removing the wire, so he explained why it was there, patiently. The walker continued with his task. 'That's your problem, not mine.' No wonder farmer's get depressed.

21 MARCH 2020

We've lived here for over 50 years and this is the first year that Canada geese have not nested on our pond. Last year they hatched five youngsters but they were hoovered up by kites within a week of being hatched. This year a pair of geese made an exploratory visit and the air above them was alive with kites and buzzards, so they must have thought better of it. The numbers of birds of prey is out of hand, but those who have all the influence can't see it.

★★★

I never thought that I would see the day, but here I go recommending a recipe to you. Before I was married and living at home, my mother used to cook for us, especially in winter, a boiled chicken. And very good it was too. She used to boil it along with vegetables, carrots and onions and the like, and pearl barley. I am not sure what pearl barley is, but it is in there as well. I've been married over 50 years, and fair play, my wife always asks what I want for tea, which is our main meal.

About twice a year for 50 years I have said that my Mother used to boil a chicken, and why can't we have one? And my wife has always replied that years ago you could buy what they called boiling fowl, and now you can't. All those years ago people kept traditional breeds like Rhode Island Reds and Light Sussex. When their laying life ended there would still be a substantial carcass that would have a value in the food chain. Today's laying hen is like an athlete, it is designed to produce lots of eggs and not to waste food producing body weight. To use a canine comparison, the laying hens of yesteryear were like bulldogs, now they are like whippets. About 20 years ago I started saying that it was true that you couldn't buy boiling fowl anymore, but where does it say that you can't boil a fresh chicken instead?

Anyway, last week she bought one, she has what is called a slow cooker and she added some carrots and onions and sage and put in some pearl parley. I thought that some peas would have given it a bit more colour but 50 years of marriage teaches you to keep quiet. The chicken was plonked on top and it was cooked, on and off, for about 12 hours. It was good, but not as good as my Mother used to cook but we'll keep quiet about that. Ann liked it as well. She paid £5 for the chicken and the vegetables wouldn't have been expensive. We had three meals each out of it. She likes the idea so much I expect that we will have it for tea three times a week, every week, for the foreseeable future. Even if I had to wait 50 years for it.

★★★

Today we turn our attention to my eldest granddaughter. She is in her first year of university. Life has not been easy for her in some respects because she suffers from dyslexia. She's a bit of a family favourite because she's not let that inhibit her aspirations and she is not afraid of a challenge. Moving from the safe, quiet environment of a farm upbringing to living in the centre of a city where she didn't know anyone, is yet another challenge she has taken in her stride. Truth be told she is a bit of a curiosity amongst her fellow students. Some of them don't even know for sure what a farm is, let alone have they ever met a farmer's daughter. She gets lots of questions, but not all of them are very demanding. They tend to be of your school-days variety, 'If a white cow gives white milk, what colour does a brown cow give?' But most of them don't know that cows give milk anyway. One girl, who pretended to know more than her colleagues, wanted to know why some cows gave milk and some gave cheese!

She shows them photographs on her phone of where she lives. On one photo there was a cock pheasant in the background. Now pheasants are the most numerous birds around here, especially in October, before the shooting season starts in earnest, but the consensus amongst the other students was that pheasants were in fact extinct and she had put the bird on the photo herself.

I am not sure what course she is on but I do know that it includes design. One piece of work she did created a lot of interest, especially amongst her lecturers and mentors. She had created the picture of a farmer's discarded dirty wellies and the legend 'not wanted anymore'. They were so intrigued, and it was so different from anything her fellow students had created, that they wanted to know more. She explained that her Dad produced beef cattle and that at the time he was selling them for about £100 a piece, less than a year ago. That there was a serious question of what sort of tariff there would be on lamb going to Europe in the future. That beef would still the same price in the shops but no one seemed to care.

And that this sort of situation couldn't go on. They listened to her story carefully, and said they had no idea. I suspect she did a lot of good with her dirty welly concept. The lack of understanding of food production amongst university students is both hilarious and alarming. If they are supposed to be the most intelligent, what do the rest know?

28 MARCH 2020

A feature of the window in our living room is that the windowsill is only about a foot high. This is a good thing because when I am sitting in my favourite armchair the sill is below my eyeline, so that I can see all of the nearby fields and I can also see all of the fields in the distance and the woods beyond them.

The dog Gomer likes this low windowsill as well because he can jump up on it and parade up and down. It's so much more than a windowsill to him, it's his stage. He can sit there and growl at everything he doesn't like, which is usually a passing cock pheasant. He goes berserk if he should see a rabbit or a squirrel. His favourite time is when the farm dogs come to have a look at him. He likes it best if it's a wet cold day. He sits there in the warm and the dry and the other dogs regard him with envy. It isn't that warm indoors, but it's warmer than it is outside.

Unfortunately, he can't get on there at the moment because there is a plant pot on it. Just over 12 months ago, my florist friend had one of those big birthdays. On each table at the party there was an orchid in a pot. These were distributed to various of the ladies present and we had one to bring home. Its flowers lasted several months and then they died back. But just when it was on its way to the wheely bin, it had a new lease of life. New buds began to appear and it was put on the low windowsill in our living room. I head for my armchair every day to watch the 1 o'clock news on TV. Most days I drift off to sleep. I might only sleep for 10-15 minutes but I don't fight it. I always wake up refreshed and ready to go.

One day last week I woke up as usual and whilst I was coming round, I looked out of the window. You know the phenomenon you get from a heat source, a sort of shimmering effect that is rising up above the fire. You often see it above someone's wood burner. Well I could see this shimmering ripple effect going up our window. I gave my eyes another rub and it was still there. My first thought was, 'That orchid is on fire!' Almost instantly my second thought was 'It can't be.' There was simple explanation. We have a lady comes in one morning a week to help with the housework. She's a good friend but she is always moving stuff around. Truth be told it's often several days after she has been before we have found everything. We don't say anything because she is also scary. She had found one of those scented candles somewhere, I think she had bought it us for Christmas. We are not big into candles, never lit one, but she had put this candle behind the orchid and lit it. I had to get up close to find it. I was so relieved: I thought that I might be seeing things, and that would never do, would it.

★★★

I know that they are all lambing around here, but they are not talking about it. I wonder why? They all scanned their ewes a couple of months ago but there was no bragging about prospective numbers of lambs; I think that overall, they were disappointed. I've never been a big fan of scanning, although I used to do it when I kept sheep. It's a good management tool, having your ewes marked so that you know just how many lambs they are carrying. Almost as important is knowing which ewes are not carrying any lambs at all. There's no prizes for guessing where most of these end up. (The price of cull ewes is at record levels, and people often ask me why. I always suggest that it is because it is probably the only part of the food chain that the supermarkets are not involved in and therefore they can't keep a lid on it.)

But I'm not a big fan of scanning because there is enough superstition in me to worry about counting your chickens before they are hatched. The week before your lambing starts can be a traumatic time. You can get abortions, dead ewes, lambs born prematurely. You can get all of these things when lambing properly starts but they are then part of a bigger picture, you get the majority of live healthy lambs and it doesn't seem so bad.

Lambing duties seem to have changed a bit since I kept any ewes. I used to sleep in the chair or on the settee for the first three weeks. It used to take a special sort of willpower to get up every couple of hours when you had got warm and comfortable and you were very tired. Especially if you could hear rain on the windows or you knew that there was snow on the ground. I know of several shepherds, who, if the lambing shed is not close to their house, install a cheap caravan in the lambing shed to sleep there if they need to. One of my friends has gone even further down that road. His ewes lamb in a shed a mile from where he lives. He had bricked-in a corner of the shed and made himself a sort of bedroom. He has put an old carpet on the floor, put in a bed, and installed a log burner. He has a fridge and a microwave and a television. He spends his evenings sitting up in bed and watching television. Close at hand is his air rifle. He uses this to shoot rats as they scamper across the wall he built. As yet we can't find out if he takes his wellys off to get into bed.

4 APRIL 2020

I'm the family lawn mower. Even using a ride-on mower, it can take two hours. One thing I have learnt over the years is not to let the lawn get on top of you. By that I mean growth that can occur in early season, for example in February. If there is a dry day in February I often give the lawns a light cut to keep on top of them. I never collect the grass I have cut; I much prefer to cut them twice a week, but I can't do with leaving a lot of cut grass on top of the lawn. Taking two light cuts weekly in the spring, when grass growth is at its maximum, alleviates this. This year, for obvious reasons, I was not able to cut the lawns in February so they got ahead of me. I was fairly pragmatic about this. You can't do anything about the weather so you just have to do your best. It's what farmers always do, it's a part of their lives.

Besides, I had had the lawn mower serviced. For over 50 years I had intended to get the various lawn mowers I have had, serviced in the winter, and this is the first time I have actually got around to it. I knew that there was a fair growth of grass on the lawns but I thought that if I cut them three times in fairly quick succession, each time setting the mower just a little bit lower, I would soon be back in control.

What I hadn't foreseen was just how much growth there had been. I've been growing grass for a living most of my life. Some of my neighbours have said I'm quite good at it. It's always been a mystery to me that every spring there is always more grass on the lawns than there is in the fields where you need it. In some places the mower had to chomp its way through grass that was at least six inches long, whereas none of our fields has grass that long. The only reason for this that I have ever come up with is that the grass is sheltered by fences and garden hedges. You often see an abundance of grass on the verges at the sides of roads in spring, possibly for the same reason. It has some shelter from wind chill.

The last lawn that I mow is my son's lawn. This lawn is close to the road and elevated so that you are above the traffic. Drivers can all see me and there is much waving and horn blowing. A lot of folks around here have these 4x4 pickups. Perhaps it's a trick of the light or it's how the windows are positioned, but you can't always see the faces of those driving so I wave at all of them in case I know them. I feel quite good with myself; I feel as if I am the centre of attention. But this good feeling doesn't last long. My next-door neighbour starts to plough the field just the other side of the road. They have a fairly new 200hp tractor and a newish 6-furrow reversible plough. Then there's me, chuffing away on my little sit-on lawn mower, and I'm not sorry when my progression of mowing takes me further and further away across the lawn.

What is happening here today is a bit like a farming career. When you first start out on a farm you are clearly the boy and you get all the mundane jobs that are usually reserved for boys. Then you get older and you move on up the ladder, with a bit of luck you might end up as the boss. Then the next generation takes over all the important jobs and you end up where you started, back doing the boys' jobs, jobs like lawn mowing. It's a bit like being an agricultural auctioneer. When you first start out selling, they get you to sell all the tat that is difficult to sell, and your audience is indifferent. But if you achieve some seniority you end up selling farms in pubs and your audience hangs on your every word.

★★★

I am just finishing my breakfast when Stephen, who works for us, calls in. He is given a cup of tea and we have a chat. We chat about farms and people, mostly about people who farm. The conversation runs its course, and I go to leave, but he says, 'What did you want to see me about?' I say that I didn't need to see him but he says that he has just had a text to say, call in. 'Not from me you didn't.' 'Yes, I did.' And so it goes on until he gets the text up on his phone and sure enough he has a text from me, asking him to call in. I know for sure that I haven't sent him a text that morning so we dig a bit deeper into his phone. We find that it was a text I sent on May 19th last year. Much of modern technology is a mystery to me and incidents like this only serve to unnerve me. Where has this text been since last May, was it stuck in a tree somewhere? Even stranger still, this text was sent on my previous phone and that phone passed away several months ago!

11 APRIL 2020

Because it's dried up a bit, I am able to drive my truck into more fields. I drive into one field slowly and steadily but I don't stop. Stopping can often cause more alarm to wildlife than if you keep moving. If you keep moving the creatures you want to see seem to assume that whatever their hiding place, it's working. There she is. A hare is squatting low in the grass. The grass is not yet long enough to hide all of her back but she doesn't know that. Her head is well down and I assume that she thinks that if she can't see me, then I can't see her. Somewhere, probably within 10 yards or so, she has twin leverets. There they are. They are the first leverets I have seen this year. They are tiny and they are vulnerable and I fear for their future. There are so many kites and buzzards and ravens about, it's a wonder they have lasted this long, never mind the foxes and badgers.

I also know that within yards there will be another hare. I've got this one down as the Dad but of course there is no way I can know this. If I was a romantic, I could be forgiven for thinking that he is on guard as well. I don't know how the mating habits of hares works; most animals in the wild come into season just as they have weaned their offspring. There 'he' is about 100 yards away. I don't think he's on guard, I think he's waiting for a mating opportunity. Sometimes these hares will breed several times a year so there is little time for romance. I have seen hares boxing often enough to know that a romantic liaison is more rough and tumble than it is chocolates and flowers.

★★★

We live in an area with a low population. Most people know most people, which is nice. And if you don't know them to speak to, you know their faces, you have seen them about. This is particularly true of shopkeepers who know by sight most of the people who enter their shops. Most of the food shops are small by modern comparison, you have to go 15-20 miles to find a nationally-known supermarket. We know the people who work in or own these local shops, they are part of our community, and over the last week or so they report that they have never been so busy. They have been busy serving strangers during the coronavirus crisis. Some of these strangers readily admit to travelling 50 or so miles to stock up.

It could be said that they have cleared their own shelves and now they are clearing ours. But I don't see it like that at all. There's plenty of food in the pipeline, nature and food production will go on with its own agenda despite this crisis. The upside is that the local shops are glad of this extra business. The downside is that if these strangers clear out a particular shelf and it is suggested to them that they put some back, they can become abusive and aggressive.

As we all sort of hunker down to the present-day restrictive regime, our landline telephone has never been so busy. I suspect that it is mostly women having the conversations they previously had at supermarket check-outs. I don't really know because I never answer the landline.

We all know what's dominating the news but the demise of singer Kenny Rogers did sneak recently into the news bulletins. He's a big thing around here. *Islands in the Stream* was the most played song on the juke box in the pub, by some distance. No matter what people's taste in music, they would frequently include it in their selection. It was a sort of village anthem. In the next village to us, their anthem is the *Crystal Chandelier*, but they are not as cultured as we are. I see that our pub is shut as a mark of respect for Kenny. When the song first came out, I can remember doing a mime duet to it at a rugby club Christmas party, and I assure you I wasn't Dolly Parton.

17 APRIL 2020

Stuff happens. There's been a lot of unexpected 'stuff' about lately. In fact, for most of us, there's never been more. I've settled into a sort of routine and like to think that I am taking the restrictions in my stride. There's nothing to be done about it so we will all just have to wait it out.

When I get up, and before breakfast, I answer yesterday's emails. I don't want to give the impression that this is a big job but I only type with one finger so it's big enough. After breakfast is reserved for writing, I write for some other publications and there is always writing to do. Early in the afternoon I venture forth to visit the cattle that we have turned out. I take my time over this as it's nice to get out and about and the views from our top land are spectacular and I never tire of them.

When I get back home I often have time to watch a film I have recorded. Films have played a strange part in my life. When you are a dairy farmer, time dictates that you only ever see half a film. 'Time to go to bed, you have to be up early in the morning.' 'Leave that film, it's time to do afternoon milking.' I've not been in a cinema for over 30 years. I discovered early on that no matter the hype and publicity, if you were patient, a new film would soon arrive on television.

This process seems to have accelerated over recent years. I thought that the present coronavirus crisis would be a good chance for me to catch up on films. But it hasn't been that straightforward. I don't record any film that includes fantasy or sci-fi or Harry Potter or a superhero. This doesn't leave many films, so I end up watching good films twice. What do I miss during lockdown? I miss going to the pub, but I don't miss it as much as if everyone else is there, but not me.

It's a strange phenomenon that. It's closed to everyone so that's OK, sort of. What I have discovered is that there are regulars in the pub that I don't miss at all. I miss going to the gym, I think that certain exercises were doing me good. What I do find strange is that sometimes, when I go to see the cattle, I often see a couple, who also go to the gym. They are taking their exercise by walking along a narrow lane, there's nobody else about so they are not doing any harm. I do find it really odd not to stop and say hello. This is my first and natural inclination and I don't like just waving and driving by.

We live one field away from a B-road, and I have never known it so quiet so I think that the shut-down is working. News comes in that a pub, not that far away, was raided by police and drinkers were found within. But what has surprised me is the number of people that have said to me just how much they are enjoying the peace and quiet. We live in what people call a tranquil area, one where peace and quiet is something of a norm. If people are enjoying it being quiet around here, what's it like elsewhere? It goes back to my contention that there are probably too many people living on a relatively small island. I'm not talking about immigration, it's just a statement of fact. But then, if there weren't people about, what would I write about? You can't have it both ways. You rarely can.

★★★

A friend wrote to me recently and reminded me that 15 or 20 years ago he had had some issues in his life and I had told him, 'You have to find positives in adversity.' It makes me cringe when I read it now. It sounds as if I am taking one of those motivational courses. It's a variation of the theme, 'Every cloud has a silver lining.'

What's the positive in the present coronavirus adversity? I've done a lot more reading, which I have neglected of late. For example I've just been reading the diaries of a Welsh farmer who emigrated to the state of Victoria in Australia in 1869. He stayed there 25 years and he spent all of those years as an itinerant worker. Except that they didn't call them itinerant workers, they called them swagmen. Like in the song about the jolly swagman; and the swag was the bag in which they carried all their belongings. There were hundreds of swagmen roaming the Australian roads looking for work and they used to walk huge distances in that search. They were poorly paid and had to do 15-16 hours of hard manual labour a day. Because the seasons in Australia are more defined and extreme than ours there were long periods when there was no work to be had.

But the real story is never told and it intrigues me. Why did a farmer of some repute go to Australia when he was 51? Why did he leave a good farm, his wife and children to live such a hard life at that age? He was an educated man; he wrote regularly to newspapers. He kept his diary every day that he was in Australia. He won prizes for his poetry at Australian Eisteddfods (there seemed to be lots of Welsh people in that area). He saved enough money to return to Wales in 1894 'to see his grandchildren and to be buried in Welsh soil.'

Why he went, we are not told. I suspect there was a woman involved but that would be sexist, or is it romantic? I forget which.

★★★

The television in our kitchen always seems to be on in the background. Since we have had lockdown most of these interviews have taken place in the celebrities' homes.

To start with mostly they were conducted in front of shelves of books, so trying to read the titles of their books was usually more interesting than the interview. Now these interviews seem to have moved to the celebrities' kitchens. All this moving the 'home office' about is only possible because most people have the know-how and the in-home technology to meet a wider audience. I don't come into that category and don't intend to do so. Last week we had a virtual parish council meeting and I was the only one who didn't get through.

These online interviews are regarded as some sort of triumph in a time of adversity but they are not. The people conducting the interviews are in awe of the people they are talking to, they treat everything that is said as if it is wisdom, which it usually isn't, and they fall about laughing at the slightest hint of humour.

But it's not like that at all. This increased exposure has shown just how shallow, in the majority of cases, the lives of celebrities and TV gurus are. They rarely have anything original to say, they clearly live empty vacuous lives and the whole thing, the celebrity thing, is a charade.

Contrast that with the people we see on farming programmes! There have never been more programmes devoted to life on the farm than there are now. The farming programmes wouldn't be on if they weren't popular. They show real people, not people trying to be flash, living hard-working lives, as they try to look after the welfare of their animals and feed the nation.

It's all so real, there's new life and just as surely there is death in the countryside. Celebrities are trivial by comparison. And it is lockdown that has exposed it.

Further rural reading from Merlin Unwin Books

Pull the Other One! Roger Evans £12 hb

Fifty Bales of Hay Roger Evans £12 hb

A View from the Tractor Roger Evans £12 hb

A Farmer's Lot Roger Evans £12 hb

Don't Worry he doesn't Bite *Tales of a Country Postman* Liam Mulvin £12 hb

Myddle *The Life and Times of a Shropshire Farmworker's Daughter* Helen Ebrey £12

Much Ado About Mutton Bob Kennard £20 hb

A Most Rare Vision *Shropshire from the Air* Mark Sisson £14.99 hb

Extraordinary Villages Tony Francis £14.99 hb

The Countryman's Bedside Book BB £18.95 hb

A Job for all Seasons *My Small Country Living* Phyllida Barstow £14.99 hb

My Animals and Other Family Phyllida Barstow £16.99 hb

The Byerley Turk *The True Story of the First Thoroughbred* Jeremy James £9.99 pb

Maynard: *The Adventures of a Bacon Curer* Maynard Davies £9.99 hb

Maynard: *The Secrets of a Bacon Curer* Maynard Davies £9.99 hb

Advice from a Gamekeeper *John Cowan* £20 hb

The Way of a Countryman *Ian Niall* £16.99 hb

The Hare *(new edition)* Jill Mason £25 hb

The Rabbit *Jill Mason* £20 hb

The BASC Game Shooter's Pocket Guide Michael Brook £7.99 pb

Available from all good bookshops
For more details of these books: **www.merlinunwin.co.uk**